Democratizing AI

Manchester University Press

CRITICAL POWERS

Critical Powers is dedicated to constructing dialogues around innovative and original work in social and political theory. The ambition of the series is to be pluralist in welcoming work from different philosophical traditions and theoretical orientations, ranging from abstract conceptual argument to concrete policy-relevant engagements, and encouraging dialogue across the diverse approaches that populate the field of social and political theory. All the volumes in the series are structured as dialogues in which a lead essay is greeted with a series of responses before a reply by the lead essayist. Such dialogues spark debate, foster understanding, encourage innovation and perform the drama of thought in a way that engages a wide audience of scholars and students.

To buy or to find out more about the books currently available in this series, please go to: https://manchesteruniversitypress.co.uk/series/critical-powers/

Democratizing AI

Annette Zimmermann

with responses from:

Chiara Cordelli
Ritwik Agrawal and
Thomas Christiano
Nadia Urbinati
Allison Stanger
Regina Kreide
Mathias Risse

MANCHESTER UNIVERSITY PRESS

Published by Manchester University Press
Oxford Road, Manchester, M13 9PL

www.manchesteruniversitypress.co.uk

British Library Cataloguing-in-Publication Data
A catalogue record for this book is available from the British Library

ISBN 978 1 5261 8361 3 hardback

First published 2026

EU authorised representative for GPSR:
Easy Access System Europe, Mustamäe tee 50, 10621
Tallinn, Estonia
gpsr.requests@easproject.com

Typeset
by Cheshire Typesetting Ltd, Cuddington, Cheshire

Contents

List of contributors vii
Acknowledgements x
Editor's introduction xi

Part I: Lead essay – Annette Zimmermann

1 Hype 3
2 Progress 15
3 Risk 27
4 Agendas 40
5 Strategies 54
6 Democracy 67
7 Future 97

Part II: Responses

8 AI, democracy, and the problem of collective disempowerment – Chiara Cordelli 121
9 Representative democracy and the harms of AI – Ritwik Agrawal and Thomas Christiano 134
10 'After the revolution'? On Annette Zimmermann's idea to democratize the AI agenda-setting – Nadia Urbinati 147
11 AI governance at a crossroads: Renovating democracy in the age of AI – Allison Stanger 161
12 Affirmative not critical: How AI language systems are changing the political public sphere – Regina Kreide 178
13 On the variety of ways of making philosophical sense of AI – Mathias Risse 194

Part III: Reply to critics

14 Reply to critics – Annette Zimmermann 209

Index 235

List of Contributors

Allison Stanger is Middlebury Distinguished Endowed Professor at Middlebury College. Together with Danielle Allen, she co-directs the GETTING–Plurality Research Network at Harvard University. She is the author of *One Nation Under Contract: The Outsourcing of American Power and the Future of Foreign Policy* (Yale University Press, 2009) and *Whistleblowers: Honesty in America from Washington to Trump* (Yale University Press, 2019). She has co-edited the open access textbook *Introduction to Digital Humanism* (Springer, 2024). Her next book, *Who Elected Big Tech?* is under contract with Yale University Press.

Annette Zimmermann is an Assistant Professor of Philosophy and an Affiliate Professor of Statistics at the University of Wisconsin-Madison, and co-leads UW-Madison's Uncertainty & AI research group. Zimmermann has held a Fellowship at Weizenbaum Institute Berlin (2024), a Technology & Human Rights Fellowship at Harvard University (2020–23), and a Postdoctoral Research Fellowship at Princeton University (2018–20). In addition to regularly providing expert advice to policy and industry audiences on cutting-edge topics in AI ethics and governance, Zimmermann is a frequent keynote speaker, such as at the AAAI/ACM AI Ethics and Society (AIES) conference (2023). Zimmermann was named on the 100 Brilliant Women in AI Ethics list (2021) and won the American Philosophical Association's Public Philosophy Op-Ed Prize (2021) as well as the Hastings Center for Bioethics' David Roscoe Award for an Early-Career Scholar's Essay on Science, Ethics, and Society (2020). Zimmermann holds a DPhil (PhD) from the University of Oxford.

Chiara Cordelli is Professor of Political Science at the University of Chicago and Affiliated Faculty in Philosophy. Her research interests focus on issues at the intersection of political philosophy and political economy. She is the author of *The Privatized State* (Princeton University Press, 2020), which was awarded the 2021 ECPR Political Theory Prize, and of *Privatocrazia* (Mondadori 2022), as well as the editor of *NOMOS* and the co-editor of *Philanthropy in Democratic Societies* (University of Chicago Press, 2016). Cordelli has held visiting positions at Stanford, Princeton, Harvard and at the École des hautes études en sciences sociales.

Mathias Risse is Berthold Beitz Professor in Human Rights, Global Affairs and Philosophy and Director of the Carr-Ryan Center for Human Rights Policy at Harvard University. His research is primarily in political philosophy and philosophy of technology, and he is currently at work on a book on Indigenous philosophies. He is the author or co-author of six books, including *On Global Justice* (Princeton University Press, 2012) and most recently *Political Theory of the Digital Age: Where Artificial Intelligence Might Take Us* (Cambridge University Press, 2023).

Nadia Urbinati is the Kyriakos Tsakopoulos Professor of Political Theory in the Department of Political Science at Columbia University. Her research interests focus on democratic theories and models of political representation via parties, populism, and lotteries. Her books include *Democratic Representation: Principles and Genealogy* (Chicago University Press, 2006), *Democracy Disfigured: Opinion, Truth and the People* (Harvard University Press, 2014), *Me the People: How Populism Transforms Democracy* (Harvard University Press, 2019), *Virtuous Hypocrisy* (Polity Press, 2025), and *The Lottocratic Mentality: Defending Democracy against Lottocracy*, co-authored with Cristina Lafont (Oxford University Press, 2024).

Regina Kreide is Professor of Political Theory and History of Ideas at the Justus Liebig University in Giessen, Germany, and one of the directors and speakers of the Collaborative Research Center 'Dynamics of Security', financed by the German Research Association (DFG). Her research interests focus on political and critical theory, especially on global (in)justice, (in)security, theory of democracy, property, and most recently AI. Her books include the *Habermas Handbook*, with H. Brunkhorst, C. Lafont (Columbia University Press, 2017) and *The Securitization of the Roma in Europe*, ed. with H. van Baar and A. Ivasiuc (Palgrave, 2018).

Ritwik Agrawal is a researcher at the University of Arizona, affiliated with the Philosophy Department and the Program in Cognitive Science. He designed and teaches the University of Arizona's first course on the Ethics of AI. He also designed and teaches a recurring core course on the Philosophy of Cognitive Science & AI for the Young India Fellowship Programme of Ashoka University and has been an Assistant Professor of Philosophy at

St. Stephen's College, India's premier undergraduate institution. He has discussed various aspects of AI on television news and as an invited speaker at several universities and corporations.

Thomas Christiano is Professor and Head of the Philosophy Department at the University of Arizona and Interim Head of the Political Economy and Moral Sciences Department. He works and teaches in moral and political philosophy. He has published papers and books on economic justice, international political theory, and democratic theory, including *The Constitution of Equality: Democratic Authority and Its Limits* (Oxford University Press, 2008).

Acknowledgements

I am grateful for support by the Vilas Faculty Early Career Investigator Award, the UW-Madison Fall Research Competition, UW-Madison's Department of Philosophy, and the OVCR. For early stage encouragement that even a fast-moving topic like AI could be a book rather than a paper, I thank Chuck Beitz and Rob Reich. For believing in my vision and supporting me to make it a reality, nobody has been more helpful than Peter Niesen and the team at MUP. Beyond my supportive colleagues at UW-Madison, I am grateful to Elliott Sober and Hayley Clatterbuck for encouraging me to impact audiences beyond academic philosophy. For giving me the best possible introduction in the US AI Policy world years ago at a pivotal moment when AI ethics and governance boomed, I am grateful to Ed Felten and Mihir Kshirsagar. For welcoming me into the interdisciplinary technology law community, I thank Ryan Calo and Ari Waldman. For insightful dialogue with interlocutors in computer science, I thank Hoda Heidari, Iyad Rahwan, Omer Reingold, and Juba Ziani. Early normative ideas underpinning this book were shaped by conversations with Ruha Benjamin, Josh Cohen, Daniel Innerarity, Hélène Landemore, Chad Lee-Stronach, Matthew Liao, José Luis Martí, Martin O'Neill, Annie Stilz, Thorsten Thiel, and Shannon Vallor. Key preparatory research happened in the context of a FAccT'24 workshop organized jointly with Nina Da Hora, Timnit Gebru, and Joana Varon. Key chapters were written during a visiting fellowship at Mila Miceli's inspiring research group at Weizenbaum Institute. Conversations with Carole Cadwalladr, Alex Hanna, Alondra Nelson and Christoph Neuberger inspired me to double down on the book's focus on questions of concrete strategic pressure points and elective political mobilization, as did audiences at AIES, Columbia, Harvard, Johannesburg, Max Planck Institute, the Simons Foundation, UC Berkeley, Yale, and other venues.

Editor's introduction

In a matter of months, the deployment of generative AI has changed the way we live. The roll-out of large language models such as ChatGPT has disrupted centuries-old practices of interaction in schools, universities, media, politics, and industry. Their virtually universal accessibility has deeply affected the common life-worlds of families, professions, associations, and political communities. Even the most inexperienced of users have witnessed the massive advances made by subsequent versions of generative AI, deployed in rapid succession. But the huge impact of ChatGPT and its competitors has only accentuated what philosophers, social theorists, and public intellectuals have long been urging: the near total pervasiveness of AI applications in everyday life makes it imperative to think about political responses to its influence. How can complex societies deal with the disruptive fallout and the huge risks unleashed by the uncontrolled provision of world-changing digital tools?

Most normative engagements with AI have so far focused on its ethical dimension; for example, on its material consequences for surveillance and discrimination, or its implications on our ideas of authenticity or creativity. In her evaluation of AI deployment, Annette Zimmermann departs from such more traditional routes of critique to launch an approach from democratic theory. According to Zimmermann, much of the problem of AI innovation results from deficits in the process of its deployment. Her key claim is built on the observation that AI companies have the power to unilaterally determine the public agenda by rolling out disruptive technologies, while leaving democratic governments and societies to pick up the pieces and deal with the consequences. She shows that the way tech companies disperse significant risks is inherently asymmetrical, that it lacks public justification and administers benefits very narrowly. Rather than evaluating particular features of AI from a normative perspective, Zimmermann asks about the political procedures in place that govern AI's deployment and the effects of AI on democratic processes of agenda setting more generally.

As Zimmermann observes, the danger of a 'tech capture' of public decision-making has massively increased thanks to a political climate hospitable to its entrepreneurs, with 'elected officials actively relinquish[ing] control to unelected tech industry leaders'. One need only point to the Trump/Musk 'DOGE' collusion of early 2025 to see the relevance of her diagnosis. The same trend is illustrated by the recent executive order on state AI regulation signed by Donald Trump in December 2025. The order seeks to halt any laws limiting artificial intelligence by the states, and creates a federal taskforce that is to challenge states' AI laws (Robins-Early and Kerr, 2025). The proposed moratorium has thus generally been regarded as a gift to a tech industry supporting right-wing policies in exchange for being given *carte blanche* in the development and management of AI and digital platforms. Zimmermann points out that even unbiased research on the 'tech capture' of political decision-making is currently endangered, since competitive research funding often comes from the very actors that should be under academic scrutiny, creating conflicts of interest and the expectation of tech-company-friendly results.

How can democratic communities regain control over their fates? Zimmermann's lead essay presents a bold new idea: by reclaiming the power to set the democratic agenda in the AI conversation. Within democratic theory, it is a deeply entrenched view that agenda-setting power should not be taken away from the people. Without such powers, how could the people influence the way their societies are heading, and how could governments be responsive to them? Yet the issue has not been explored theoretically with regard to the extraordinary impact of AI deployment, and has never been linked to the power of out-of-control tech companies.

The heart of the lead essay is a powerful philosophical reflection on agenda-setting, which is bound to inspire future democratic theory and practice. Zimmermann understands agenda-setting power as a way of increasing the public salience of a topic. This is more than just making sure certain proposals are out there for discussion: it is increasing the likelihood that a public body will take a decision on them. Of course, the decision could still go either way, but without the agenda-setting power of the people, their proposals will be 'crowded out' by the effective consequences of tech deployments in the first place. Zimmermann shows why neither top-down decisions over deployment nor voluntary self-regulation of the tech industry can be fully trusted, and instead puts her hope in institutions that ensure the anticipatory and permanent contestation of AI development. These innovatively designed institutions are what she calls 'informed sub-constituencies', to be equipped with a number of key powers. Such sub-constituencies would be made up of two very different kinds of expert citizens. Both groups would have AI-specific experience, either in virtue of advanced technological understanding and experience, or 'in virtue of possessing lived experiences that give them enhanced epistemic access to the nature, scope, and asymmetrical dispersion of relevant risks and harms', i.e. those on the receiving end of its potential prejudiced, discriminatory, misleading, or dangerous fall-out. These bodies – think of local or centralized citizens' assemblies, randomly made up of the two kinds of experts – are to have powers to audit companies, suggest revisions to safety standards, and access unreleased technology with a view to spotting risks. They would scrutinize developments such as the city-wide implementation of facial recognition surveillance, or the use of algorithmic decision procedures in the judiciary. Additionally, Zimmermann is prepared to entrust part of the regulatory agenda to citizen referenda, or at least keep the possibility of holding referenda in the background as a permanent threat to the industry. She puts her trust in the people rather than political officeholders because she thinks it 'much more likely that a small group of human decision-makers will disenfranchise and exploit the rest of the *demos* by deploying and benefitting from advanced AI tools, than it is that *demoi* will choose to delegate significant authority to AI proper'.

Despite Zimmermann's sustained warnings over democratic delegitimation through technological advances, she is no tech-skeptic. She insists that the demands that AI development imposes on us are unprecedented, but she rejects the defeatist attitude that AI cannot possibly be understood by the wider public, or that it would be impossibly complex to regulate its deployment. She is confident that democratizing AI will promote broader 'democratic resilience' and vice versa.

As Chiara Cordelli points out in her response to the lead essay, Zimmermann's conception of democracy is quite ambitious: she is not just concerned about fighting domination, but insists on re-establishing collective autonomy over our fates. What this means is brought out in an exchange with Cordelli and Regina Kreide on the 'world-disclosing' potential of AI. Both Cordelli and Kreide build their cases on insights from social philosophy, which they argue precede democratic theory and our thinking about justice. While Cordelli stresses that citizens are collectively disempowered by the 'alienating' character of techno-capitalist societies, Kreide claims that AI's inbuilt 'affirmative' tendencies reinforce conformist user behavior, thus moving us in an authoritarian direction. In reply, Zimmermann asserts the priority of political autonomy and unfettered democratic participation over ethical conceptions of non-alienated, nonconformist lives, and professes her neutrality as to the outcome of robustly democratic AI regulation processes. The openness of democratic futures is also a theme in the debate with Mathias Risse. Risse brings in alternative intellectual genres and traditions that may be thought helpful in addressing the future of humanity under the influence of AI, such as the Amish tradition or East Asian political thought. He doubts whether philosophy can come up with a unified, democracy- or justice-based theory to face its challenges. His approach stresses AI's unavoidable impact on the changing self-understanding of humankind. Zimmermann agrees, but stresses that the democracy-based arguments she offers do not by themselves logically imply anything about the normative desirability of further AI innovations. She remains therefore agnostic with regard to the direction in which oversight of AI deployment may steer democratic societies, asserting that 'the goal of democratizing AI is not necessarily linked to any particular evaluative view about whether further technological innovation in this area is all-things-considered desirable'.

In the debate with Allison Stanger's more tech-optimistic approach, as well as with Ritwik Agrawal and Thomas Christiano's political–economic reflections, Zimmermann agrees that income and power inequalities would have to be comprehensively addressed under any progressive approach. Stanger and Agrawal and Christiano point out the real-world harms of AI deployment in referring to impending mass layoffs or the havoc that independent weapons systems are causing, and therefore stress the need for strong top-down regulation. They suggest that international alliances will be necessary to rein in tech oligopolies, that federal AI governance frameworks need to be erected, unaccountable 'technocratic centralization' as in DOGE thwarted, and the tech capacities of office-holders and civil servants increased. These points are further reinforced by Nadia Urbinati's worry about the socioeconomic sources of asymmetrical risk distribution in AI agenda-setting. Recapitulating the moderately successful tech regulation approach in the European Union, Urbinati stresses the non-utopian character of Zimmermann's proposal. Her résumé is that 'economic and social inequalities are not beyond our amending proposals and are not so deep as to make asymmetry a factual blackmail that ordinary citizens cannot escape'.

If there is a common theme addressed in the six responses by philosophers and democratic theorists, it is how the nature of the questions raised by AI should impact on the embedding of Zimmermann's procedural suggestions in the skewed power structures of contemporary market societies. In her response to interlocutors, Zimmermann addresses the danger that has also been raised in recent anti-oligarchy literature (Arlen, 2019; Bagg, 2024): that exclusively proceduralist innovations, though feasible and not utopian in the negative sense of the term, could be helpless against structural asymmetries of power, dependent on undistorted processes of opinion-formation that are nowhere to be found. Is it not illusory to believe that democratic institutions will be capable of addressing the massive dangers emanating from unregulated AI deployment? Zimmermann flanks her account with recommendations of more traditional political tools, such as the unionizing of tech workers or the implementing of antitrust measures, and fields objections from assumptions of low citizen engagement or competence. She is very much aware of the regressive politics and fatigued mentalities of our day. Yet she counters that a more destructive 'illusion [is] that they [the people] are fatally uninformed and ultimately powerless against oligopolistic AI deployers'.

In sum, Zimmermann's bold and original approach is best understood as an essay in 'democratic underlaboring' (White, 2006; Patberg et al., 2025). She clears away some of the toxic underbrush of prejudice and attacks a mentality of helpless submission, gives a spirited defense of our democratic expectations even under transformed conditions, and develops problem-sensitive institutional suggestions. As Urbinati highlights, the challenges of our times create the need for intellectuals to raise their game on the technical side and acquire the expertise necessary to get involved in AI debates, for which Zimmermann herself could serve as a role model. At the same time, she joins Risse in insisting that philosophers should not assume the authority of experts, to which they have no further claims than all other democratic citizens. Zimmermann treats AI development not as our destiny, but as a complex tool. If it is to remain that, its deployment and implementations should be judged not for their own sake or the material interest of the industry, but by the human projects they serve.

Peter Niesen

References

Arlen, G. (2019), Aristotle and the problem of oligarchic harm: Insights for democracy. *European Journal of Political Theory* 18, no. 3: 393–414.

Bagg, S. (2024), *The Dispersion of Power. A Critical Realist Theory of Democracy*. Oxford University Press.

Patberg, M., Ahlhaus, S., and Eberl, O. (2025), The democratic underlabourer. From the domestic to the international level. *Journal of International Political Theory*, OnlineFirst.

Robins-Early, N. and Kerr, D. (2025), Trump signs executive order aimed at preventing states from regulating AI. The *Guardian*, 12 December. Available online at: https://www.theguardian.com/us-news/2025/dec/11/trump-executive-order-artificial-intelligence (last accessed April 8, 2026).

White, S. (2003), *The Civic Minimum: On the Rights and Obligations of Economic Citizenship*. Oxford University Press.

Part I

Lead essay

1

Hype

1.1 Gold rush

Trial-and-error, accidents, and surprises have always been a central component of innovation. This much is indisputable. In 1928, when Alexander Fleming returned from a holiday to his rather untidy laboratory, he made a surprising discovery. Before his departure, he had been negligent enough to leave a petri dish containing cultures of staphylococcus bacteria unattended on a laboratory bench. The petri dish was supposed to be stored in an incubator but had been left outside accidentally. It quickly became apparent that while Fleming was on holiday, the bacterial cultures had happened to become contaminated by a fungus, which was able to grow only because the petri dish had remained outside the incubator: *Penicillium notatum* mold.

As Fleming discovered during a series of experiments during the subsequent years, the fungus had powerful antibiotic properties not found in other molds. Penicillin could therefore be used to achieve something previously thought to be entirely infeasible by the wider public: quickly and effectively treating a large number of patients for a wide range of life-threatening bacterial infections, thus preventing diseases from spreading rapidly.[1] This is not the only example of surprising, rapid, and beneficial scientific innovation. Seemingly aimless experiments that throw caution

1 It is worth noting, of course, that public attitudes about the unforeseeable and surprising nature of this and other innovations do not necessarily track more contextually nuanced attitudes in the scientific community. Scholarly experts, unlike ordinary members of the public, might have seen Fleming's discovery as part of a more gradual – though not always perfectly predictable – process of innovation in this field, dating back at least to Paul Ehrlich's work on the concept of a 'magic bullet', and continuing on to a relatively long journey towards large-scale deployment in the 1940s, largely thanks to significant war-time public investment in fermentation methods that finally enabled the production of Penicillin at scale. For detailed discussion of the historical context of this case, see Bud (2007).

(or, in Fleming's case, tidiness) to the wind have often made the impossible possible, giving rise to sudden technological progress.

Obviously, not all forms of innovation take the route of similarly fortuitous accidents. Many high-risk scientific discoveries and innovations have, after they have been developed and deployed, triggered calls for regulation and even outright bans from the public and from their creators alike, such as in the case of genome editing and nuclear weapons technology. AI is no exception to this: there has been a cascade of public controversies surrounding AI innovations, from cases of algorithmic bias replicating social injustices and stereotypes, to concerns about unpredictable errors and misinformation; from deepfakes and other deceptive AI-generated content, to invasive data collection practices; from exploitative labor conditions experienced by content moderators and other tech workers, to increasing concerns about the environmental harms created by massive data centers requiring huge amounts of energy and finite natural resources.

These kinds of cases have bolstered calls from citizens, experts, and public officials to put regulatory guardrails on this technology. But at the same time, there is a widespread sense that AI has an almost 'magical' quality, one which, if channeled correctly, could change the world for the better – like other scientific advances have before. For that reason, many seem to think, we ought to be very cautious not to unduly stifle AI innovation. Tech industry leaders are not the only ones championing guardrail-free deployment: many regular citizens, too, tend to see AI as an *exceptional* phenomenon, one which can and should be exempt from the confines of regulation. And regulators themselves seem to feel that they cannot possibly keep up with such a rapidly evolving technology, often pointing out that ordinary mechanisms of institutional oversight and control are much too sluggish to meaningfully constrain AI. And so the AI gold rush continues – for now.

How did we get here? November 2022 marks a key trigger point for the most recent instantiation of the ongoing AI gold rush. Prior to that, Big Tech companies and start-ups had already been competing in a largely unregulated market to rapidly deploy algorithmic decision-making tools for relatively narrowly circumscribed use in specific social domains, like hiring, education, transportation, healthcare, criminal justice, and finance. But the rise of generative AI, such as large language models (LLMs), changed the game: generative AI made it possible to design much more sophisticated tools that could be deployed for all sorts of purposes to solve all sorts of different problems, rather than developing tools tailored to a pre-defined problem space, the latter of which by definition limits scalability and thus potential profit (Brown et al., 2020; Bender et al., 2021). This supercharged a deployment logic that had already existed to some extent in the AI market, but that crescendoed to an unprecedented pace that November with the successive mass deployment of ChatGPT, Bing AI, and competitor tools: *deploy first, ask for democratic control later* – if at all. When workers at OpenAI received instructions to build a chatbot as quickly as possible in November 2022, ChatGPT was deployed within thirteen (!) days (Roose, 2023). This reportedly triggered a 'Code Red' for Google, pushing the company to focus on deploying a competitive LLM shortly after the controversy over its LLM-based chatbot LaMDA (which, contrary to what a former Google engineer falsely claimed at the time, could not plausibly be construed as 'sentient' (*The Washington Post*, 2022))[2]. 'SOTA-chasing', the phenomenon often observed in the tech industry as part of which companies compete aggressively to try to achieve and maintain the 'state of the art' (SOTA) with their product, ensued: a relatively small number of companies able to avail themselves of the vast resources required to compete in this space further accelerated this deployment momentum, releasing tools like Claude (Anthropic) and Llama (Meta).

It is noteworthy, however, that rapid AI deployment is often part of a nervous dance between rushing to market and quickly pulling back entirely. When a demo of Meta's Galactica started generating false (yet authoritative-sounding) and stereotype-laden outputs in the winter of 2022, Meta took it offline a mere few days later (*Ars Technica*, 2022). This echoes Microsoft's earlier 2016 decision to deploy-but-immediately-take-down its 'teen-girl' chatbot Tay, which within hours of deployment started spewing racist and sex-related content (*MIT Technology Review*, 2016).

But despite these examples of Big Tech occasionally backtracking on deployment, it is important to appreciate that a decision to deploy powerful technology is not always easily reversible. Consider the example of DukeMTMC, a dataset of two million video frames recorded in public spaces on Duke University's campus and released publicly without proper privacy protections for people featured in the videos. In the aftermath, controversial research on computer vision-based surveillance technology utilized this data, and following public backlash, it was taken down in June 2019. Nonetheless, within the following year, at least 135 research papers utilized that dataset – and others derived from it – *after* it had been taken down (Peng, 2020). And even in scenarios involving more cautious deployment, in which a company or research team deploying AI does manage to reverse their deployment decision *and* successfully block public access to data and tools after that decision, it will not necessarily be true that such backtracking will stop competitors from developing similar tools. If anything, one deployer's choice to backtrack clears the market, thus opening up more opportunities for others to fill the vacuum.

2 For critical philosophical discussion, see Chalmers (2023).

Despite the dazzling speed and scale of recent generative AI deployment decisions, echoing earlier iterations of 'moving fast and breaking things', change is afoot. In a May 2023 Senate committee hearing, OpenAI's CEO Sam Altman explicitly asked US lawmakers to regulate generative AI deployment by creating a new oversight agency, modeled after existing federal institutions like the FDA, and imposing a novel licensing policy, which would restrict AI deployment capabilities to a small group of tech industry actors who meet a demandingly high bar of computational capabilities and resources. Both proposals, which were broadly well-received across the political spectrum, signify a radical shift in attitude towards government regulation of emerging technologies. In this way, they approximate (though they do not neatly overlap with) ongoing, more overt efforts to comprehensively regulate high-risk AI tools in other world regions, such as via the European Union's new AI Act.[3] Meanwhile, in a surprising and controversial move that seemed to contradict well-established, risk-friendly ideological leanings in the tech industry, a large number of industry leaders – including Elon Musk – recently called for a six-month deployment moratorium of AI in an open letter (Future of Life Institute, 2023), while individual countries pushed ahead with more heavy-handed, though temporary, bans (Robertson, 2023).

These developments have been the subject of much debate amongst scholars, industry practitioners, regulators, and the wider public. Increasingly, philosophers as well as political and social theorists have also started to focus on interrogating conceptual and normative issues

3 While my starting point for reflecting on generative AI deployment dynamics is the US context given the powerful global impact of US tech companies' deployment decisions, and while a book of this scope cannot claim to offer a *comprehensive* global comparative analysis of all contemporary generative AI deployment decisions and associated regulatory frameworks, the essay's normative arguments are not necessarily limited to the US context. Briefly, other examples of top-down AI regulation efforts across the world include the UK's strategy of empowering *existing* regulatory agencies – such as the Information Commissioner's Office (ICO), the Financial Conduct Authority (FCA), and the Competition and Markets Authority (CMA) – with more domain-specific oversight responsibilities rather than passing more comprehensive, cross-agency regulatory frameworks; as well as China's recently adopted binding legal frameworks pertinent to AI, such as the 2022 *Algorithmic Recommendation Regulation* and the 2023 *Generative AI Regulation*. Key American regulatory counterparts, which so far have been less focused on passing binding federal laws, as evidenced in President Biden's 2023 *Executive Order on Safe, Secure, and Trustworthy AI* as well as the *Blueprint for an AI Bill of Rights* released by the White House Office of Science and Technology Policy in 2022, the National Science and Technology Council's 2023 update to the *National AI Research and Development Strategy*, and the National Institute of Standards and Technology's *Artificial Intelligence Risk Management Framework* (2023).

regarding AI, including AI's potential to spread misinformation and propaganda, to exacerbate social biases and inequalities, to yield unexplainable results, and to lure vulnerable, suggestible users into damaging behavior. While most contributions have focused on applied *ethical* questions in this area, there are a few notable recent examples that have put – as I plan to do in this essay – a stronger emphasis on the *political* philosophy of AI (Buolamwini and Gebru, 2018; Eubanks, 2018; Noble, 2018; Zuboff, 2018; Benjamin, 2019; Bender et al., 2021; Crawford, 2021; Reich et al., 2021; Zerilli, 2021; Risse, 2023; Simons, 2023; Coeckelbergh, 2024; Vallor, 2024).

In addition, philosophical commentators have focused on the question of whether generative AI might at some point move us closer to AI consciousness (although many experts take the view that current models are far from that) (Chalmers, 2010), and what this would imply for the moral status of hypothetical future artificial agents (Liao, 2020) – as well as about the *long-term* consequences of AI development and deployment for existential risks for humanity. This is a worry not only articulated by philosophers (Bostrom, 2014), but also by voices in the effective altruism community as well as prominent tech industry leaders: 'Godfather of AI' Geoffrey Hinton, after leaving his position at Google, warned in a BBC Newsnight interview that '[b]etween 5 and 20 years from now there's a probability of about a half that we'll have to confront the problem of [AI] trying to take over' (BBC Newsnight, 2024). Similarly, a public statement by the San Francisco-based Center for AI Safety – signed by the CEOs of DeepMind, OpenAI, and Anthropic, amongst others – declares: '[m]itigating the risk of extinction from AI should be a global priority alongside other societal-scale risks such as pandemics and nuclear war' (Center for AI Safety, 2023). Palantir CEO Alexander Karp's July 2023 guest essay for *The New York Times* calls this 'our Oppenheimer moment', although instead of embracing the idea of halting deployment increasingly popular in some long-term AI safety circles, he swiftly follows this up with a plea to instead double down on the 'AI arms race' to safeguard 'Western liberal democracy' by fostering close cooperation between tech industry and governments when it comes to deploying military and intelligence AI tools (Karp, 2023).[4]

4 Obviously, Karp's claims here exemplify a rather specific political view which the public would do well to subject to critical scrutiny – it is far from clear whether accelerating an 'AI arms race' between the West and other geopolitical forces, rather than aiming for enhanced global cooperation, is at all desirable; nor is it in any way obvious that close proximity between the tech industry on the one side and the governmental intelligence and security apparatus on the other, as championed by Karp, would make us more rather than less free.

Arguably, such alarmist and ideologically specific statements by tech industry leaders like Karp are not exactly representative of the views of philosophers and other scholars working on assessing long-term AI risks. But even in light of more nuanced philosophical contributions, other scholars have – in my view, reasonably – worried that discourse around hypothetical future forms of AI may unduly inflate contemporary AI's real capabilities, a problem exacerbated by the fact that tech companies often lack incentives to communicate AI's limitations in a sober and balanced way (Narayanan and Kapoor, 2024). And they have compellingly argued that there is a risk of diverting our attention away from an equally – if not more – important and urgent question: what about the shorter-term, immediate impact of AI on society, which often sharply exacerbates social injustices? After all, that impact is visible and well-documented right here, in the present moment, unlike uncertain future harms that may never eventuate, and that do not harm currently existing people (Birhane and Van Dijk, 2020; Gebru and Torres, 2024). I am broadly sympathetic to this approach in terms of urgent moral and political priorities, though I do not think that this requires us to deny that more speculative AI safety research is warranted, too. More widely, I think we have good reasons to resist the strict dichotomy between 'short-term' and 'long-term' research foci with respect to AI: after all, issues considered by those allegedly adopting a 'short-term' perspective often pertain to notoriously complex, long-lasting, structural problems in society, such as structures of racism, sexism, and other forms of oppression. Arguably, failing to address those problems will, in the long run, have deeply corrosive – and, yes, possibly existential – consequences.

One urgent question highlighting societal risks that have *both* this short-term *and* this long-term character is the one motivated by my earlier discussion: what are the political and moral implications of rushing generative AI to market prematurely and at scale here and now – and whose current and future interests in shaping our joint future are best served by the current generative AI gold rush? That question is philosophically underexplored, and it will therefore take center stage in this essay as I work towards making progress on the complex question of why and how to subject AI to real democratic control.

1.2 The tools and their makers

Due to the specific technological features of generative AI tools, this powerful new technology raises new and pressing philosophical questions in its own right, and thus merits sustained philosophical scrutiny itself.

One thing that makes generative AI different from previous, more narrow forms of AI and machine learning – focused on solving tasks in specific domains such as algorithmic decision-making in criminal justice, healthcare, insurance, and transportation – is the fact that generative AI is a domain-unspecific technology. We can use generative AI tools to solve complex, varied tasks across different domains of application, and to do so at an unprecedented scale and speed; and most importantly, to move from simply making predictions about a circumscribed dataset to creating entirely new content based on data on which the tool was trained. For this reason, the magnitude of generative AI's impact on people's lives may well be greater and more multifaceted in comparison to other forms of AI – and so also the associated risks and benefits.

At the same time, we must not forget to consider the more immediate, less technology-focused problem of how to think about the *people* who have vast amounts of power over how this technology is developed and deployed. What do they believe – and what are their normative and strategic goals?

When an earlier version of ChatGPT, GPT-2, was released in 2019, OpenAI initially blocked full public access to the tool, on the grounds that the technology was 'too dangerous to release' (the *Independent*, 2020a). Since then, a radically different deployment strategy has taken hold in Big Tech: deploy as quickly as possible and as publicly as possible – without much (or any) red tape. Tech practitioners tend to justify this by arguing that improving this technology, and mitigating the risks associated with it, requires massive amounts of data in the form of user feedback. Microsoft's Bing Blog states in a recent post:

> The only way to improve a product like this, where the user experience is so much different than anything anyone has seen before, is to have people like you using the product and doing exactly what you all are doing. We know we must build this in the open with the community; this can't be done solely in the lab. Your feedback about what you're finding valuable and what you aren't, and what your preferences are for how the product should behave, are so critical at this nascent stage of development (Microsoft Bing Blogs, 2023).

That is one way of putting it. Another way is this: the status quo in the AI market is that technology companies who have oligopolistic control over generative AI further increase their wealth and power by benefiting from the fact that a growing number of members of the wider public voluntarily use, and thus help optimize, their products – for free. This *disperses the risks* associated with rolling out and improving these tools maximally widely, while allowing actors empowered with developing, deploying, and procuring these tools to *concentrate* – and maintain control over – *the profits* resulting from generative AI innovation (Acemoglu and Johnson, 2023).[5]

Tech industry practitioners might reply that that itself does not mean that Big Tech is engaged in *unfair advantage taking* when it comes to improving generative AI post-deployment. After all, generative AI innovation may ultimately benefit *all of us* in many ways – in fact, the benefits for humanity may be 'so unbelievably good that it's hard for me to even imagine', says Sam Altman, OpenAI's CEO, in a recent *NYT* interview. If that is the case, then a wide distribution of risks coupled with an initially narrow distribution of benefits looks less objectionable, as long as those benefits trickle down eventually.

Whether they will, however, is far from clear. Given the current regulatory vacuum and minimal public oversight over rapid generative AI deployment, oligopolistic actors have little incentive to allow themselves to be curtailed and held to account by governments and the wider public later. It would better serve public interests, then, to shift from passively observing rushed deployment efforts and hoping for widespread, beneficial downstream effects later on, towards actively determining whether there are any domains of AI use in which rushed deployment needs to be restricted.

1.3 Taking control

While the diagnosis that contemporary AI is subject to some type of democratic legitimacy deficit is an intuitively plausible one, a more specific analysis of this problem is arguably available. Ongoing dynamics of AI deployment are philosophically and politically interesting because they are,

5 It should be noted that this point does not imply a predictive claim to the effect that the development and deployment of AI will necessarily continue to proceed in a highly concentrated market. Instead, my view is simply that there currently exists an oligopolistic concentration of power and wealth amongst a few key corporate actors (at least in, though possibly not limited to, the US context) that possess the kinds of vast computational capacities needed to design and deploy state-of-the-art generative AI. However, this may very well not be the case going forward: the future trajectory of present-day oligopolies will be in part a function of regulatory and democratic interventions into the AI deployment landscape. Therefore, my aim here is not to predict – or to merely assume as an undefended premise – that oligopolistic power in Big Tech will persist long-term, but rather to offer an analysis of what kinds of democratic agenda-setting interventions are available, and what their respective future consequences might be for democratic constituencies' ability to keep oligopolies in check. For an in-depth empirical analysis of concentrations of wealth and power amongst tech industry actors, see Acemoglu and Johnson (2023).

as I will argue in this essay, a particular instance of undemocratic *agenda-setting*. AI deployers, who are usually corporate actors not subject to direct democratic authorization and accountability, are currently able to unilaterally set technology regulation and technology ethics agendas simply by developing tools and granting public access to them, while simultaneously offloading responsibilities for *ex post* harm mitigation onto government actors and democratic constituencies.

This turns a core tenet of democratic control over decisions that affect *demos* members' morally and politically weighty interests on its head: rather than merely issuing reactive policy and regulatory decisions *ex post* in response to decisions made by corporate actors, democratic constituencies – ideally – seek to exercise active, *ex ante* control about which policy options and choices require democratic deliberation and contestation. Once democratic constituencies relinquish the power to effectively set agendas, and find themselves locked in a dynamic of reacting to a (possibly unduly narrow and risky) cluster of options presented to them by an unrepresentative and excessively powerful subset of the democratic constituency, they relinquish an essential feature of democracy itself: the right to exercise free and equal control over the nature and scope of decisions shaping their shared future. Rather than uncritically accepting *AI exceptionalism*, the view that AI is a highly unusual policy domain that cannot possibly be subjected to democratic contestation and control, we – as democratic constituencies – must identify ways of taking charge, inspired by the ways in which *other* complex policy domains have been democratized.

There is a rich body of work in political philosophy and democratic theory focused on interrogating the conceptual and normative dimensions of agenda-setting in democratic constituencies more generally. However, no contribution to this well-established literature to date has explored the full potential of utilizing these theoretical foundations to systematically analyze how contemporary processes of *AI* deployment may align with, and differ from, *other* instances of (un-)democratic agenda-setting; to articulate which specific democratic *values* ought to guide efforts to subject AI deployment to democratic control; and to specify which concrete *political practices and institutional transformations* can best approximate such values. This essay seeks to address each one of these urgent research gaps, both in the lead essay and in conversation with interlocutors.

1.4 The roadmap

My argument proceeds as follows. Chapter 2 ('Progress') explores what those who have outsized power over the direction of state-of-the-art AI say they *believe*: about innovation, about caution, about AI's potential to benefit – or endanger – everyone. Experimenting, tinkering, and shaking up the status quo has long been at the core of the Silicon Valley mindset, painting a straightforward picture of why tech industry leaders like to deploy new technologies fast and deal with the consequences later. But now that moving fast and breaking things is not the only game in town anymore, and at least some Big Tech CEOs are suddenly professing a desire for nuanced regulation, what can we learn from the ways in which ideas of technological progress have been evolving – and from the extent to which those ideas have been (mis-)aligned with actual deployment choices?

Such ideas, I argue, signal a superficial shift in publicly expressed attitudes – which distracts from, and possibly obfuscates, the fact that AI deployment dynamics remain largely under the control of industry actors. Chapter 3 ('Risk') explores in more depth why the locus and direction of market power continue to pose not just a moral, but also a political problem for AI deployment. *Dispersions* of risk associated with generative AI and related technologies, coupled with intensifying concentrations of power, wealth, and information amongst an oligopoly of industry actors, create a pernicious *asymmetry* in society: one that indicates a persistent democratic legitimacy deficit in current AI policy. Building on widely held philosophical views to the effect that even the imposition of *mere risks* can be wrongful, I argue that specific distributions of such risks exacerbate such wrongs. Risk dispersions of this kind stand in need of much more thorough public justification and democratic control – even if they coincide with, as a common point of view suggests, wide societal dispersions of AI-related benefits.

Chapter 4 ('Agendas') provides the theoretical building blocks for tackling the democratic legitimacy deficit created by the present asymmetry. Here, I build on, and extend, conceptual and normative resources in political philosophy and democratic theory concerning one particular democratic participation pathway: *agenda-setting*. After motivating the basic intuition that legitimate democratic participation extends far beyond participation in highly regulated *electoral* processes, I show why the decision to deploy some new AI tool can itself be an instance of exercising significant agenda-setting power. For this reason, current dynamics of AI deployment pose a distinct and philosophically interesting democratic problem, given that industry-based deployers are usually neither directly nor indirectly democratically *authorized* and given that they *de facto* have largely *uncontested* agenda-setting power: AI deployment is currently a highly anti-competitive agenda-setting environment. What, then, should democratic constituencies do in response? I argue that democratically legitimate AI deployment requires the implementation of *fair participatory procedures* in conjunction with minimal outcome constraints and with mechanisms that are sensitive to asymmetrical dispersions of risk.

Before developing an account of what such procedures ought to look like in practice, we must interrogate which strategies are currently being adopted to subject AI deployment to greater control – and what their respective shortcomings are. Chapter 5 ('Strategies') analyzes the complex landscape of different deployment regulation strategies proposed recently, identifying two heterogeneous clusters. On the one hand, there are strategies focused on regulating deployment *itself* by utilizing the top-down power of government regulators, such as licensing and pre/post-deployment safety review models, possibly under the auspices of newly created government agencies and institutions, or – in contrast – heavy-handed deployment moratoria. On the other hand, there are strategies focused on *changing, ex post,* how democratic constituencies *respond* to existing or ongoing deployment decisions, possibly by opening up channels for bottom-up democratic input and by trying to initiate larger-scale legal transformation on the basis thereof. Besides that, I also identify – and set aside – a third, half-baked strategy: voluntary self-regulation by tech industry actors. My preferred view departs from all of the former strategies, though it incorporates elements of the first two to chart a more productive path. That path, I argue, better serves the end of democratic legitimacy in a rapidly evolving policy environment.

How can this theoretical alternative, designed to enhance opportunities to exercise democratic agenda-setting counterpower, be realized in real political practice? Chapter 6 ('Democracy') develops a *playbook* for achieving this aim. As it turns out, from harnessing the power of non-traditional intermediary associations and direct participatory mechanisms to strengthening worker power while keeping oligopolistic power in check, democratic constituencies can – but have so far largely chosen not to – avail themselves of a wide range of already available political strategies. I show that several of these strategies have already proven to be successful in other complex, high-stakes policy domains, but their resources remain dangerously untapped. Meanwhile, *AI exceptionalist* thinking further takes hold, distorting our political imagination of how much democratic control is already possible. In response to this problem, I explore and defend the view that more meaningful democratic control over AI is within reach, even in our imperfect, messy, and unjust real-world political arenas – if we collectively choose to take action now.

Chapter 7 looks beyond the current moment in generative AI deployment. I identify larger-scale normative implications of my view on democratizing AI deployment that will remain applicable for future iterations of next-generation AI innovation and related emerging technologies. While any given wave of AI innovation, in keeping with Moore's Law, has unfolded at an ever-increasing pace, and while future AI innovations are predictable only to a limited extent, I argue that we can draw more general, value-based insights from an analysis of current AI deployment dynamics that equip us with a better conceptual toolbox for subjecting AI deployment to critical scrutiny. This also reveals a number of philosophically rich open questions that call out for further conceptual and normative inquiry, including by my interlocutors in this volume.

2

Progress

'Microsoft has had clear competitors in the past. It's a good thing we have museums to document that.' (Bill Gates: Computer History Museum, 2004)

'We believe markets are generative, not exploitative. [...] The techno-capital machine works for us. We believe in making everyone rich, everything cheap, and everything abundant.' (Andreessen, 2023)

To those not actively involved in the technology industry, generative AI's rapid rise may have seemed like a sudden yet inevitable occurrence. Following its deployment in November 2022, ChatGPT was suddenly everywhere: regular citizens who had not thought much about AI before started using it to write authoritative-sounding work emails and witty social media captions, to generate workout plans, dad jokes, and sheet music, and to help write clever essays for their college classes. Soon, it became impossible to ignore generative AI: not only because of its benefits to users without any computer science background, but also because it predictably triggered concerns about whether these tools are simply 'too smart', and whether they might make vast numbers of jobs redundant.

Either way, the public response to ChatGPT and tools like it acknowledged that simply opting out of interacting with generative AI was becoming less feasible by the minute. Most internet users became aware that any image, text, or audio they encountered online may possibly be AI-generated. AI took over work and education, too: businesses and universities started integrating generative AI into their standard workflows and encouraging employees to use AI-powered productivity tools, such as Microsoft's Co-Pilot, deployed since March 2023 across all MS Office applications. And the structure of ubiquitous everyday online activities changed forever: when Google rolled out its AI search feature in May 2023, online search shifted from a task requiring users to read and evaluate a number of top-ranked sources one by one to being presented with an

AI-generated summary of search results at the very top of the screen right in the search interface.

In short, generative AI is now everywhere, all at once. Is this a selfless act of service, on the part of major tech companies, in pursuit of ease, universal access, and abundance for all? Unsurprisingly, the story is more complicated than that. Just because cutting-edge tools are at our fingertips, that does not mean that they are truly in our hands. 'Democratizing AI' requires more than giving everyone the ability to use it in some way.

This chapter proceeds from the claim that a closer look at which visions of progress drive AI deployment decisions, and which political ideologies underpin them, proves instructive for analyzing ongoing AI deployment dynamics in more depth. Exploring examples of public expressions of beliefs about AI regulation by key tech industry leaders will provide the basis for the basic descriptive claim that there is a widely shared current (though possibly changing) attitude amongst tech industry practitioners and decision-makers that favors unilateral, speedy, scaled-up, and not comprehensively regulated generative AI deployment (Crawford, 2021: 211–227; Reich et al., 2021: 3–24).

As it will turn out, however, recent public statements by Silicon Valley thought leaders also exhibit a number of complex political and philosophical shifts and ruptures. In this sense, 'Silicon Valley ideology' is not plausibly a monolith anymore. Currently dominant lines of thinking include *right-wing libertarianism* and different forms of *longtermism*, such as *effective altruism* and *effective accelerationism*. Recent public statements by tech leaders depart significantly, and in increasingly different political directions, from the simpler, older, and more homogeneous version of 'move fast and break things' ideology, thus complicating the view of Silicon Valley that has long taken hold in the public imagination.

Nonetheless, despite recent nuanced shifts, examining the larger philosophical context of different influential political orientations amongst tech industry practitioners reveals that important similarities remain across seemingly opposing camps. Unfortunately, these similarities point to a view of society and technological progress that, from the perspective of democratic legitimacy, risks taking us backwards. More specifically, they provide evidence in support of this thesis:

> THE SHIFT: In the past, most tech industry practitioners used to be hostile to technology regulation on the grounds that the latter may stifle innovation. But in the wake of the generative AI deployment rush, many have started to advocate for regulatory interventions, from precision regulation to heavy-handed deployment moratoria. This seems to signal a considerable attitudinal shift. However, this shift has not fundamentally curbed unilateral, fast-paced, and scaled-up deployment dynamics. In fact, these dynamics have intensified.

2.1 Beliefs and choices

Despite the widespread impression that generative AI simply *happened to us*, all of a sudden and with full force, the truth is that someone *made* generative AI happen in this way. The fact that generative AI tools are now so ubiquitous is no accident. It is the result of a series of deliberate decisions – decisions that could have turned out differently, and that could have been made by different decision-makers. The decisions resulting in the AI deployment dynamic in which we *currently* find ourselves were made primarily by tech industry leaders rather than regulators or citizens. This raises two questions. Descriptively, what do those who have the power to deploy state-of-the art generative AI believe? And, conceptually, what do the decisions they have made so far – as well as the roads they chose *not* to take – tell us about the notions of technological and societal progress that are driving much current AI deployment dynamics?

Of course, it would be much too quick to say that the fact that some agent endorses some set of political and philosophical beliefs about AI is necessarily a *causal explanation* for why that agent ends up taking any particular action regarding AI deployment. This is true in a more general way: people take all sorts of actions that have no direct causal link to their background beliefs and assumptions. Entirely external influences and constraints can force our hand when choosing what action we actually take (Amy can disagree strongly with tax laws but still end up begrudgingly paying her taxes to avoid legal repercussions), and external influences can make us fail to successfully align our actions with our own beliefs even if we want to do so (Amy can wholeheartedly believe that she should not drink alcohol under any circumstances, and nonetheless end up drinking alcohol due to overwhelming peer pressure).

Nothing in my analysis, then, hinges on whether, in all cases or even in any specific case, there is in fact a direct *causal* relationship linking some set of *actions* – such as the decision to deploy AI fast and at scale – to some set of political and philosophical *views* – be it libertarian normative beliefs about the limited scope of permissible state regulation and the power of the market; be it effective altruist beliefs that AI safety concerns may warrant temporary deployment moratoria, but that prospective future benefits of deployment could ultimately outweigh present-day risks of harm; be it effective accelerationist beliefs that AI should be deployed even faster and without regulatory hindrances despite salient risks of harm; or be it more general beliefs about the comparative importance of unconstrained innovation.

Although deployment actions often do seem to align closely with political and philosophical views articulated by tech industry leaders, attesting to their outsized power to pursue their goals even if those goals do not always track the broader public's preferences, the fact that one deployment decision is made over another may not always be solely and directly attributable to deployers' beliefs. *External*, non-ideological factors may also drive deployment decisions, such as market dynamics of competition.[1] And in any case, it is not always possible to know to what extent a given tech CEO's public statements are an *accurate* reflection of their actual beliefs.

Even if a clear causal link between prevalent beliefs and actual deployment decisions is not discernible beyond the shadow of a doubt in all cases, this does not undercut the *descriptive* claim that views about AI deployment publicly endorsed by Silicon Valley decision-makers do often map onto a larger background of specific philosophical and political views. While the analysis of ideologies is admittedly not particularly *en vogue* in contemporary analytic political philosophy, I think that it is hard to deny that real-world decisions to deploy AI at a specific time, speed, and scale *de facto* overlap with a lot of the broader stated beliefs and background assumptions of those with the power to shape AI deployment. This includes beliefs and assumptions about technology's role in improving human life, about the comparative value of unrestrained liberty in relation to other values, like justice and wellbeing, and about our supposed strengths and flaws as humans, which may or may not be enhanceable by advanced technology. The point is that ideas are not just ideas – they give us useful *context* for understanding the actions taking in pursuit of (and in opposition to) them and understanding why recent actions taken to *deploy* generative AI may have followed such an accelerated and reckless pattern.

The *normative* claim motivated intuitively by the descriptive claim above, and to be explored in more depth in the coming chapters, is simply that the locus and direction of the power to deploy AI *matter*, and that they matter specifically from the standpoint of democratic legitimacy. Much like ideas and beliefs do not simply float in a consequence-free political vacuum, decisions about where, when, and why to deploy technology do not either. Such decisions track higher-order normative commitments, whether explicit or implicit. Rapid, large-scale AI deployment is not the only possible option to be chosen; other forms of deployment are in principle available. Each decision, at any given point in time, to deploy some new AI tool *in this way* signals a commitment to a particular set of *goals*, and alignment with

1 Here, I allow for the (in my view, likely) possibility that in general not all market choices have an ideological component, though many dynamics in the *generative AI market* specifically – such as SOTA-chasing – do seem to be driven by actors who also voice support for ideological beliefs about the moral and political importance of accelerating AI deployment.

particular visions of what the *purpose* of technological progress is, neither one of which is necessarily politically neutral.[2]

2.2 Freedom, speed, and ... long-term caution?

Over the past few decades, Silicon Valley has adopted a relatively straightforward public image: a haven for young, nerdy, and entrepreneurial-but-well-intentioned tinkerers. Those who championed what scholars have called 'the Californian Ideology' combined an ethos of experimentation with a commitment to the view that technological progress can and will be beneficial to society (Barbrook and Cameron, 1995).[3] On this view, government regulation objectionably stifles the freedom to experiment and innovate,[4] and that disruption by the bold few is preferable to long-winded deliberation by the unduly cautious many.[5] A characteristic combination of economic libertarianism and social progressivism, at least in a thin 'diversity and inclusion' sense, has long aptly characterized Silicon Valley and beyond: both with respect to tech leaders' stated views, and with respect to the public's perception.[6]

But things have changed. For one, tech industry leaders have been less and less concerned about signaling public support for socially progressive positions and candidates. Elon Musk has invested 75 billion dollars into his

2 For a canonical statement of the view that technologies can reflect political assumptions and preferences, see Winner (1980: 121–136). On the related, more general argument that entirely 'value-free' objectivity in scientific reasoning more broadly is neither possible nor desirable, see influential contributions by feminist philosophers of science such as Douglas (2009: esp. 115–155), and Longino (2004: 127–142).

3 This foundational text in early critical technology studies champions a conclusion well-aligned with the spirit of my own argument: 'It is now necessary for us to assert our own future – if not in circumstances of our own choosing. [...] We need to find ways to think socially and politically about the machines we develop. While learning from the can-do attitude of the Californian individualists, we also must recognize that the potentiality of hypermedia can never solely be realized through market forces.'

4 For an influential early statement of this view, see Barlow (2019: 5–7). It was written largely in response to the Telecommunications Act of 1996, which expanded the reach of US regulatory power to internet communications for the first time.

5 In an influential essay, Peter Thiel states that '[t]he fate of our world may depend on the effort of a single person who builds or propagates the machinery of freedom that makes the world safe for capitalism' (Thiel, 2009).

6 A recent study by Broockman et al. (2019) focusing on the attitudes of over 600 tech leaders supports my analysis of the standard social progressivism–economic libertarianism nexus that used to characterize tech elites.

pro-Trump 'America PAC', which is supported by a cluster of influential tech founders and venture capitalists (*The Washington Post*, 2024). While the tech industry as a whole has of course not universally moved to the right, it is noticeable that popular industry views have undergone a shift. For example, classic libertarian skepticism of state authority and governmental overreach, traditionally a core component of Silicon Valley ideology, does not attract near-universal support anymore: Palantir CEO Alex Karp explicitly supports state authority – as long as it is Western state authority – while also mirroring the 'anti-woke' rhetoric characteristic of the contemporary alt-right:

> I think the central risk to Palantir and America and the world is a regressive way of thinking [...] corrupting [...] our institutions that calls itself 'progressive,' but actually – and is called 'woke' – but is actually a form of a thin pagan religion. [...] There are lots of questions about why we are so active in defending the values of the West, that our belief that the West is a superior way to live, and our ways of organizing around that are the reason why our products are transformative' (Palantir Technologies Inc., 2024).

While it would be too hasty and overly general to attribute extreme-right views to tech leaders as a group, influential libertarian figures like venture capitalist Marc Andreessen do signal some alignment with the ideological foundations of right-wing *authoritarianism* when he approvingly paraphrases a 1909 Italian 'Futurist Manifesto' (Marinetti, 1909) that would go on to become a key reference point for Mussolini's fascist movement:

> Beauty exists only in struggle. There is no masterpiece that has not an aggressive character. Technology must be a violent assault on the forces of the unknown, to force them to bow before man (Andreessen, 2023).

Relatedly, venture capitalist Balaji Srinivasan has argued that San Francisco's tech industry should embrace utilizing the power of coercive state authority, and bribe politically friendly members of law enforcement to drive 'woke' progressives out of the city and out of local government (Republicans, by contrast, would still be tolerated):

> What I am really calling for is something like tech Zionism. [...] Take total control of your neighborhood. Push out all Blues. Tell them they're ... unwelcome. [...] Reds should be welcomed there. [...] A huge win would be a Gray Pride parade [...] That would start to say: 'Whose streets? Our streets!' [...] Grays should embrace the police, okay? All-in on the police. What does that mean? That [means] banquets. That means every policeman's son, daughter, wife, cousin, you know, sibling, whatever, should get a job at a tech company in security (Moment of Zen Podcast, 2023).

Another increasingly popular Silicon Valley libertarian line of thinking involves creating *new* state structures ('network states': Srinivasan, 2022) rather than instrumentalizing the brute force of existing ones: the problem, on this view, is not state authority itself, it is that the wrong people have authority. In response to this problem, supporters of this view quietly buy up swaths of land in the Bay Area, preparing to create independent cities in which tech elites will be able to live and work in luxury while being governed by industry-friendly officials (*The New York Times*, 2023). Similarly, Thiel-backed initiative *Praxis* aims to 'build the future of the west' and to become 'the next America, built on the internet' (Praxis website, n.d.). Prospective Praxis members pledge to 'build a nation that embodies strength, virtue, and innovation together, for our present and our children's future', and to relocate to an independent new city-state in the Mediterranean 'when the time comes' (Praxis Citizen Pledge). Overall, it is clear that the normative core of Silicon Valley right-wing libertarianism is still right-wing; but it is far removed from the spirit of old-school libertarianism as such.

In addition, the – very different – view of *effective altruism* (EA) continues to enjoy considerable popularity in Silicon Valley. The view was originally focused on our moral duty to maximize good outcomes when engaging in charitable giving to fix global problems – but it, too, has evolved. It now prioritizes our duty to mitigate long-term existential risks posed by AI, while deprioritizing other problems. As longtermist Nick Bostrom puts it:

> A non-existential disaster causing the breakdown of global civilization is, from the perspective of humanity as a whole, a potentially recoverable setback: a giant massacre for man, a small misstep for mankind (Bostrom, 2009: 196).

Effective altruism's cautious attitude to AI safety in light of fears concerning existential risks has triggered an increasingly vocal backlash: *effective accelerationism*, the view that we should throw caution to the wind and advance AI as fast as possible. Andreessen, a key thought leader in this movement, couples this view with the deterministic claim that this will be to everyone's benefit in a more civilized, superior future:

> We are told to denounce our birthright – our intelligence, our control over nature, our ability to build a better world. [...] Technology is the glory of human ambition and achievement [...] We can advance to a far superior way of living, and of being. [...] Productivity growth, powered by technology [...] improv[es] the material wellbeing of the entire population. [...] This is why we are not still living in mud huts, eking out a meager survival and waiting for nature to kill us [...] this is why our descendants will live in the stars (Andreessen, 2023).

This is not just a normative view about technology's place in society. It is also a normative view about human nature, or – in Andreessen's words – our duty to 'become technological supermen'; one that is noticeably chauvinistic:

> We believe in the natural human drive to make things, to gain territory, to explore the unknown [...] we are *conquerors*. We believe in nature, but we also believe in *overcoming* nature. We are not primitives, cowering in fear of the lightning bolt. We are the apex predator; the lightning works for us. We believe in *greatness* [...] in the romance of technology [...] the eros of the train, the car, [...] the neural network, the rocket, the split atom (Andreessen, 2023).

These developments, too, indicate a significant attitudinal shift to the right end of the political spectrum, away from earlier and somewhat less grandiose versions of Silicon Valley ideology.

2.3 One step forward, two steps back

Ultimately, although the political and philosophical views distinctively popular amongst tech industry decision-makers covered in this chapter are part of a rather wide political spectrum, and although they point to – sometimes dramatically – different normative conclusions regarding emerging technologies and their place in society, they do share a number of important similarities (Gebru and Torres, 2024),[7] beyond the general observation that these views are normally held by people who benefit (or might hope to benefit) personally from the concentration of power and wealth around innovative technology.

First, and most obviously, supporters of several dominant Silicon Valley ideologies explicitly endorse a deterministic view of the positive power of the market.[8] Both effective accelerationists and right-wing libertarians (the latter of which may, but need not, be accelerationists) think that

7 In virtue of these and other similarities, Gebru and Torres – as part of a much more extensive argument – group the views discussed in this chapter as well as a number of other views under the label 'TESCREAL': 'transhumanism, extropianism, singularitarianism, cosmism, rationalism, effective altruism, and longtermism', arguing that these views are 'overlapping and interconnected' (Gebru and Torres, 2024).

8 In critically exploring different tech industry beliefs about the virtues of unrestrained markets, I need not commit myself to the view that market competition *as such* is objectionable. In fact, my view – which I expect to be relatively uncontroversial, and therefore not in urgent need of a standalone defense – is that fair competition is generally preferable to oligopolistic and monopolistic *erosions* of fair competition. The fact that the views critically discussed here claim to champion competition, but often fail to offer normative grounds to resist outcome distributions that undermine their own stated aim, is another reason to subject them to critical scrutiny.

technological progress will, guided by the (ostensibly inherently objective) invisible hand of the market, be a *net positive* for society. Even if innovation requires the imposition of some type of harm on some subset of the population, the thinking goes, the benefits of doing so will far outweigh its moral costs, because the market will fix larger-scale societal problems like poverty, lack of knowledge, entrenched conflict, hard labor, and so on.

It does of course seem like contemporary effective altruists focused on AI safety are the one ideological outlier in this context, given that many of them have publicly urged for far-reaching guardrails on AI design and deployment, even if market dynamics forcefully push against deployment restrictions and regulations (MacAskill, 2022).[9] But it is worth noting that earlier forms of effective altruism preceding the movement's (now dominant) focus on AI and associated existential risks adopted a remarkably uncritical perspective towards market power: leading effective altruists like MacAskill have long championed ideas like taking up a highly paid profession such as investment banking or management consulting to maximize one's ability to improve society through efficiently allocated donations ('earning to give'). In a compelling critique of this concept, Amia Srinivasan argues that early forms of EA relied on the idea that we can – and crucially, *should* – simply instrumentalize market dynamics for good, rather than challenging us to question and change them on a deeper level (Srinivasan, 2015).[10] This diagnosis presumably also extends to contemporary EA to some degree: if it turned out to be the case that a massive concentration of power, wealth, and information amongst a small group of people as a result of unfettered market forces is what enables society to mitigate existential risks hypothetically posed by advanced AI, or perhaps to harness the power of AI to maximize value for everyone, then so be it. EA does not offer *principled* reasons to resist such concentrations.

9 Interestingly, influential effective altruists like MacAskill have until quite recently been less concerned about technological acceleration. In his 2022 book, he writes that 'a period of stagnation could increase the risks of extinction and permanent collapse' (MacAskill, 2022). Elon Musk, who endorsed the idea of blunt AI deployment moratoria mere months later, wrote on X that MacAskill's book is 'worth reading. This is a close match for my philosophy.' @elonmusk post on X (8/22/2022).

10 '[MacAskill's book] *Doing Good Better* is a feel-good guide to getting good done. It doesn't dwell too much on of global inequality, and sidesteps any diagnosis of its causes. [...] MacAskill is evidently comfortable with ways of talking that are familiar from the exponents of global capitalism: the will to quantify, [...] the obsession with productivity and efficiency, the conviction that there is a happy convergence between self-interest and morality, the seeming confidence that there is no crisis whose solution is beyond the ingenuity of man' (Srinivasan, 2015).

Second, none of the dominant views discussed here are particularly well-equipped to offer and prioritize a sufficiently nuanced analysis of the *structural* nature of many problems that plague contemporary society, in that they tend to adopt a reductive lens on how best to address those issues and on who ought to lead those efforts. To illustrate, consider accelerationist Andreessen's claim that

> [w]e believe intelligence is in an upward spiral [...] as more smart people around the world are recruited into the techno-capital machine. [...] We believe that there is no material problem – whether created by nature or by technology – that cannot be solved with more technology. [...] Give us a real-world problem, and we can invent technology that will solve it (Andreessen, 2023).

And despite their staunch opposition to accelerationism, even effective altruist views sometimes push into the same direction: consider, for example, Anthropic CEO Dario Amodei's claim in a self-published essay titled 'Machines of loving grace' that

> [AI-related risks] are the only thing standing between us and what I see as a fundamentally positive future. I think that most people are underestimating just how radical the upside of AI could be. [...] Many things cannot be done without breaking laws, harming humans, or messing up society. An aligned AI would not want to do these things. [...] [Widely shared human] intuitions [...] lead eventually to rule of law, democracy, and Enlightenment values. [...] AI simply offers an opportunity to get us there more quickly (Amodei, 2024).[11]

One reason for this shared shortcoming, across considerable ideological divides, is that the three clusters of views – irrespective of their differences – are biased towards one particular, narrow *type* of longterm perspective on evaluating AI's impact on society. By this, I do not mean that every tech industry practitioner *explicitly* endorses longtermism, and I also do not mean to insinuate that all possible forms of longtermism are equally *objectionable*. Rather, my claim is simply that influential industry figures who support effective altruism and effective accelerationism – both of which are explicitly longtermist – or right-wing libertarianism – which is not explicitly longtermist, but many versions of which *de facto* rely on a longterm vision of the role of capitalist markets to structure well-functioning societies and to, as a collateral consequence thereof, ameliorate social welfare – prioritize uncertain longterm benefits and risks associated with AI innovation over certain present-day harms, such as racial and gender bias in AI. Even worse, as I have argued in Chapter 1, they tend to misconstrue the latter as purely 'short-term' concerns. In doing so, they fail to pay due attention to the present and

11 See also Amodei (2023).

(crucially) long-lasting moral weight of structures of social injustice potentially exacerbated by AI deployment, and they gloss over the deeper political question of whether it is legitimate to attempt to address these problems as a mere trickle-down effect of the bold deployment efforts of the enlightened, disruptive few.

Finally, these views tend to, at least implicitly, rank the normative goals of freedom and wellbeing higher than the value of equality, and most importantly for our purposes here, the value of *political equality* in a framework of well-functioning and fair democratic processes. More specifically, the dominant views surveyed here fail to appreciate the value of actual, direct democratic participation. Instead, they tend to prioritize the widespread availability of AI and the role of 'domain experts',[12] which they tend to construe unduly narrowly as highly skilled technological and scientific elites.[13] This entrenches social relations that are at odds with democratic equality in a broad sense: rather than embracing the idea that all of us have the right to shape the direction of technological innovations that affect all of us, these views stipulate that tech elites, as our benevolent caretakers, have not only a right, but also a *duty* to chart our collective path for the benefit of the clueless masses. This is clearest in the case of libertarianism and accelerationism. Andreessen's manifesto, which mentions 'abundance' twelve times (and 'equality', predictably, zero times), states that

> we believe any deceleration of AI will cost lives. Deaths that were preventable by the AI that was prevented from existing is a form of murder. [But] we have enemies. Our present society has been subjected to a mass demoralization campaign – against technology and against life [...] our enemies are [...] social responsibility, stakeholder capitalism [...] collectivism [...] socialism [...] vetocracy [and] the ivory tower (Andreessen, 2023).

Meanwhile, Thiel condescendingly warns that

> the great task for libertarians is to find an escape from politics in all its forms – from the totalitarian and fundamentalist catastrophes to the unthinking demos that guides so-called 'social democracy' (Thiel, 2009).

12 It is telling that in the aforementioned essay, Amodei defines democratization as mere public access rather than public control: 'this technology is becoming democratized, is getting built into products that people are able to use without a ton of technical expertise'.

13 In a self-aware nod to his own agenda-setting power, Amodei muses that '[o]ne thing writing this essay has made me realize is that it would be valuable to bring together a group of domain experts (in biology, economics, international relations, and other areas) to write a much better and more informed version of what I've produced here. It's probably best to view my efforts here as a starting prompt for that group.'

While not all supporters of such views are quite as explicitly anti-democratic as accelerationists like Andreessen and libertarians like Thiel are, they all at least *deprioritize* political equality as a value. And even the less obviously objectionable 'impartial' perspective underpinning effective altruists' basic claim that we have a moral duty to maximize good outcomes in an agent-neutral way is susceptible to this. EA focuses on harnessing the data-driven expertise of virtuous and educated elites for the wellbeing of all rather than on creating real-world mechanisms that empower everyone to articulate and pursue their own conception of wellbeing. If one thinks that we are facing an apocalyptic AI doomsday that renders participation on free and equal terms a luxury we cannot afford, that makes sense: after all, emergencies have often been used to justify incursions into the realm of democratic equality (Honig, 2011). In my view, we should not let this assumption stand uncontested. This is especially important because the mere fact that there are stark differences between the three views discussed here risks distracting from the fact that all three are actually misaligned with one and the same higher-order goal: the goal of enabling the democratic participation of political equals.

Overall, my brief commentary on the philosophical underpinnings of prevalent beliefs amongst powerful tech industry actors cannot hope to – and need not – provide a comprehensive empirical ideology analysis. The main upshot, for now, is that while the ostensible attitudinal SHIFT away from moving fast and breaking things has not fundamentally changed AI deployment dynamics, the fact that there is a greater heterogeneity of tech industry views voiced recently about AI deployment has to some degree obfuscated the extent of this problem. To get a firmer grasp of what the political and moral stakes are for different actors in society when it comes to deploying sophisticated generative AI tools, the following chapter turns to a deeper analysis of market power and its connection to asymmetrical dispersions of risk associated with AI.

3

Risk

'[Interviewer:] There is a balance between innovation and risk. How do you balance those two?'
'[Jeff Bezos:] When you're doing these experiments, winners pay for thousands of losers.' (Geek Wire, 2018)

Tech insiders are not the only ones to emphasize that embracing risk is central to innovation. Anyone wanting to create genuinely new and ground-breaking tools, tools that push the horizon of what we thought possible, must be ready to accept a higher degree of risk than those who would rather play it safe – this much is clear.

The trouble is that the risk borne by bold innovations does not always exclusively affect those who initially decided to take on that risk. Of course, tech entrepreneurs trying to develop a novel AI tool may fail to secure enough venture capital or fail to sell and scale their product effectively, ultimately suffering the financial repercussions. But there are yet other, larger risks at play:[1] many AI tools may exhibit major biases, they may hallucinate and spread misinformation, they may be vulnerable to misuse by malicious

1 This is not an exhaustive list of possible risks associated with generative AI – doing so would be well beyond the scope of this essay. As I have pointed out above, philosophers of AI differ in their respective focus on various types of risk, from risks that are already clearly present here and now to risks that are subject to a greater degree of uncertainty in the longer-term future (such as hypothetical existential risks posed by AI). What motivates my discussion here is predominantly a concern about the former, given that they are the most salient in present-day AI policy efforts and the most plausible targets for immediate democratic intervention. For the purposes of this essay, however, I do not commit myself to a *principled* view as to whether or not the latter might be a productive locus of democratic agenda-setting, or whether focusing on one may be unproductively pulling away resources and attention from the other – largely because, as I have argued earlier, I am skeptical that a commonly drawn distinction between short-term and long-term risks can be drawn quite so clearly.

actors attempting to jailbreak them, and they require staggering amounts of energy (Luccioni et al., 2024: 85–99). In that case, the financial risk to the original deployers pales in comparison to the second-order risks that arise once the tool is out there and its capabilities become known, including to other would-be deployers. These second-order risks affect everyone in society, not just the entrepreneurs who so boldly chose to embrace some degree of personal risk in the first place.

Generative AI deployment, and the deployment of other powerful technologies, disperses second-order risks in this way even if entrepreneurs do *not* fail. In fact, the longer a 'winner' deployer operates successfully and makes more and more advanced technology widely available, possibly without sufficient safety testing or without being able to fully predict potential adverse outcomes in the future, the more opportunities there are for the aforementioned risks related to bias, misinformation, and misuse to become dispersed in society. And as AI deployment accelerates further, systemic effects on the environment accelerate too – this is an area in which Big Tech's outsized power to exploit natural resources and economically vulnerable populations has become especially apparent. Tech companies have been buying cheap land in various countries in the Global South to build the gigantic data centers required for running next-generation AI tools. But the imposition of environmental risks associated with that is starting to attract bottom-up democratic pushback: to give just one example, in 2023, a planned Google data center in southern Uruguay that would require millions of liters of water every single day for cooling and energy production was met with protests as Uruguay had been facing its worst drought in a century that year, which severely limited its citizens' ability to access clean drinking water (the *Guardian*, 2023a). Industry attitudes about these problems have been noticeably cavalier, centering the techno-solutionist idea that *further* AI deployment is our best shot to mitigate these risks. 'We're not going to hit our climate goals anyway', former Google CEO Eric Schmidt said in a September 2024 fireside chat on AI and energy, 'Yes, the needs in this area will be a problem, but I'd rather bet on AI solving the problem rather than constraining [AI deployment]' (Schmidt, 2024).

Risk dispersions are not innocuous – even if not *every* member of society ends up suffering actual, tangible harms as a result of AI innovation. The basic claim that imposing a mere risk on someone can *morally wrong* that person, even if that person does not suffer actual harm, has been explored in depth by moral and legal philosophers. But, as I argue in this chapter, there is another reason why exposure to risk can be objectionable – it is objectionable on *political* grounds, if and when risk exposure is distributed in specific ways in society. Contextualizing dispersions of risk with an analysis of market power currently held by oligopolistic actors in the tech industry (§3.1), thereby adopting a macro-level lens on risk that goes beyond the individual, reveals that we need to think about the philosophical problem posed by risk in a more nuanced way (§3.2). As my argument will show, when dispersions of risk are asymmetrical and lack sufficient public justification, they are subject to a democratic legitimacy deficit. At the same time, widespread views in Silicon Valley and beyond like the one surveyed in the previous chapter suggest that even if risks linked to the deployment of cutting-edge AI are objectionably dispersed, they bring considerable benefits with them, too – benefits for the many, not just the few. An underlying assumption of many 'techno-optimist' positions seems to be that if benefits are dispersed alongside risks, the presence of a democratic legitimacy deficit ceases to pose an important problem. As I will show, however, this claim does not stand up to scrutiny (§3.3).

3.1 Market power

On an intuitive level, I have already motivated the claim – in Chapter 1 – that there is a concentration of AI-related benefits amongst a handful of powerful deployers of generative AI coupled with a wide dispersion of associated risks across society. But this analysis of supply-side market power warrants more detailed exploration. Isn't the AI sector a rollercoaster anyway, a rapidly evolving environment in which disruptive new start-ups unexpectedly rise to the top all the time? Clearly, it would be too quick to simply *assume* the lasting presence of a Big Tech oligopoly. Rather, the oligopoly claim is a substantive one that warrants a standalone defense. Here is the more precise, narrowly construed claim I wish to defend:

> THE ASYMMETRY CLAIM: currently, there exists an oligopolistic concentration of wealth, power, and information (in short, *benefits*) associated with innovative AI deployment amongst a handful of Big Tech companies, many of which are located in the United States, and which have unmatched computational capabilities – that is, the kinds of vast material and technological resources required to train and deploy next-generation generative AI tools. Meanwhile, *risks* associated with innovative AI deployment are currently not similarly concentrated. Instead, they are dispersed widely in society.

In a nutshell, if AI deployment goes poorly, it goes poorly for everyone. And if it goes well, it might go well for everyone, too – but it will go vastly *better* for a small number of people than it will for everyone else. The combined wealth of the world's ten richest tech entrepreneurs (all of whom happen to be US citizens), for instance, is currently estimated at around 1.62 trillion dollars (Forbes, 2024b).[2] Obviously, in comparative terms, the rest of the population has benefited to a much lesser degree from successful AI innovation. In the current AI market, then, risks do not perfectly track benefits.

All this, of course, may change in the future – this is why the ASYMMETRY CLAIM is constrained to a description of current market power, though it is worth considering that even if disruptive *new* tech companies enter the generative AI market, oligopolistic structures may remain in place while the *composition* of the oligopoly shifts. Additionally, distributions of market power may differ across geographical contexts: oligopolies and monopolies may be more or less pronounced in different regions of the world.

However, in support of my analysis of our current status quo, particularly in the US, the fact alone that there has been a recent wave of antitrust lawsuits and regulatory interventions explicitly citing oligopolistic and monopolistic market power proves instructive:[3] in the 2024 ruling of the US District Court for the District of Columbia in *United States v. Google LLC* (2020), the court stated firmly that 'Google is a monopolist, and it has acted as one to maintain its monopoly', striking anticompetitive deals with Apple and other tech companies to maintain its dominance in the search engine space rather than merely offering a superior product that naturally led to an outsized market share. In the ongoing case of *FTC v. Amazon.com, Inc.*, the FTC alleges that Amazon 'engages in a course of exclusionary conduct that prevents current competitors from growing and new competitors from emerging' (Federal Trade Commission, 2023), and similarly, the US Department of Justice, in its ongoing lawsuit against Apple (*United States v. Apple, Inc.*), alleges that 'Apple has maintained monopoly power in the smartphone market, not simply by staying ahead of the competition on the merits, but by violating federal antitrust law' (Office of Public Affairs, Department of Justice, 2024).

In a nutshell, as Allen and Weyl compellingly put it, generative AI tools and other advanced technologies that outperform humans in complex tasks 'seem almost perfectly designed to concentrate power with a technical elite [...] the investment scale required to develop [generative foundation]

2 This is the combined net worth, as of September 2024, of Elon Musk, Jeff Bezos, Larry Ellison, Mark Zuckerberg, Bill Gates, Larry Page, Sergey Brin, Steve Ballmer, Jensen Huang, and Michael Dell (all of whom are US citizens) as publicly reported in Forbes.

3 Recent antitrust lawsuits against tech companies in general have focused on claims surrounding monopoly power rather than oligopoly power. This focus is plausible for many segments of the technology industry. However, the generative AI market specifically is best understood as one characterized by oligopolistic concentrations of power, given that a small number of AI companies have been in an ongoing race to achieve and maintain SOTA.

models and the race dynamics around that development threaten to enable concentrations of democratically unaccountable power' (Allen and Weyl, 2024: 147–162); this diagnosis is bolstered further by recent scholarly contributions across a wider range of disciplines (Pasquale, 2019: 285–296; Calo and Citron, 2021: 797–846; Sadowski et al., 2021: 169–171; Viljoen et al., 2021: 1–13; Conyon et al., 2022: 1205–1224; Cofone, 2023; Hua and Belfield, 2023: 596–605; Risse, 2023; Lazar, 2024: 198; Aytac, 2024; Sitaraman and Narechania, 2024).

3.2 Mere risk

At first blush, the mere presence of risk seems morally and politically innocuous. After all, risks may well never eventuate in harm, so it is not clear that risk itself is necessarily harmful or otherwise morally objectionable. And even if it were, it is simply *impossible* to escape risk in our everyday lives: all of us are constant risk imposers and risk bearers. Therefore, if there was a duty to avoid imposing risks on anyone else at all times, we would not be able to do much at all. My act of breathing on the subway imposes a small risk on other passengers of possibly contracting a viral infection – after all, I might have a cold coming on that I have not even registered yet. My choice of eating at any restaurant stops me from exercising the full control over the food preparation process that I would have in my own kitchen – there is a small chance that my dinner will contain something that might trigger an upset stomach. My decision to leave my apartment brings with it the risk that I might physically bump into someone else, possibly causing them a small amount of pain. In short, it would be overly demanding to expect all of us to avoid imposing any risk at all on others, and it would be unreasonable of us to complain about such risks being imposed on ourselves, especially if the potential harm associated with such risks is not particularly severe.

But even if it were more serious than a cold or an upset stomach or a bump, exposure to mere risk (and, indeed, risk that *does* eventuate in harm) seems perfectly justifiable to most people in other cases. Every car ride involves a non-negligible risk of serious accidents, but we accept this because we *voluntarily choose* the trade-off of risks and benefits associated with cars. Every surgery involves some risk of possibly dangerous complications, and most of us find it acceptable for doctors to perform surgeries on patients even if patients cannot voluntarily choose to have the surgery (think of emergency cases), on the grounds that those risks are *unavoidable*.

However, risks are not always morally unobjectionable in the ways these earlier examples suggest. To avoid getting sidetracked by the hype and doom surrounding AI, and to see the force of this intuition in a more general way, let us first consider a case *not* involving AI:

> *Amy's Private Stash*: Brianna has a headache, and her grumpy mood is getting on Amy's nerves. Brianna's mood is now Amy's problem: Amy would benefit from Brianna's headache magically disappearing. Amy routinely carries around a stash of over-the-counter pain medication in her handbag, so she offers Brianna one of the pills from her bag. Both Amy and Brianna know that Brianna is also an asthma sufferer, and that taking Aspirin rather than Tylenol would be potentially dangerous for her. Amy thinks that her loose pills are most likely Tylenol, which would help alleviate Brianna's headache while not triggering an asthma attack. Rather than alerting Brianna to the possibility, however small, that the pill might in fact not be Tylenol, Amy simply hands Brianna the pill: 'Just have this and you'll feel better', she says. 'Are you sure?' Brianna asks, 'What even is this?' Amy brushes her off, insisting: 'Don't overthink it, it's fine. It's just a Tylenol!' Brianna takes the pill, her headache fades, and she does not get an asthma attack. 'Oh, good,' says Amy, 'there was a slim chance of that actually being Aspirin. That would have ended badly. Lucky us.'

Here, Amy has imposed a non-trivial risk of harm (a potentially serious asthma attack) on Brianna. However, Brianna did not actually suffer an asthma attack. In other words, the risk in this case remained a 'pure risk' and did not eventuate in harm (Thomson, 1986: 173).[4] In fact, Brianna benefited (her headache disappeared), and Amy benefited, too. But none of that changes the fact that Amy *wronged* Brianna by imposing a non-trivial, avoidable, and not fully voluntarily assumed risk on her. Like all people, Brianna has a morally weighty interest in autonomy. Not being provided with sufficient information about the risks attached to taking Amy's pill when deliberating about which course of action to choose undermines Brianna's interest: in Oberdiek's words, Amy has 'normatively foreclosed formerly safe possibilities' for Brianna (Oberdiek, 2017: 87).The formerly safe option of 'taking a Tylenol' is now a much less safe option: 'take a pill that might be a Tylenol'. Brianna's morally weighty interest justifies a correlative moral duty on Amy's part not to undermine those interests.

4 Here, I follow standard terminology in the ethics of risk literature. Thomson introduced the conceptual distinction between pure risks – which do not eventuate in harm – and impure risks – which do eventuate in harm (Thomson, 1986: 173). Thomson and others have argued that imposing pure risks can be wrong. I endorse this general view. While some philosophers have tried to explain the wrongness of pure risk impositions by conceptualizing pure risks as *harms* themselves (see, for instance, Finkelstein [2003]), I do not commit myself to this more specific view; my view allows for *other* wrong-making features of pure risk besides harm.

Amy's risk imposition on Brianna – the choice to persuade her to take the pill despite her lack of certainty about the type of pill and her knowledge of the associated safety risk – wrongfully breaches that moral duty (Raz, 1986: 166ff).[5] Crucially, Amy therefore wrongs Brianna even if they are 'lucky' and no harm results from the risk imposition.

The choice to deploy powerful AI tools at scale can create risk imposition scenarios of a similar normative structure. Even if you do not fall prey to some machine hallucination that gives you mistaken investing advice or non-existent case law, your exposure to the risk of doing so still matters. Even if you do not encounter disturbing AI-generated images that deeply hurt you because they insultingly stereotype a feature of your own identity, the fact that you could have easily encountered them is not morally trivial. Neither can such pure risks plausibly be construed as 'unavoidable', such as the car driving or surgery cases with which we started: exposure to these pure risks is the result of explicit choices that someone – the deployer – has made. And to make matters worse, AI deployment involves plenty of well-documented *impure* risks resulting in actual harm, too;[6] though the crux of my argument here is that the problem of AI-associated risks is more complex and extends much *further* than the scope of dispersed impure risks.

So far, my analysis has followed existing philosophical work on the ethics of risk in centering the idea that risk impositions are morally objectionable if and because they wrong individual risk-bearers. However, intuitively, the *distribution* of risks in society matters, too. To see the force of this intuition, consider first a modification of our earlier case:

> *Amy's Private Stash**: Both Brianna and Camila are grumpy due to their headaches, to Amy's chagrin. Unlike Brianna, Camila does not have asthma, so Aspirin is not dangerous for her. Aspirin does however slightly upset her stomach. Amy gives both of them a mysterious pill, not being completely sure whether it is Tylenol. 'I bet it is Tylenol, though,' insists Amy, 'just go ahead.'

Amy imposes the same kind of risk on Brianna and Camila – negative health consequences of some kind, should the pill turn out to be Aspirin not Tylenol – but the severity of harm associated with this risk is much worse

5 The same will not be true, of course, for trivial interests with little or no moral weight – to use my earlier example, an interest in 'never being bumped into and experiencing a small amount of pain as a result' cannot plausibly justify the imposition of a *duty* on others to not ever impose such risks, though it may well justify a much more minimal duty to *try* one's best to avoid doing so.

6 Here, I follow many other moral philosophers in endorsing the interest theory of rights, though space constraints prevent me from offering a standalone defense of this general theory. For what is arguably the most influential version of this theory, see Raz (1986: 166ff).

for Brianna. More broadly, two people or groups could be exposed to the same *kind* of risk, but the risk exposure could *differ* across the two in terms of the severity of potential harm associated with the risk, thus creating an unfair risk distribution. And even more perniciously, two people or groups could be exposed to the same kind of risk *and* to the same level of severity, but – depending on how social institutions and political practices are set up – still be plausibly subject to an unfair risk distribution if one of them suffers from a *different* level of vulnerability to the specific potential harm at play. This can give rise to an important political, not just moral, problem.

This distributive dimension of wrongful risk, too, applies directly to the context of AI deployment. Current AI-related risk dispersions are often unfair, and this is a wrongness-exacerbating feature of wrongful risk impositions via AI. When tech leaders justify a speedy and experimental approach to deployment, they often downplay the risks: 'When you're balancing the risks,' Amazon founder Jeff Bezos says, 'you say the most I can lose is the cost of the experiment. And the value of the invention could be uncapped' (*Geek Wire*, 2018). But that misrepresents the stakes of risk-laden choices to deploy. The deployer might 'lose the cost of the experiment' – but others stand to lose much more, given that risks *could* eventuate in severe harm. Deploying a generative AI tool that allows malicious actors to dramatically scale up the production of malware, weapons, or political misinformation may merely cost the deployer her upfront investment into the new tool (since benevolent actors will not buy it, and malicious actors will simply steal it), but it may cost everyone else in society basic societal stability and security.

And even in cases involving less severe (but still wrongfully imposed) impure risks, or indeed 'mere' pure risks, problems remain. Consider any AI tool that exacerbates pre-existing social stereotypes and inequities: say, an AI tool designed to assist law enforcement in screening online conversations for potential violent or extremist content, and to interact with users through natural-sounding conversations to gather additional information pertinent to identifying potential threats. Even if all those interacting with the tool have roughly the same probability of mistakenly getting flagged as potential violent instigators, mistakenly getting flagged will involve a bigger risk of harm for some rather than others: members of specific racial and religious minorities who are already unfairly harmed by biased law enforcement practices now unfairly face potentially more serious repercussions. For people already viewed with unduly high levels of suspicion, being labeled as a potential threat may provoke a particularly aggressive intervention by law enforcement in such cases but not others, thereby further exacerbating the wrongness of the initial risk imposition. Notice that this remains a moral and political problem even if none of the risks eventuate (i.e. nobody gets mistakenly flagged): the distribution of risks of harm is *itself* unfair. This point generalizes: everyone is wronged by the imposition of risks of harm associated with an inaccurate or misleading AI tool, but if and when risk distributions affect different groups differently – be it because of pre-existing social inequities or because of some other reason – some people are wronged more seriously than others.

You might think that deployers bear these risks, too: the very fact that AI-related risks are dispersed in society means they are not exempt from potentially unfair dispersions of risk. But people with outsized power to steer AI deployment decisions often also have outsized social power due to their membership in privileged social groups and their ample resources, so unfair societal distributions of risk are unlikely to not play out in their favor in comparison to other members of society: Jeff Bezos is much less likely to get mistakenly flagged as a violent threat in comparison to people with a different name, race, zip code, way of speaking, and so on.

And even more importantly, risks can be dispersed unfairly between a group of deployers and the rest of society, rather than simply being dispersed equally amongst all members of society. What I have in mind are cases in which deployers take unfair advantage of everyone's free use of some AI tool, which in turn drastically improves that tool in a way that benefits the deployer first. Consider the recent wave of large language models deployed at scale: data on how users interact with some new and imperfect tool free of charge is immensely beneficial for companies' efforts to improve those tools and possibly to create gatekept commercial versions thereof later. Consider also the environmental footprint of such tools: everyone will be impacted by climate change, a lack of clean water, diminishing natural resources, and spreading conflict and diseases, but ultra-wealthy tech leaders are well-positioned to shelter themselves – and elite groups of their choice – from these risks of harm. Mark Zuckerberg has been building a 270 million-dollar compound including an apocalypse bunker in Hawaii (Wired, 2023), while Jeff Bezos's company Blue Origin champions the 'vision of millions of people living and working in space for the benefit of Earth', presumably with tech elites first in line (Blue Origin, n.d.).

Having covered the wrong-making and wrongness-exacerbating features of risk distributions, we can now return to the normative core of the problem at the heart of the Asymmetry. Consider:

> *Amy's Good Deed:* Amy has access to other substances, including a supplement that claims to improve cognitive capacities. Amy thinks that everyone should benefit from this miracle innovation, so she publicly announces that she will spike her city's entire water supply with the supplement. The supplement has not undergone rigorous scientific testing, so there is a risk that it may in fact harm people rather than benefiting them. Suppose that even though

Amy does not try to conceal her plot, nobody has the power or resources to stop her, and Amy's plot succeeds: the water supply gets spiked.

Amy's choice to spike the water supply lacks joint *public justification* by everyone else involved. Even if the supplement actually benefits people, there is still a moral problem: no one else had the opportunity to participate in this decision that impacted a formerly safe public resource. Everyone's morally weighty interest in autonomy was thereby set back. By contrast, had everyone in her city decided together in a fully informed and voluntary way to try out the supplement, and to do so by authorizing Amy to spike the city's water supply, Amy's act would not be wrongful because her risk imposition on others would not involve setting back their interest in autonomy.[7] The larger point applicable to widely and often unfairly dispersed risks associated with ASYMMETRICAL AI deployment is that deployers typically lack such explicit collective authorization following a fair process of deliberation and justification.

3.3 Can't everyone win?

Skeptical readers may object at this point that my analysis of what is *wrong* with a dispersion of risk along the lines of the ASYMMETRY CLAIM is uncharitably one-sided. What if, they may wonder, considerable *benefits* associated with generative AI deployment are dispersed in society at large, alongside risks, making all of our lives easier and more abundant (Andreessen, 2023)?

But the mere presence of benefits resulting from widespread AI deployment does not provide sufficiently compelling reasons to abandon the ASYMMETRY CLAIM. Even if important benefits are dispersed alongside risks, there is still a morally and politically troubling asymmetry with respect to the *scale* of benefits. Consider

Amy's Million Dollar Drug: Amy develops a new drug that could potentially save the lives of thousands and make Amy a rich woman. But Amy's drug

7 One may object that it is implausible to say that Brianna is wronged on the grounds that Brianna still *chose* to take the pill – Amy did not exactly force her to take it. However, the 'voluntary choice' objection is not persuasive in this case: Brianna did not have a full understanding of what she was agreeing to do, given Amy's choice to conceal her own uncertainty. Therefore, Amy wronged Brianna by imposing a risk in a way that set back Brianna's interest in autonomy. This is still the case even if Brianna was also neglectful in her *own* responsibilities, such as a self-regarding duty to check more carefully what pills she was taking.

> needs to be tested first before that happens: the drug could have serious potential side effects. Amy makes the untested drug available for free to anyone who would like to take their chances and test it. Brianna, Camila, and many others eager to improve their daily lives opt in. Amy closely observes how Brianna and Camila use the drug. Both survive the drug trial unharmed, but their respective drug use experiences prompt Amy to make crucial changes to the publicly recommended dosage. Amy could not have made the drug ready for successful large-scale deployment without their help. Amy ends up earning one billion dollars. 'Brianna and Camila have nothing to complain about', Amy says. 'They now live in a world in which they and everyone else gets to benefit from the fact that my miracle drug is now widely available! My innovation benefits everyone.'

The distribution of benefits associated with Amy's innovation remains highly asymmetrical: yes, everyone benefits, but Amy benefits vastly more than everyone else. Similarly,[8] in the hypothetically possible case of universally beneficial AI innovation under current market power distributions, the scale of benefits will be skewed towards the few who control the development and deployment of these tools, and the fact that benefits associated with AI might 'trickle down' in society will be a small consolation only given the continued presence of worsening wealth inequality.[9]

But even if the distribution of benefits associated with AI innovation were *not* distributed quite as asymmetrically between AI deployers and AI users, there would still be a democratic legitimacy deficit – and that would

8 Obviously, the scenario in *Amy's Million Dollar Drug* also exhibits some important dissimilarities with AI deployment. First, drugs are a tightly regulated market in most jurisdictions, whereas the AI market is not (yet). Second, whether next-generation AI can be plausibly *likened* to a life-saving drug remains to be seen, to put it mildly. Third, *Amy's Million Dollar Drug* stipulates that A imposes a risk on B and C which B and C *voluntarily* assume, which – as per *volenti non fit injuria* – renders the risk imposition on B and C much less morally troubling (for a discussion of the philosophical stakes of this intuitively plausible legal principle, see Feinberg (1989), whereas members of the public exposed to AI-related risks are usually not able to voluntarily assume the latter: companies often have unilateral deployment power, and even if they did not (that is, if the public had significant control over deployment), the public may not fully understand the risks involved, thus blocking their ability to assume them in a truly voluntary way.

9 Obviously, enhanced democratic input into the question of what kinds of dispersion of risk/concentration of power ASYMMETRIES are justifiable need not yield the result that democratic constituencies choose to *reduce* wealth inequalities. Instead, they could decide to accept existing distributions. In such a case, those ASYMMETRIES may still be objectionable for other normative reasons (connected to broader questions of distributive justice, for instance), but they would cease to lack democratic legitimacy.

be politically objectionable in and of itself. To see the force of this intuition, consider an extension of *Amy's Million Dollar Drug:*

> *Amy's Drug Empire*: Due to the massive earlier success of Amy's drug, Amy's company now has the biggest market share in the pharmaceutical sector. Amy's company sells most of the most common drugs that people in her country need. Amy sets the R&D priorities in that society when it comes to pharmaceuticals, hiring the best scientists, funding major drug trials and research projects, sending her lobbyists to regulators to influence healthcare policy, and acquiring potential competitors who dare to venture in new research areas that Amy's company is not well-positioned to tackle. In short, Amy has outsized influence on the question of which issues to prioritize in pharmaceuticals R&D in her country, not just inside her company. Neither other companies nor government regulators can feasibly influence Amy's decisions – in fact, Amy influences theirs. As it turns out, Amy is an excellent decision-maker and sets the best possible R&D priorities, amassing more wealth by selling more and better drugs, and even convincing regulators to support her with public funds because she is the most well-positioned actor to execute cutting-edge research projects. Everyone's quality of life increases. 'See, everyone?' Amy gloats, 'I got it right. You're welcome. It's not a problem that none of you had any input into this – it all worked out in everyone's favor, didn't it?' As a bonus, Amy regularly donates 90% of her vast income to assist the poor and the sick in her society.

Here, widely dispersed risks (the threat of potentially charting the wrong R&D course or developing unsafe drugs) did not eventuate, and instead, everyone – not just deployer Amy – was blessed with widely dispersed benefits (better health outcomes for all). Even in this case, though, something of political and moral value has been lost. The fact that everyone else never had the opportunity to shape drug innovation priorities that affect everyone, not just Amy and her company's customers, means that citizens were put in an inferior position of passively receiving the fruits of Amy's magnanimous decision-making. In *Amy's Drug Empire*, everyone else becomes a patient, with Amy as their benevolent caretaker: Amy's disproportionate power to dictate the course of action blocked everyone else from taking charge of an important element of their shared future. Yes, everyone ultimately benefited in terms of the healthcare outcomes achieved. Yet everyone paid the price of not being able to *decide together* on shared goals and possible actions in pursuit of those goals, freely and on truly equal terms; everyone continued to be vulnerable to the risk of Amy messing up one day, since it was impossible to impose checks and balances on her to enforce her accountability to the public; and, everyone remained vulnerable to the possibility that Amy's generosity might at some point dry up.

At its best, unilateral, rapid, and large-scale deployment of generative AI by a small group of tech industry actors could mirror *Amy's Drug Empire*: generative AI might, on balance, make all of our lives better. I do not commit myself to any speculative predictions about how likely this is. Suffice it to say that AI's future trajectory is much less certain than the successes of Amy's wise decision-making that we swiftly stipulated for the purposes of this example. The crux is that, as I have shown here, even if the future of the AI age is as bright as techno-optimists and accelerationists would have us believe, the current lack of genuine democratic control remains a problem either way.

These observations alone, of course, do not give us a decisive reason to endorse the positive claim that, all things considered, democratizing drug deployment in *Amy's Drug Empire*, and – by extension – democratizing AI deployment would render ASYMMETRIES present in those domains morally and politically *unobjectionable*. A lack of democratic legitimacy concerning the distributions under those ASYMMETRIES is but one relevant normative problem, and other problems – such as larger background structures of injustice and domination – may well remain.[10]

My modest aim in this chapter has been to make salient what is *lost* when impactful decisions lack democratic legitimacy, even in best-case scenarios in which everything 'works out', at the level of benefits received by all. In what follows, we turn to the question of which actions democratic constituencies can take to reclaim their power, and to recover what is lost.

10 See Chapter 6.2 for in-depth discussion of this matter.

4

Agendas

'It is our responsibility to educate policymakers and the public about what we think is happening, what we think may happen, and to put technology out into the world so people can see it.'
(Sam Altman: *TIME Magazine*, 2023)

As we have seen so far, recent AI deployment decisions have been characterized by an asymmetry between the way in which they widely disperse AI-related risks, and the way in which they narrowly concentrate AI-related benefits. This asymmetry is politically and morally troubling, because it is subject to a democratic legitimacy deficit. This status quo stands in stark contrast to increasingly louder, though often rather vague, calls for subjecting AI deployment decisions to some type of democratic control.

Articulating concrete and action-guiding strategies for successfully democratizing AI deployment, especially during particularly frantic deployment cycles like the current generative AI race, requires identifying *the right pressure points* in a precise way. A pressure point can be any juncture of a larger-scale societal decision sequence that is in principle open to some form of democratic participation, but that is currently subject to democratically illegitimate forms of influence. My view is that the specific pressure point that is the most tangible and promising, in this context, is *the power to set democratic agendas*. We cannot tackle the ASYMMETRY and the democratic legitimacy deficit associated with it if we fail to interrogate the following questions: when it comes to AI, who has the power to determine what we make collective decisions about in the first place, and at what point in time? Have we responded with undue deference to powerful actors who simply deploy and make it our problem later – and how can that response be improved?

Agenda-setting is an underappreciated pressure point not only in AI policy, but in contemporary democratic practice more generally. Here, I explore this problem theoretically by mobilizing conceptual resources from an important early body of work in democratic theory that has recently been somewhat dormant. These conceptual foundations help us see more clearly why an appropriately demanding and comprehensive picture of what democracy is and what it requires reveals what we, as democratic constituencies, can do differently if and when collective decision processes fall short of legitimacy (§4.1) (Whelan, 1983; Goodin, 2007: 40–68; Song, 2012: 39–68).[1]

Even though powerful individuals in the tech industry have spent the ongoing generative AI wave publicly signaling a striking attitudinal shift with respect to greater AI oversight, these shifts are rather superficial. They do not fundamentally alter the lack of democratic legitimacy created and sustained by recent AI deployment decisions. Crucially, however, this does not mean that there is no hope for successful AI deployment democratization. Instead, I argue, we are currently witnessing a valuable *window of opportunity* in this space. As democratic citizens, it is our responsibility to seize this opportunity before the window closes. To identify politically desirable and feasible ways of doing so, I offer an analysis of why the power to deploy is *itself* an instantiation of the power to set agendas, and why AI policy in particular is currently a highly anti-competitive agenda-setting environment (§4.2). The positive counterpart to my critique is a substantive account of agenda-setting that is appropriately sensitive to the deployment dynamics characteristic of the AI industry, and a substantive account of democratic legitimacy that is appropriately sensitive to risk asymmetries intensified throughout the generative AI boom (§4.3). Both of these provide the normative foundation for the democratization strategies defended in the subsequent chapters.

4.1 Thick democracy

When asked what democracy involves, most regular citizens might respond, at first blush: 'electing a candidate', 'voting for some proposition on a ballot', 'our newly elected representatives passing a law', and so on. And it is true that taking part in regular and highly formalized electoral mechanisms, as infrequent as they may be, is a central aspect of democracy. It is tempting, then, to view democracy simply as the practice of choosing, as part of scheduled collective decisions, one option from a menu of possible choices. Call such a view:

> THIN DEMOCRACY: in a democratic state, all those who are members of the democratic constituency have the right to participate in collective decisions in the form of free and fair elections, which in turn authorize representatives to pass legislation.

1 See §6.2 for in-depth discussion of this matter.

But on closer inspection, THIN DEMOCRACY captures only one facet of democratic politics. Of course, political philosophers and theorists do not usually view democracy in such a thin way – but many members of the wider public, as well as tech industry insiders commenting critically on the perceived perils of subjecting technology to democratic oversight, seem to adopt this narrow frame when they worry that efforts to democratize will be stifling, sluggish, and unduly complex, at the cost of brilliant rogue individuals who could otherwise make bold decisions outside of the confines of publicly accountable procedures. Peter Thiel, in a 2007 essay commenting in depth on ideas by figures popular within contemporary neo-reactionary and antidemocratic movements – Carl Schmitt, Oswald Spengler, Leo Strauss – critiques 'the political paralysis embedded in our open system of government: [...] a direct path forward is prevented by America's constitutional machinery. By "setting ambition against ambition" with an elaborate system of checks and balances, it prevents any single ambitious person from reconstructing the old Republic. [...] [T]he project of the Enlightenment perhaps always came at too high a price of self-stultification' (Thiel, 2007).

Even if THIN DEMOCRACY matches what many people might intuitively focus on when thinking about the concept of democratic politics, it is worth adopting a more broad-minded perspective. The more compelling view, I think, is the one that acknowledges that democracy is not exclusively, and perhaps not even primarily, about voting. Voting in national and local elections is one mechanism for democratic decision-making and participation – albeit an important one, but nonetheless one amongst many. Processes of public deliberation amongst members of the *demos* can take a myriad of forms. Many of them are considerably less formalized than electoral procedures. Many of them happen long before, or after, some electoral procedure takes place – and they have significant yet intractable effects on the menu of possible options that eventually end up on democratic ballots.

Think, for instance, about a small, non-violent public protest happening a year before an election – any protest, not necessarily a protest about AI, given that the dynamic of interest here is a more general one which applies to any political process within or outside of AI policy. Suppose that some group of regular citizens is motivated by some political issue, and they have opted in on putting that issue on other citizens' radar. For now, this is just a classic case of bottom-up democratic activism, which may or may not remain a one-off event, and the larger-scale impact on democratic decision-making is unclear. But suppose that the protest does trigger (counter-) protests in other locations, which end up amplifying the public *salience* of the original issue at stake. Next, more organized actors in civil society, such as advocacy and expert groups, NGOs, and think tanks start adding arguments to the public discourse on the original issue, thereby increasing public pressure on elected representatives. They may start actively lobbying for particular viewpoints on the issue, for instance by simply informing the wider public, or by addressing democratic representatives and institutions directly – in open letters, white papers, and submissions to hearings soliciting expert testimony. Elected representatives, in turn, may see this as an electoral threat or an electoral opportunity. They may solicit public input by hosting town halls or by strategically consulting experts and affected communities, or they may simply tailor policies to real or perceived public preferences without a direct consultation process. They may start campaigning on newly shaped policy platforms, supported by a well-oiled campaign finance apparatus. Wealthy donors and powerful corporations may make their policy preferences known, sending lobbyists and offering financial support to secure particular outcomes, or simply to shift attention away from an inconvenient issue.

A number of non-trivial things have happened here. Before the next election even happens, the political landscape surrounding the original issue has been fundamentally transformed by a large variety of actors, without a single vote being cast. And on election day, the menu of future policy horizons that voters will have in mind when deciding for or against some candidate will have been shaped not only by directly democratically authorized representatives, but also – in large part – by whichever person or group has managed to influence public discourse, in a way that tangibly changes its direction and focus, whether correctly or incorrectly, and whether rightfully so or not. Finally, at this point, the activists who originally made some issue 'happen' in a public way may not even recognize their initial political goals amongst the slate of offered policy responses. If powerful political actors with competing aims have succeeded in impacting public awareness of the protesters' initial goals, the former may have simply been crowded out of the wider political conversation. This may prompt the protesters and their supporters to continue pursuing the issue independently of electoral cycles, imposing *ex post* sanctions on representatives by calling for their impeachment.

In short, the full spectrum of democratic participation reaches far beyond electoral processes and top-down regulation by elected representatives. At a basic, ecumenical normative level, democracy is about realizing in practice the principle that all members of the democratic constituency ought to have a free and equal say in that constituency's decisions. But realizing that normative goal typically involves the pursuit of multiple political practices by multiple political actors. Not least, it also involves the mere act of *setting a political agenda*: the act of circumscribing, and iteratively reshaping, the proper scope of issues that fall within the domain of public deliberation and decision-making.

Given the broad spectrum of political practices observed above, a view like Thin Democracy will not cut it. The following conception more aptly describes real democratic practice, which 'incorporates society into systematic political analysis without reducing society to a body of voters' (Carpenter, 2023: 193–212, 208):

> Thick Democracy: Democracy is about more than citizens occasionally participating in electoral processes and public officials regulating in a top-down way. In a democratic state, all those who are members of the democratic constituency have the right to participate by engaging in activism, advocacy, and specific forms of lobbying; campaigning and campaign financing; expert consultation and civic deliberation; elections and post-election sanctions; and crucially, the *setting of political agendas*.

How we approach democracy *conceptually* has clear implications for how we will approach the *normative* requirements of successful democratization. A prior commitment to Thin Democracy might make us think that democratizing some issue simply means finding a way to put it up for a vote and being done with it. Under Thick Democracy, democratizing some issue means democratizing it at the agenda-setting stage already – early, and often. Thick Democracy means democracy all the way down, all the time.

While Thick Democracy does not *limit* us to democratizing the agenda-setting stage – in fact, it calls for a democratization of the full spectrum of political practices – it does put it center stage. If we cannot effectively democratize our collective decision sequences at their initial stage, everything that follows is diluted by external influences that fail to faithfully track the real values and preferences of those authorized to decide for themselves.

Agenda-setting as a distinct participatory mechanism which, when done right, instantiates the more general moral right of all constituency members to participate in shaping the trajectory of collective decisions is a long-standing area of focus for political philosophers and democratic theorists. Contributors to this debate are under no illusions that agenda-setting does not only have positive democratic potential, but that it can also nefariously entrench already powerful interests. Dahl's pathbreaking work on agenda-setting focused to a large degree on how powerful agenda-setters can undermine democratic processes in local constituencies (Dahl, 1961). And as Bachrach and Baratz argue, 'power is also exercised when A devotes his energies to creating or reinforcing social and political values and institutional practices that limit the scope of the political process to public consideration of only those issues which are comparatively *innocuous* to A' (Bachrach and Baratz, 1962: 947–952, 948).

But despite the enduring threat of democratically illegitimate agenda-setting, there is hope. At its best, agenda-setting can offer pathways for regular members of the democratic constituency, including marginalized groups therein, to engage in bottom-up democratic counterpower that reshapes political agendas in a way that better reflects the public's value and policy preferences.[2] Of course, before making that hope a reality in the domain of AI policy, we must examine how agenda-setting currently shapes – and distorts – collective societal decisions about AI.

4.2 To deploy is to set agendas

The small number of technology companies that turned out to be the main actors in the generative AI gold rush did not suddenly enter the market at the beginning of this wave – they already had oligopolistic control over cutting-edge AI before the wave started. Not all of them were 'old' tech companies that were already highly salient in the public's mind under the FAANG umbrella (Facebook, Amazon, Apple, Netflix, Google) or the label 'Big Five' (also known as MAAAM: Meta, Alphabet, Amazon, Apple, Microsoft) throughout the social media boom over the previous fifteen years. Newer companies focused specifically on generative AI rather than on a larger range of technology products, like OpenAI and Anthropic, were amongst those who had the computational resources and financial backing to act as key players from the very beginning of the wave. Arguably, this was possible only because newer AI companies were supported by older members of the Big Tech oligopoly though: Microsoft currently owns 49% of OpenAI's equity, and Amazon is a minority stakeholder in Anthropic, following an investment totaling four billion dollars in 2024.

Similarly, tech companies creating not just generative AI models themselves but rather products and services facilitating the rapid deployment thereof, have joined forces with 'old' members of Big Tech. Such products and services include model repository platforms for developers like Hugging Face, on which both Big Tech companies and startups build their generative AI tools, and on which Meta's Llama 2 and Stability AI's Stable Diffusion are stored, amongst others. Hugging Face raised 235 million dollars in a 2023 Series D fundraising round via investments from Google, Amazon, Intel, IBM, Nvidia, and Salesforce (CNBC, 2023).

Other key products and services also include the physical backbone of AI innovation, such as next-generation chips powering the vast data

2 For related work on countervailing powers and the value of democratic contestation, see Galbraith (1952), Rosenvallon (2006), and Pettit (2012).

centers required to train new models: Nvidia, which owns a staggering 92% market share in the data center GPU market, announced in March 2024 that it would intensify its existing partnership with Microsoft with the explicit aim of 'help[ing] developers speed time to market of performance-optimized production AI applications', thus ultimately 'turbocharg[ing] AI deployments' (Nvidia Newsroom, 2024). Meanwhile, Dell Technologies – previously known mainly for PCs and data storage solutions – announced in May 2024 that it was building an AI Factory with Nvidia and developing generative AI tools and services in collaboration with Hugging Face, Meta, and Microsoft (*VentureBeat*, 2024). IBM, in turn, has formed new partnerships with SAP, Amazon, Adobe, Microsoft, Salesforce, and others since May 2023 alone (Forbes, 2024a), and launched a new AI Alliance with Meta that focuses on open AI innovation, and that includes Dell Technologies and Hugging Face, but notably excludes Amazon, Google, and Microsoft (IBM Newsroom, 2023).

This tight-knit web of powerful collaborators explains why AI 'power players' have successfully kept newer, smaller companies out of this market during the generative AI deployment wave. The current AI oligopoly has further cemented its power,[3] although it may seem like entirely new companies – in comparison to the companies that constituted Big Tech in the golden age of social media platforms in the early 2000s – are dominant now.

Normally powerful corporate actors shape agendas simply by exerting outsized influence on public discourse, financing political campaigns or simply crowding out rival policy ideas with their own. But in addition to adopting that standard approach, AI power players have also dictated AI policy agendas in a *distinctive* way.

Members of the AI oligopoly have the power to – unilaterally, or in competition or collaboration with other power players – determine whether to deploy, when to deploy, and how fast to deploy. Whoever has this power is able to shape what regulators try to regulate, what questions they (and the general public) ask, what concerns and priorities they have (and lack), and, possibly, what decision outcomes concerning AI regulation they ultimately reach. Exercising the mere power to *deploy* AI, then, is *itself* an instance of exercising agenda-setting power: it is not just that Big Tech companies make explicit regulatory proposals for which they attempt to secure

3 I focus on US AI companies here because the US oligopoly is also, to a large extent, a global oligopoly – although there are a few smaller European competitors (e.g. Aleph Alpha), and there are other kinds of concentrations of power in other regional markets, such as the Chinese one.

legislators' support,[4] they also set regulatory agendas merely by making AI tools publicly available, which in turn forces an *ex post* regulatory response.

Both of these paths of industry-driven agenda-setting pose a democratic problem. AI deployers – primarily, already powerful tech industry actors – are neither directly nor indirectly *authorized*, and they have largely *uncontested* agenda-setting power: AI deployment is therefore currently a highly anti-competitive agenda-setting environment. On the one hand, industry actors are able to disproportionately benefit from a concentration of wealth, power, and information, which – as we have seen – *in itself* threatens core democratic institutions and procedures. On the other hand, on a more practical note, governments' and citizens' responses to tech industry leaders have signaled a lack of *willingness* to implement meaningful checks and balances when it comes to corporate AI agenda-setting – even if more intervention is already possible. Is there a way for democratic constituencies to overcome this state of affairs, and to take control of AI deployment agendas – and in what way would doing so get us closer to the goal of greater democratic legitimacy?

4.3 Agenda-setting and democratic legitimacy

4.3.1 Disruptive ideas

Much like emerging technologies disrupt markets, ideas can disrupt policy menus – by reshaping initial decisions about what properly counts as an issue for us, collectively, to decide on (Schattschneider, 1960; Romer and Rosenthal, 1978: 27–43). For our purposes here, we will define agenda-setting power (in general; that is, both in a democratically legitimate and illegitimate form) as follows:

> AGENDA-SETTING POWER: Agent A has agenda-setting power in democratic constituency C if A has the ability to effectively increase the public *salience* of a policy proposal P in a way that increases the likelihood that members of C will make *decisions* about P.
> This account is scalar, such that A's level of agenda-setting power is comparatively *stronger* if, and because,
> (i) P's salience influences the substantive *content* of C's decisions in a way that matches or approximates P more than proposals P* by other agents B, and
> (ii) P's salience effectively crowds out *alternative* initial agendas proposed by B.

4 See Chapter 5 for detailed analysis of such cases.

In the context of AI policy, exercises of agenda-setting power via the mere act of deployment have taken the following basic form: an oligopolistic actor develops and deploys a new tool. Then, the deployer publicly contextualizes what that act of deployment might mean for policy while endorsing ideas that benefit the supply side. Public claims of this kind are often presented – somewhat deceptively – as 'educational', like Altman's quote above suggests. To achieve this, deployers often publicly discuss a *limited* range of policy proposals – say, P_1 and P_2, selected from a larger possible policy menu $P_1, \ldots, P_n$. Agenda-setting power has been exercised effectively when democratic constituencies and their elected representatives respond to this by simply *accepting* the newly circumscribed policy menu:

DEPLOYER:	Now that this tool is out in the world, we can choose either P_1 or P_2.
CONSTITUENCY:	Ok. Previously, we were leaning towards P_1, but now that we have learned that P_2 is an option preferred by domain experts, we suppose we, too, prefer P_2. And we do not need to give further thought to yet other options P_3 and P_4 – clearly, they do not seem to be part of a feasible policy menu anyway.

Interestingly, agenda-setters can make particular options *salient* not just by publicly lending strong support to a specific P, but also by underselling some option P as 'infeasible' or 'unrealistic'. Decisions to deploy AI are frequently framed as an inevitable event rather than as a deliberate, agenda-setting decision by deployers: one popular argument by industry leaders is that it is necessary for them to deploy some tool first, before it inevitably falls into the hands of 'bad actors' who will deploy it anyway (Karp, 2023). This kind of claim is an instance of what political and social epistemologists have called *cryptonormative judgments*: statements of the structure 'It's not that I think Φ-ing [e.g. implementing P_1-type AI regulation] isn't the right thing to do – it's just that Φ-ing isn't possible in these circumstances' (Worsnip, 2017: 3–24).

While such a claim seems to merely convey a descriptive statement about which policy choices are in fact feasible, it has a hidden normative component in that it artificially, and possibly self-servingly, reduces the scope of P_n. This, in turn, insulates the agenda-setter making the cryptonormative claim from public pushback – others are less likely to contest what seems like a purely fact-based statement rather than a value-based one. An absence of such pushback further increases the salience of the agenda-setter's preferred option P_1.

Clearly, this is potentially insidious if what we care about is having policy choices that actually serve the interests of all constituency members, not just those of a select few. As I will argue later, democratic constituencies can and should resist unduly narrow AI deployment agendas by critically interrogating the interests, values, and ideologies underpinning such cryptonormative judgments, and by exploring whether the range of salient options adequately reflect the full scale of possible policy choices P_n.

4.3.2 *Procedures, guardrails, and risk*

Agenda-setting is a *necessary* component of the democratic process: we must first come to a view about which questions and proposals warrant a collective decision before actually making the latter decisions. Yet not all agenda-setting is *necessarily* 'democratic'. First, agenda-setters need not be members of the democratic constituencies that they influence. They could be foreign actors, including foreign state governments and foreign companies. Second, agenda-setters need not be directly or indirectly democratically authorized: they can be powerful corporate actors, or private individuals who enjoy an outsized public influence due to their economic or social capital. Powerful tech CEOs, for example, do not participate in agenda-setting *merely* as private citizens, who (like any other citizen) have equal rights of voice and deliberation. Third, agenda-setters can end up shaping democratic decision outcomes in ways departing significantly from median voter preferences, thus distorting deliberative processes (Romer and Rosenthal, 1978).

In contrast to these three types of agenda-setting with limited or no democratic legitimacy, there are in principle two types of actors who can in engage democratically legitimate agenda-setting – irrespective of which *substantive* view of democratic legitimacy one endorses. Either agendas are set bottom-up by a set of democratic constituency members, or they are set top-down by representatives who are either elected and thus directly democratically authorized, or who hold an unelected public office that plausibly counts as indirectly democratically authorized because it is a part of a broader legitimate public institution.[5]

5 Note that membership in either one of these two groups is merely a *necessary*, not a sufficient, condition of democratically legitimate agenda-setting. And of course, this basic way of partitioning the field of legitimate agenda-setting brackets a number of non-ideal factors that can objectionably distort even agenda-setting pathways that are *in principle* legitimate. Unfortunately, those factors are ubiquitous and hard to eradicate fully. They include propaganda, mass misinformation campaigns online, unchecked campaign finance activities, and other acts of political wrongdoing such as corruption and electoral interference. However, the presence of factors like these obviously does not undermine my general claim that the *ideal* of democratically legitimate agenda-setting requires the participation of specific actors.

But beyond that general observation, which substantive view of democratic legitimacy is best? One possible view is that what is decisive for legitimacy is the question of whether some decision *outcome* serves the values that the democratic constituency wishes to safeguard – say, a free and just society:

> Pure Instrumentalism: Only the quality of decision-making outcomes is decisive for legitimacy.

If democratic decisions fall short of the instrumentalist standard, they do not count as legitimate (Arneson, 2003: 122–132). In fact, instrumentalism would deliver a strong argument against democracy *tout court* in such cases (Brennan, 2016). What is attractive about this view is that it captures a common intuition: democracies often make terrible decisions. Decisions that disenfranchise parts of the population – people of color, women, felons, for example – or decisions that infringe on people's moral and legal rights in other ways are decisions that ultimately undermine the very normative commitments that motivate the implementation of democratic procedures in the first place (Dworkin, 1996). And if democratic decision-making ends up being self-defeating, a benevolent dictator might be a preferable decision-maker than the fallible, biased, and insufficiently knowledgeable democratic constituency at large.

However, instrumentalists need not view democracy's ability to generate high-quality outcomes with quite as much pessimism. Whether instrumentalism is hostile to democracy depends on an empirical issue, not a normative one: are democratic collectives better or worse than other collectives or individuals at making good calls? If democratically made decisions were in fact the ones that delivered the best possible outcomes, instrumentalism would imply that we *should* make decisions democratically rather than via some other decision mechanism, and those decisions would then count as legitimate (Barry, 1965; List and Goodin, 2001: 277–306; Estlund, 2008; Landemore, 2013).

In short, instrumentalism either implies that democratizing any domain (including AI) will *necessarily* lead to the best decision outcomes available, or it fails to offer a justification for *democratic* decision-making whatsoever. Both are implausible in my view: I foresee the possibility that, realistically, democratic constituencies may lack relevant information about AI and adopt suboptimal AI policy on that basis. But I also object to the view that fair democratic procedures have no intrinsic value, beyond the outcomes they produce – and to the view that we must adopt a monistic approach to democratic legitimacy which hinges on a singular standard such as outcome quality (Christiano, 2004: 266–290). Luckily, philosophers have articulated alternatives to instrumentalism, which detach outcome quality considerations entirely from questions of legitimacy:

> PURE PROCEDURALISM: Only procedural features of decision-making are decisive for legitimacy.

On this view, the reason why we should make decisions democratically rather than in some other way is that doing so fairly treats each citizen as a public equal, in voice and in deliberation, which is intrinsically valuable (Waldron, 1999; Kolodny, 2014: 195–229). But while the public equality point is compelling, pure proceduralism fails to address instrumentalists' reasonable worry that fair procedures often give rise to substantively unjust outcomes that leave citizens' rights at the mercy of capricious and biased democratic majorities. To resolve this problem, Christiano has developed a *moderate proceduralist* view, which combines the public equality defense of fair democratic procedures with minimal outcome constraints that protect the rights of democratic constituency members via constitutional rights protections and institutionally secured mechanisms of contestation and recourse:

> MODERATE PROCEDURALISM implies that the democratic process has intrinsic value but it recognizes limits beyond which some restraints must be placed on the process in order to accommodate a minimum of the interests which are at the foundation of the ideals of democracy. [...] The need to avoid the creation of permanent [vulnerable] minorities is a further requirement of public equality. The minimum outcome standard is a way to satisfy the requirement of public equality in collective decision-making while avoiding a state of affairs that is clearly inconsistent with public equality (Christiano, 2008).

I endorse this general view on the grounds that it is the only view that plausibly explains a central fact of real-world democratic practice: the fact that democratic constituencies sometimes make unjust (or otherwise bad), but nonetheless procedurally legitimate decisions.[6] Detaching outcome quality from the value of procedures in this way is appealing because it allows moderate proceduralists to capture the intuition that something of value is lost when we give up on fair procedures that allow all of us, as free equals, to collectively author the rules and standards governing society, while at the same time being clear-sighted about the possible limitations of this form of collective decision-making.

6 Of course, the question of whether such democratically legitimate decisions should *in fact* be implemented all things considered in an unconstrained way will be dependent on whether other important normative goals, such as 'justice' or 'high outcome quality', offer countervailing reasons to constrain such decisions. See §6.2 for further discussion.

Yet despite moderate proceduralism's *prima facie* appeal, the view can be further strengthened by modifying it in a *risk-sensitive* way. This is particularly important when it comes to developing an account for democratizing AI, given the pernicious ASYMMETRY created by current AI deployment; but I view this risk-sensitive extension as a broader philosophical claim that applies to democratic practice more generally, not just to AI-related decision-making. Any decisions taken within – though (crucially) not necessarily by all members of – democratic constituencies can *disperse* morally and politically weighty risks amongst the constituency's members, while *concentrating* the benefits or profits arising from the imposition of such risks amongst a subset of that constituency. Some examples of such decisions include decisions about climate change, the patenting and licensing of medical and scientific innovations, defense, transportation, and – most importantly for the context of this particular proposal – the decision by corporate actors to deploy generative AI at scale. My view is that such ASYMMETRIES must be factored into our assessment of whether some decision process within a democratic constituency counts as democratically *legitimate*, given that such asymmetries can adversely impinge on moderate proceduralism's core requirements: a fair process, public equality, equal opportunities for citizens to participate in speech and deliberation, and so on. If there are fair procedures and plausible minimum outcome standards in place, but objectionable ASYMMETRIES persist nevertheless, something is still missing: outcomes reached under such conditions cannot count as fully democratically legitimate, if and because such ASYMMETRIES undermine the foundations of democratic legitimacy in the first place.

Risk-sensitivity can be built into moderate proceduralism in at least two ways. First, we can tailor *minimum outcome standards* with the explicit aim of ameliorating the ASYMMETRY. One way of doing so would be to strengthen citizens' rights to hold oligopolistic actors liable for deceptive or anticompetitive behavior that wrongfully sets back consumer interests. Another way would be to draw on existing constitutional rights protections to create new legal frameworks blocking the deployment of some tool for morally objectionable purposes that would infringe on the rights of vulnerable minorities. Or constituencies can create better safeguards against corporate regulatory capture at the agenda-setting stage that risks further entrenching ASYMMETRIES, by implementing revision, oversight, and sanctions mechanisms for cases in which there are legitimate concerns that some top-down regulatory proposal has been subject to undue corporate influence.[7]

7 §6.1.1 – especially sub-section (4) – explores concrete examples of all three of these.

Second, we can identify ways of enabling those most adversely affected by the ASYMMETRY to take a leading role in agenda-setting, and getting the rest of the constituency to appropriately value these deliberative contributions.[8] Importantly, prioritizing specific potential agenda-setters in this way does not mean deviating from the core democratic value of 'one person – one vote' political equality. Under risk-sensitive moderate proceduralism, all constituency members retain access to free and equal participation mechanisms, but at the same time, the view emphasizes the importance of *prioritizing* the perspectives of affected communities in order to productively address the ways in which ASYMMETRIES undermine the ideal of a society of free equals – not just on paper, but in real political practice.

More broadly, risk-sensitive moderate proceduralism suggests that we must pay greater attention to the fact that treating the status quo as reasonably just risks obfuscating the presence of ASYMMETRIES. Free and fair procedures open to all public equals are valuable – but they occur in a political arena in which different actors participate from a fundamentally uneven baseline, making it easier for already-powerful actors to push their preferred agendas. This in itself impedes the kind of public justification citizens are owed when ASYMMETRIES arise, and at the same time, the assumption that the baseline is not uneven makes it harder to discern the degree to which powerful agenda-setters drive larger-scale public deliberation. In a nutshell, risk-sensitive moderate proceduralism explicitly directs our attention to how risk dispersions create discrepancies between *de jure* mechanisms of equality in deliberation and voice, and their *de facto* counterpart, and it provides a theoretical foundation for participatory models that stand a chance at mitigating those effects.

8 §6.1.1 – especially sub-section (1) – explores the practical implications of this thought in depth.

5

Strategies

'There's a lot here to be excited about. […] I think this could be very positive for our society and economy.'
(Mark Zuckerberg, and viral TikTok meme, 2021)

AI innovation, in the best possible case, promises us an optimized future in which our lives are easier, safer, more prosperous, and more fulfilling. Democracy, construed in an appropriately 'THICK' sense, promises to deliver a society in which all of us are the *co-authors* of our joint future, and the *co-owners* of the fruits of our collective potential.

These are promises, not predictions. Neither one of them is guaranteed, or even particularly likely – haphazard and largely unfettered AI innovation at its worst may end up propelling us into an unpredictable and authoritarian tech dystopia, and blind trust in democratic procedures without due attention to how they might be corrupted or how they might neglect or overrule parts of society may lull us into thinking, falsely, that we have done enough to establish a free and equal society. These are urgent threats. In light of both, it is clear that neither the promise of AI innovation nor the promise of an appropriately comprehensive and inclusive form of democracy will remain within realistic reach unless we, as in-principle free and equal members of democratic constituencies, take deliberate action towards these goals now.

What do *existing* attempts to subject AI deployment to better democratic control and regulation look like, and how successful are they? 'Success', of course, is not purely a prudential matter; that is, it is not enough for a given AI deployment policy proposal to *in fact* be implemented, possibly despite persistent controversy over its merits, in order for it to count as successful. Instead, a successful attempt must meet the *normative* bar that the previous arguments have set. In other words, to what extent do these attempts actually get us closer to a world in which the political and moral problems we have identified so far are being meaningfully addressed: a world in which power and wealth concentrated in the AI industry become more accessible to the wider democratic constituency currently excluded from it; in which serious risks associated with rapid AI innovation cease to be widely dispersed in society without meaningful public justification; and in which all members of democratic constituencies have real opportunities to participate in democratically legitimate decisions about when, how, and how fast to deploy AI? And if existing AI deployment policies risk frustrating these normative standards, which new directions should democratic constituencies take to chart a better course?

This chapter begins by identifying two increasingly popular and competing sets of AI regulation and democratization approaches that have each shaped AI policy agendas. Interestingly, this analysis reveals that several ostensibly opposed approaches are actually aligned with similar strategic and normative goals. But more importantly, my analysis also reveals that even though both broad sets of approaches have their own respective virtues, each one of them exhibits significant shortcomings that risk undermining the broader goal of democratic legitimacy. In response, I explore an alternative strategy for putting control over AI deployment in the hands of the people, motivated by my preceding arguments about conceptualizing agenda-setting as a key pressure point for democratization efforts under the 'THICK DEMOCRACY' view.

5.1 Two-and-a-half strategies

The European Union has been at the forefront of subjecting cutting-edge AI, including generative AI, to thorough regulation. The EU AI Act, in effect since August 1, 2024, imposes far-reaching reporting and compliance obligations on AI deployers, based on different levels of risk associated with different AI applications. Despite this regulatory leap forward, and counterintuitively, even the EU is experiencing a significant regulatory vacuum at the moment: most provisions in the Act will be enforced only two years later, starting August 2, 2026. In the meantime, while EU member states scramble to set up national institutions and procedures designed to enforce the Act's provisions, responsible AI design and deployment continue to largely be at the mercy of industry actors. The US, in turn, has been more hesitant to impose comprehensive and binding regulation at the federal level. Both states of affairs are the outcomes of non-neutral decisions to proceed with one particular type of caution: caution about stifling innovation too much and too soon. By comparison, both regulatory contexts have exhibited less of a sense of caution about the potential adverse consequences of *failing* to regulate these tools, although regulators in both regions have frequently emphasized the moral and political urgency of doing so.

Current regulatory gaps cannot plausibly be attributed *exclusively* to industry actors' outsized influence on AI policy: as Reich et al. aptly put it 'government is complicit in the absence of regulation' (Reich et al., 2021). In fact, industry actors *themselves* are increasingly urging democratically authorized public officials to design clearer, more ambitious rules concerning AI deployment. A US Senate subcommittee hearing in May 2023, mentioned in Chapter 1, provides a rich set of illustrative examples for the dynamics at play, which are worth exploring in detail.

Witnesses at this hearing proposed an overwhelming flurry of competing AI regulation approaches (Senate, 2023). AI needs '*precision regulation*', IBM's spokesperson Christina Montgomery and OpenAI CEO Sam Altman agreed: the kind of cautious regulation that does not block innovation via blunt deployment bans, but rather surgically intervenes into AI deployment to impose 'different rules for different risks' associated with AI (Senate, 2023: 30). Despite unsurprisingly broad agreement amongst the three invited speakers – beyond Montgomery and Altman, this included vocal AI critic and academic Gary Marcus – on the basic idea that industry and government should collaborate on regulation in some broad sense, all three noticeably disagreed on what, precisely, should be regulated, and to what end: what the nature of these risks of harms might be (Senate, 2023: 6–13).[1]

All three invited witnesses also stated some degree of support for the idea of making tech companies apply for *licenses* to develop and deploy highly sophisticated generative AI. A licensing regime would tie the ability to deploy such tools to the company's computational capacities. Altman advocated for this idea – not particularly known or popular in AI policy circles before the hearing – very explicitly: 'Number one, I would form a new agency that licenses any effort above a certain scale of capabilities and can take that license away and ensure compliance with safety standards' (Senate, 2023: 32). Those with vast computational resources, the thought goes, have the ability to build cutting-edge generative AI safely, and holding a license to do so would keep 'bad actors' out of the market while subjecting the 'good guys' to reporting and oversight obligations. Meanwhile, the related idea that the US should create an entirely *new federal agency* to oversee AI deployment received mixed support, on the grounds that some witnesses thought that *existing* agencies could meaningfully regulate already in this area, and that creating a new agency would be too slow (Senate, 2023: 34, 41f). But despite some disagreement at the hearing, a wide range of US lawmakers were convinced by the broader licensing idea championed by industry. Mere months after the hearing, Senators

1 Altman and Montgomery largely focused on the risk of generative AI for existing jobs, whereas Marcus focused on problems like bias and misinformation.

Blumenthal and Hawley unveiled a bipartisan AI policy framework that called, first and foremost, for 'establish[ing] a licensing regime administered by an independent oversight body' (Blumenthal and Hawley, 2023: 1).

Another possible policy approach – the idea of imposing outright deployment bans on specific AI tools – was criticized even by Marcus, who argued that focusing on articulating clear ethics and safety standards for AI was more important than banning specific tools (Senate, 2023: 50), and Montgomery – articulating a common tech industry view – stated that 'we need to use the time to prioritize ethics and responsible technology as opposed to pausing development' (Senate, 2023: 51). In contrast, public discourse outside of this hearing had – in a turn of events atypical to otherwise staunchly anti-regulation, pro-deployment tech industry circles – recently warmed up to deployment moratoria (temporary ones, at least), particularly following the release of a heavily publicized Open Letter by the Future of Life Institute in March 2023. The letter, signed by tech leaders like Elon Musk and ex-Google 'godfather of AI' Geoffrey Hinton, stressed that AI may pose unforeseeable and possibly existential risks to humanity, calling for 'all AI labs to immediately pause for at least 6 months the training of AI systems more powerful than GPT-4' (Future of Life Institute, 2023). Against this view, and much like Montgomery and Marcus,[2] Altman dismissed this kind of idea to impose a targeted deployment moratorium – ostensibly not on principled grounds, but on the basis of the claim that AI risks were not severe enough yet: 'We don't see reasons to not train a new [model]. For deploying, [...] there's all sorts of risky behavior, and there's limits we put. [...] we don't see something that would stop us from training the next model, where we'd be so worried that we'd create something dangerous' (Senate, 2023: 50).

This approach is embedded in a larger context in earlier AI policy: the Open Letter's demands dovetailed with immensely controversial earlier efforts to impose deployment bans on specific AI tools before the generative AI boom, most notably facial recognition tools in law and immigration enforcement. In 2019's *Stop Secret Surveillance Ordinance*, following bottom-up activism by criminal justice advocates, San Francisco locally banned facial recognition tools in law enforcement settings on the grounds that their use violated civil liberties and had a disparate racial impact (City and County of San Francisco Board of Supervisors, 2019: 103–119).

2 Months later, Marcus publicly stated that he had been 'too soft' on Altman at this hearing: 'I found Altman surprisingly engaging. [...] he seemed genuine, and I recall saying as much to the senators at the time. We both came out strongly for AI regulation. Little by little, though, I realised that I, the Senate, and ultimately the American people, had probably been played' Marcus (2024).

Shortly thereafter, multiple American cities followed suit. In a surprising turn of events, several tech companies – during a time in which Big Tech was still much more overtly anti-regulation, prior to The Shift – including Amazon and IBM decided to impose deployment moratoria on themselves in 2020, citing concerns about their own ability to make those tools safer and fairer under conditions of pervasive racial injustice (Amazon Blog, 2020; IBM, 2020).[3]

In sum, recent AI deployment policy discourse has been flooded by a wide range of competing and deeply controversial regulatory approaches. At the same time, contributions to this discourse that have gained a particularly high degree of public salience have – in my view, misleadingly – conveyed the message that democratically legitimate AI regulation is a relatively straightforward task: one which can be accomplished without unduly extensive state intervention that would stifle innovative companies' ability to continue to set deployment agendas. And even more importantly, currently influential policy proposals have gained their high level of salience precisely *because* they have received public support from industry actors at key policy events facilitated by elected representatives. At these events, regulators' support for these proposals has failed to critically reflect on – and publicly communicate – the degree to which current AI policy agendas at the level of articulated preferences, not just deployment decisions themselves, have been shaped by powerful companies. At the Senate Committee hearing, lawmakers were fawning over their witnesses, seemingly desperate for their help in regulating this powerful technology, as this exchange illustrates:

Mr. ALTMAN.	We can give your office a long other list of the things that we think are important there, but specific tests that a model has to pass before it can be deployed into the world.
Senator KENNEDY.	Can you send me that information?
Mr. ALTMAN.	We will do that.
Senator KENNEDY.	Would you be qualified, if we promulgated those rules, to administer those rules?
Mr. ALTMAN.	I love my current job.[4]
[Laughter.]	

3 For IBM's letter to Congress pledging to self-impose a facial recognition deployment moratorium for reasons related to racial justice in 2020, see IBM (2020).

4 After being fired by OpenAI's board for a few days over ethical concerns and eventually getting reinstated, Altman reshaped the board and consolidated his power inside the company. As of now, only two of OpenAI's eleven founders (one of which is Altman) are still actively working at OpenAI (*Bloomberg*, 2024).

Senator KENNEDY.	Are there people out there that would be qualified?
Mr. ALTMAN.	We'd be happy to send you recommendations for people out there, yes.
Senator KENNEDY.	Okay. You make a lot of money, do you?
Mr. ALTMAN.	No. I'm paid enough for health insurance.[5] I have no equity in OpenAI (OpenAI website).
Senator KENNEDY.	Really?
Mr. ALTMAN.	Yes.[6]
Senator KENNEDY.	[...] You need a lawyer or an agent.
Mr. ALTMAN.	I'm doing this because I love it.

Altman's positions on AI regulation were well-received not only in the US Senate, but also across the world. In the month after the hearing, Altman went on a world tour, traveling to Israel, Jordan, Qatar, the United Arab Emirates, India, South Korea, Japan, Singapore, Indonesia, and Australia to speak to regulators about AI policy (Foreign Policy, 2023). Meanwhile, in the EU context, big tech companies exerted considerable influence on lawmakers, too. OpenAI, Microsoft, and Google all lobbied EU lawmakers to dilute restrictions imposed by the AI Act, warning about 'unduly burdening innovation'[7] (The Software Alliance, 2023), and threatening to cease their operations in Europe unless regulators complied with their demands. Even though these threats were later walked back (Reuters, 2023), some of these lobbying efforts successfully altered the final version of the Act. For instance, as freedom of information requests filed with the European Commission by journalists at *TIME* magazine reveal, OpenAI supported the late introduction of the separate concept of 'foundation models' because adding that conceptual category meant that the Act did not frame all generative AI models as inherently 'high risk' – which is exactly the view that OpenAI supported in its *own* unpublished White Paper on the AI Act, sent directly to European regulators in September 2022 (Perrigo, 2023). Similarly, in a letter addressed to EU commissioners obtained by transparency group Corporate Europe Observatory, Google had argued that '[g]eneral-purpose AI systems are purpose neutral: they are

5 This answer omits the fact that Altman owns equity in Y Combinator, which in turn has a stake in OpenAI. See 'Our Structure' (OpenAI website, n.d.)

6 This answer may be subject to change in the future. As part of ongoing plans to restructure OpenAI as a for-profit company, OpenAI considered giving Altman a 7% stake in the company, which would increase his net worth by billions (*Bloomberg*, 2024). Altman denied this the following day at an OpenAI all-hands meeting: 'Sam Altman tells OpenAI staff there's no plan for him to receive a "giant equity stake" in company' (CNBC, 2024).

7 This claim appears in a statement by the Software Alliance, a lobby group founded by Microsoft. Other members, amongst others, include IBM, Oracle, and Salesforce.

versatile by design, and are not themselves high-risk because these systems are not intended for any specific purpose' – and has got the result it wanted (Schyns, 2023).

Given this complex AI policy landscape, how can we systematically analyze and evaluate competing AI democratization and regulation proposals? As it turns out, paying closer attention to the explicit and implicit goals of recent proposals reveals that some seemingly *opposing* policies actually target similar objectives, in the sense that they aim to push on the same kind of pressure points. Given this, we can group the wide range of currently influential proposals concerning the democratization and regulation of AI deployment into two broad strategies that are currently dominant in US AI policy as well as in the EU context.

The first strategy consists of a heterogeneous cluster of approaches to regulating *decisions* to deploy AI *themselves*. This includes licensing rules, institutionalized mechanisms for pre- or post-deployment safety review via newly created public agencies, or – in stark contrast to the first two – heavy-handed deployment moratoria imposed in a top-down way either from government or from industry actors. Despite the fact that supporters of each of the former – especially fans of deployment moratoria and fans of much less heavy-handed 'precision regulation' – strongly disagree with each other, each of them actually serves the pursuit of the same higher-order goal: to shape and direct deployment itself rather than responding to it later. This strategy most closely tracks Altman's view cited at the beginning of Chapter 4, which does go beyond relying exclusively on tech companies' sense of societal responsibility, but which frames industry-based deployers as the ones who must first *educate* regulators and the wider public on which policy proposals might be best suited for mitigating dispersions of risk associated with AI deployment. Call this:

> Strategy A: Regulate new AI deployment decisions themselves by utilizing top-down mechanisms to impose more or less restrictive deployment constraints.

The second set of approaches focuses instead on *changing* how democratic constituencies *respond* to already-existing or currently ongoing AI deployment, as in the bottom-up activism example leading to San Francisco's temporary local ban on facial recognition tools. More generally, this kind of strategy includes the exercise of bottom-up agenda-setting counterpower – via activism, advocacy, or lobbying – with the aim of shifting deployment goals and constraints *ex post*, but it can also include initiating large-scale top-down legal transformations that seek to redress regulatory gaps in the AI space, possibly as a result of bottom-up activism. Call this:

Strategy B: Redirect existing AI deployment agendas by utilizing bottom-up mechanisms to contest policy preferences articulated, and agendas set, by industry-based deployers, possibly followed by regulatory change if bottom-up agenda-setting succeeds.

5.2 Hunting bugs

Each of these two broad strategies, (A) and (B), is subject to significant pitfalls when implemented in isolation. First, (A) risks *further concentrating power* and preventing AI deployers in Big Tech from being subject to public accountability.[8] For instance, if licenses are tied to a company's ability to avail itself of vast computational resources above a high threshold, then only a handful of companies will be able to obtain such licenses. This immediately clears the market of competitors potentially threatening to disrupt oligopolistic structures, such as start-ups and less well-funded research teams. This is in the interest of a few corporate actors, but not necessarily in the interest of the democratic constituency at large, given that the latter's interests are likely better served by fair market competition.

Second, (A) offers few opportunities for meaningful *bottom-up* participation, and it will possibly depart quite significantly from broader political preferences in the constituency as a whole (Mansbridge, 2018: 298–338). Since (A) focuses not on contesting agenda-setting via deployment, but rather on making binding regulatory decisions which constrain deployment, its preferred mechanism of intervention must be a top-down one. A risk-sensitive moderate proceduralist perspective on democratic legitimacy suggests that any exclusively top-down form of democratic decision-making is intrinsically objectionable, on the grounds that such an approach lacks fair procedures that are accessible to all citizens and that publicly express their equal political status. In this sense, (A) is another troubling instance of a problem persuasively diagnosed by Urbinati: the phenomenon that contemporary representative democracies may optimize for *isonomia* – equality in lawmaking – but fail to realize or approximate the ideal of *isegoria* – equality in deliberation and voice (Urbinati, 2006).

Third, (A) may be hard to implement *well* in the absence of global cooperation. Even if one country or region R succeeds in passing comprehensive top-down AI regulation, this will not necessarily stop a deployer operating in a global market from continuing to deploy elsewhere, which in turn

8 For an extensive analysis of pitfalls associated with components of (A) that adopt a logic of 'approval regulation', such as an 'FDA for algorithms' and licensing approaches, see Carpenter and Ezell (2024).

could have feedback effects on the well-regulated constituency R: unconstrained deployment in other regions could make high-risk AI capabilities accessible to hostile actors aiming to destabilize R.

On the other hand, (B) risks being *slow* and *reactive*. Waiting and seeing what agendas are set by industry via the very act of deploying some new tool, and attempting to tackle the repercussions of that only after the fact, unduly limits the scope of democratic control in this area. It also puts regular citizens in a passive position: one in which they do not take action until they are confronted with a new status quo – one from which it may be difficult to backtrack post-deployment.

(B) can also easily result in *patchy* regulation: when bottom-up agenda-setting counterpower succeeds, some AI tools may be banned in some local jurisdictions, and that may be normatively desirable from the perspective of local democratic legitimacy. However, these kinds of interventions do not result in regulation that can cut across different local jurisdictions and different domains of application. For that reason, they fail to give proper consideration to the morally weighty interests of *all* members of the democratic constituency at large in a way that realizes their status as public equals. Unless other local constituencies copy the successes of those who have successfully implemented (B), we cannot expect (B) by itself to deliver the *comprehensive* democratic control that is needed when it comes to rapid and large-scale AI deployment.

Relatedly, (B) suffers from an additional weakness: it is not realistic to expect that all members of democratic constituencies will be perfect model citizens, who actively intervene in public deliberations over AI policy, without there being clear participatory pathways that facilitate better bottom-up agenda-setting concerning AI. It is more likely that bottom-up input into ongoing deployment processes will primarily include a small subset of citizens who are already highly politically mobilized, and that such participation will be triggered by one-off controversies over some particular AI use case. This, again, results in a patchwork approach to democratizing AI, rather than enabling bigger-picture value-based public deliberation on AI's societal purpose and future direction. Each of these factors makes (B), when implemented in isolation, an inherently reactive and insufficiently comprehensive strategy.

Before we continue, a caveat is in order. Astute followers of recent public discourse on AI regulation will have noticed that one further strategy notorious for its own pitfalls has been missing in my analysis so far. This is the strategy of *voluntary self-regulation* by industry actors. This can take the form of company-internal ethics pledges, or codes of conduct by tech-related professional organizations modeled after a Hippocratic Oath, or non-binding agreements between public officials and tech CEOs to adhere to ethical goals like 'trustworthiness' and 'safety' – such as the EU's AI Pact accompanying its AI Act (European Commission, 2024), or the Biden administration's ethics pledge with the US' leading tech CEOs (The White House, 2023).

More specifically, this strategy aims to align AI – both with respect to the ways in which tools are designed, and with respect to when and how they are deployed – with political and moral values that the larger democratic constituency is *assumed* to hold, or (perhaps) with values that industry teams, given their domain-specific expertise, deem appropriate irrespective of their assumptions about whether other citizens *in fact* endorse those values. A charitable reconstruction of this strategy suggests that its supporters may hope that successfully implementing this strategy will lead to a new status quo in which democratic constituencies consider the deployment of some AI tool legitimate in at least a thin sense, even if they had no direct control over deployment, on the grounds that industry deployers have demonstrated good intentions to build tools that align with values that regular citizens would *hypothetically* endorse. Call this:

> Strategy C: Rely on deployers to self-impose legally unenforceable value-based constraints on their own AI deployment decisions, and to responsibly reflect on what kinds of agendas they have the power to set merely by publicly articulating AI policy preferences and by having the power to decide to deploy some generative AI tool at time T and scale S.

In all fairness to those who champion voluntary self-regulation in the tech industry, few seem to think that strategy C is *sufficient* for achieving democratically legitimate AI, or even just *reasonably good* AI that does not exhibit major biases and egregious errors. (C) is less of a political strategy and more of a wishlist. As earnest as they may be, lofty aspirations to 'innovate responsibly' do not get us very far, given that countervailing market pressures may crush those aspirations at any moment.

Many contributions to public discourse thus acknowledge explicitly that (C) is a less-than-optimal band-aid whenever other forms of oversight and regulation seem impossible or insufficient. But irrespective of whether (C) supporters think that (C) is a mere substitute for other, better strategies, or whether they (more ambitiously and less plausibly) think that (C) is actually all-things-considered preferable to the other strategies, my view is that (C) remains fundamentally inadequate if the goal is to achieve democratically legitimate AI deployment decisions, and that we can therefore disqualify it from further consideration as we proceed in our evaluation of plausible solutions for democratizing AI. These efforts – if driven by genuinely good intentions rather than by PR goals – are laudable, but they are inherently unenforceable, and recent history suggests that they are often short-lived.

Consider, first, Google's decision to remove its own 'Don't Be Evil' motto from its internal code of conduct in 2018 (*Gizmodo*, 2018). This leaves one to wonder whether even this remarkably minimal ethical bar was unduly restrictive. Consider also the self-imposed 2020 facial recognition deployment moratoria discussed above: Amazon had first extended the moratorium on police department contracts involving such tools *indefinitely* in 2021. However, as of 2024, reports suggest that Amazon is now selling these tools to the FBI (*Computer Weekly*, 2024). IBM, three years after sending a letter to Congress pledging to self-impose a facial recognition deployment moratorium for reasons related to racial justice (now deleted from the company's blog), signed a $69.8 million contract with the UK government to provide facial recognition tools for law and immigration enforcement purposes (UK Home Office, 2023). Consider, finally, that public agreements like the Biden administration's ethics pledge with leading tech CEOs do not include any particular *deadlines* or *reporting and disclosure obligations*. While existing enforcement bodies like the FTC could in principle utilize existing consumer protection law to investigate breaches of the pledge under the framework of *deceptive practices*, it is unclear how a breach would be defined given the remarkably capacious language of such pledges (*The Washington Post*, 2023b).

5.3 A new path

Which democratization approach amongst the competing models covered above is ultimately *preferable* from the perspective of democratic legitimacy? Risk-sensitive moderate proceduralism suggests that, ultimately, the decisive question is which approach is best suited to address the dispersion of risk/concentration of power ASYMMETRY's bad effects on fair participatory procedures instantiating our status as political equals. As we have seen, that ASYMMETRY cannot be mitigated effectively by either one of the two approaches alone, given their respective flaws. Nonetheless, we can draw action-guiding insights from each one to identify a better solution: one that puts more power in the hands of the people, and one that targets the right pressure points in larger-scale societal deployment decision processes, thus offering better prospects for keeping oligopolistic concentrations of power and wealth in Big Tech in check.

Let us get more concrete. On this new view, rather than abandoning either one – or both – of the currently dominant democratization approaches entirely, we can incorporate some of the motivating claims of each one, and chart a more promising path forward.

From supporters of the heterogeneous cluster of approaches targeting deployment decisions *themselves* – Strategy A – we can learn that such responses will work only if they are backed by concrete institutional and regulatory transformation rather than lofty declarations of self-imposed, non-binding ethical responsibility. Further, we can learn that democratically authorized representatives – not just regular citizens – have an important role in democratizing AI deployment, despite the agenda-setting perspective's close alignment with empowering bottom-up civic participation. Crucially, however, such institutional and regulatory transformations must not be the result of decision-making agendas shaped in large part by oligopolistic actors themselves, as current versions of (A) often are.

From supporters of the approach that focuses on changing our *response* to ongoing deployment decision processes – Strategy B – we can learn that the ability to question and critique such decisions, to refuse to simply accept them as inevitable, and to demand recourse for any resulting harm can trigger the formation of new and possibly dramatically different deployment agendas – even through democratic actors that lack deep technological or regulatory expertise. At the same time, it remains a key priority, from the perspective of democratic legitimacy, not to rely too heavily on the often unrealistic expectation that ordinary citizens will consistently and reliably opt into processes of public deliberation and contestation over some AI tool. And most importantly, our earlier examination of (B) has shown that any strategy that fails to fundamentally alter the 'deploy first, ask for control later' dynamic that gave rise to the Asymmetry in the first place will remain inadequate. A better alternative strategy must avoid replicating B's inherently reactive nature. A new view combining these insights, at its most basic level, looks like this:

> Strategy D: *Anticipate* and *iteratively contest* AI deployment agendas by utilizing democratically legitimate bottom-up participatory mechanisms in combination with top-down regulatory interventions by democratically authorized representatives to (i) comprehensively shape deployment agendas; to (ii) legally secure safeguards against the creation and exacerbation of Asymmetries; and (iii) to enforce citizen's value-based political preferences concerning the implementation of those agendas.

(D) achieves multiple intuitively plausible goals. First, it combines the appealing elements of top-down regulation and bottom-up participation included in (A) and (B). The view motivating this hybrid approach is that bottom-up participation remains toothless in the absence of meaningful regulatory change at the level of institutions and procedures, and that top-down regulation remains ill-equipped to evade the influence of corporate power in the absence of impactful avenues for citizens to demand public accountability. By contrast, when these two elements are implemented in conjunction, they mutually support each other. In that way, they open up more direct participation pathways without sacrificing the important goal of upholding and creating well-defined, enforceable rules and protections at the institutional level.

Second, (D) captures the intuition that the task of democratically legitimate agenda-setting is never done (Reich et al., 2021: 59).[9] The earlier members of democratic constituencies can intervene in agenda-setting, the better: on the (D) view, it is not enough to merely *respond* to agendas that have been set already, either by AI deployment decisions themselves that force a specific regulatory response, or by disproportionately salient policy preferences voiced by tech industry leaders. Instead, democratic constituencies must strive to anticipate what might be at stake, at the level of competing political and moral values, in deployment decisions yet to come, and to articulate policy preferences on that basis. Further, good agenda-setting harnesses the power of revisiting our decisions, and of *changing our minds* if needed. Current dynamics of market competition disincentivize companies from publicly disclosing sufficiently comprehensive information about their products. This means that public access to agenda-relevant information often follows a slow, incremental path. But as soon as new information comes to light that alters the political and moral stakes identified in previous iterations of agenda-setting, (D) prompts democratic constituencies to be ready to tailor agendas to new realities as frequently as needed, and to not fall back into political complacency on matters of AI policy.

9 Other commentators on AI policy have emphasized the need for this iterative dimension given AI's rapid evolution. See, for example, Reich et al.'s proposition that 'our rules must be as dynamic as the technologies they are designed to regulate' (Reich et al., 2021: 59).

6

Democracy

'I no longer believe that freedom and democracy are compatible. [...] Since 1920, the vast increase in welfare beneficiaries and the extension of the franchise to women – two constituencies that are notoriously tough for libertarians – have rendered the notion of "capitalist democracy" into an oxymoron.' (Peter Thiel, 2009)[1]

6.1 Power to the people

What, then, can democratic constituencies do in concrete terms to redesign participatory political processes and to take control of AI deployment agenda-setting, along the lines that (D) articulates? My view is that an important part of resisting the kind of *AI exceptionalism* that has taken hold in AI policy and that I have critiqued at earlier junctures of this essay is to examine *other* policy solutions outside of the domain of AI. This will help us identify successful cases of democratic innovations that have strengthened democratic participation regarding other complex collective decision problems, and that have the potential to provide tangible, action-guiding models for future efforts to democratize AI deployment.

In what follows, I explore possible policy interventions which would better secure citizens' right to voice, on more equal terms, their political preferences about what kinds of deployment-related *problems* need to be on the collective decision agenda. Each intervention would thus provide a much-needed counterweight to industry-driven agenda-setting by enabling *value-based* and *public* deliberations about AI's proper purpose within a given democratic constituency.

1 Following pushback against this claim, Thiel added to his earlier remarks, stating that '[w]hile I don't think any class of people should be disenfranchised, I have little hope that voting will make things better. [...] Politics is about interfering with other people's lives without their consent. [...] Thus, I advocate focusing energy elsewhere, onto peaceful projects that some consider utopian' (ibid.).

My aim is not to provide an *exhaustive* list of possible policy interventions – it is possible that there are many other agenda-setting pathways aligned with (D). The goal is to illustrate simply that more democratically legitimate agenda-setting concerning AI deployment, in comparison to the status quo, is *already feasible*. It is feasible even in the imperfect and complex democratic institutions we have right here and right now.[2] Even better, it is feasible to approximate (D)'s normative goals from different angles, building on participation pathways that take *many different forms*. In short, my aim is to describe an AI democratization PLAYBOOK, not a blueprint: democratic constituencies and their elected representatives can choose multiple options from a menu of legitimate and potentially transformative moves, opting to prioritize some strategies over others depending on context-specific feasibility constraints in a given constituency, such as the amount of available resources and expertise, or the degree of political polarization hindering effective public discourse.

Implementing *each* of these pathways would contribute to ameliorating the existing ASYMMETRY in generative AI deployment. By doing so, citizens would gain meaningful opportunities to reclaim some of the decision-making power currently concentrated amongst Big Tech companies, and to publicly contest the wealth accumulation associated with these technologies. These interventions would also facilitate value-based public deliberation on how much AI-related risk dispersion democratic constituencies wish to accept.

But in addition to that, each pathway also has the potential to amplify *other* pathways' positive impact with respect to making more and better democratic input into AI deployment possible for more people. Having access to a wider range of democratic participation opportunities provides important safeguards for democratic constituencies: it's a way to *hedge* against the risk of corporate overreach, and thus to make fair democratic procedures resilient against attempts to unduly influence them. Even if oligopolistic industry actors successfully capture agendas with respect to one particular deployment domain or procedure, other participation pathways

2 Obviously, this restricts the scope of my argument to constituencies in which democratic procedures are *already* in place in some capacity, such that they can feasibly be enhanced in a way that bolsters legitimate agenda-setting pathways. Developing a standalone account of how to newly democratize decision procedures within constituencies in non-democratic (i.e. authoritarian) states, and to then democratize the specific pressure point of agenda-setting concerning AI deployment within those same constituencies, would be far beyond the scope of this essay, because doing so involves a plethora of additional complicating geopolitical and cultural factors. I invite others, including my interlocutors in this volume, to take up the task of making progress on this complex issue.

may still offer opportunities for citizens to exercise agenda-setting counterpower. For this reason, the interventions identified here target different types of decision sequences using different participatory mechanisms and centering different types of actors, while paying special attention to the value of agenda-setting contributions by specific *sub-constituencies* and *intermediary actors*. Bolstering agenda-setting in line with (D) thereby creates healthier democratic institutions overall, in which democratically illegitimate influences in one or some participation pathways need not spell disaster for the larger goal of democratically legitimate agenda-setting more generally.

6.1.1 *The playbook*

(1) Empowering informed sub-constituencies to enforce accountability and to make binding decisions

Perhaps surprisingly, industry and government actors have made some real efforts to seek the public's input into their AI deployment decisions, and they have used AI in interesting ways to further this aim (Fung and Cohen, 2021: 23–61, 25).[3] OpenAI has solicited feedback from educators on the role of generative AI (OpenAI, 2023b) as well as soliciting funding proposals for experimental projects aimed at 'setting up a democratic process for deciding what rules AI systems should follow' (OpenAI, 2023a), and Anthropic has used the open-source platform pol.is – which uses machine learning to facilitate deliberative processes at scale – to include the input of a demographically diverse group of 1,000 Americans to provide input into the principles shaping its 'Constitutional AI' (Anthropic, 2023).[4] Meanwhile, teams in federal agencies, such as NAIAC (the National Artificial Intelligence Advisory Committee within NIST, the National

3 Whether technological innovation is more likely to hinder or to promote democracy has been subject to some debate amongst political theorists. Fung and Cohen reach the intuitively plausible conclusion that this is a fundamentally *open* question to which there is no context-independent answer: 'the democratic exploitation of technological affordances is vastly more contingent, more difficult, and more dependent on ethical conviction, political engagement, and good design choices than the technological determinists appreciated' (Fung and Cohen, 2021: 23–61, 25).

4 It is worth noting that these powerful companies are not the only ones using AI to facilitate deliberative processes – there has been an explosion of 'participatory AI' projects led by researchers and non-profits proposing to use technology to enhance democratic processes. For an example from the European context, see the 'Virtus' project (funded by the German government and developed as part of the 'House of Participation' research center, https://hop.fzi.de/projekte/virtus/) which used

Institute of Standards and Technology), have been particularly proactive in hosting meetings that feature AI experts but that are also accessible to members of the wider public (The White House, 2021), and bodies like OSTP and the FTC have regularly requested public comments on draft policies (Office of Science and Technology Policy, 2023a, b). Similarly, the European AI Office regularly hosts multistakeholder consultations on issues pertaining to the AI Act, which explicitly champion the idea of implementing an 'inclusive and transparent process' on the grounds that any member of the public can join them in principle (European Commission, 2024a).

These efforts usefully combine elements of top-down agenda-setting concerning AI deployment (A) with bottom-up participation opportunities (B). For that reason, they are aligned with (D) to some extent. But they do not go far enough. Input is not the same as binding decision-making power – and while mere input *can* shift agendas, it can easily be disregarded entirely. Therefore, mere input can fail to be a meaningful agenda-setting pathway whenever strong Asymmetries persist in society. More troublingly, powerful actors can easily use the fact that some public input was solicited as part of what Sloane et al. have aptly called 'participation-washing': stifling critique of their deployed tools by pointing to the fact that some public input was considered prior to deployment (Sloane et al., 2022: 1–6).

By contrast, a *binding decision* at some juncture of a process forces other political actors to grapple with a new status quo, which makes it a more impactful tool for setting future agendas. Similarly, having the ability to not only provide input, but also to *audit and critique* the deployment choices of other actors, means having the ability to hold others publicly accountable, which is crucial for determining how future agendas should be redirected: democratic constituencies need to first have tools to uncover what might have gone wrong in a given case of AI deployment before they can identify publicly beneficial AI policy issues that no other political actor – such as industry leaders – is incentivized to feature on agendas.

In my view, we can best achieve these stronger forms of democratically legitimate agenda-setting power if we do not rely exclusively on democratic

immersive extended reality (XR) applications to facilitate real-time bottom-up participation. For a discussion of use cases, see Stein and Fegert (2024). I concede that these kinds of approaches could be a good addition to other (not AI-enabled) forms of democratization, but my earlier concerns about any model that does not move from bottom-up input to bottom-up binding decisions still apply here. For a more general analysis of 'augmented deliberation' models designed to utilize technology to boost participation, including a balanced assessment of their potential weaknesses, see Weyl and Tang (2024).

constituencies as a whole, and instead focus on harnessing the power of *informed sub-constituencies*:

> INFORMED SUB-CONSTITUENCIES: Technical expertise is not the only relevant criterion for counting as an 'expert' within the context of AI deployment. Informed sub-constituencies leading the way in democratically legitimate agenda-setting surrounding AI deployment include, broadly, members of democratic constituencies who have domain-specific expertise, either by virtue of possessing specialized technical knowledge *or* by virtue of possessing lived experiences that give them enhanced epistemic access to the nature, scope, and asymmetrical dispersion of relevant risks and harms.

Informed sub-constituencies can contribute to agenda-setting aligned with (D) in multiple ways. They can operate within voluntary intermediary associations, such as professional organizations, labor unions, or civic interest groups focused on specific domains like criminal justice or healthcare or housing. As a growing number of political philosophers and democratic theorists have pointed out, such intermediary associations are well placed to serve as a catalyst for enhancing public deliberation on specialized policy domains, representing diverse citizen preferences, contesting regulatory decision-making, and holding corporate actors accountable (Urbinati, 2006; Mansbridge, 2018: 298–338; Carpenter, 2023: 193, 212).[5] Furthermore, empirical research shows that participation in intermediary associations can itself enhance one's domain-specific expertise, thus boosting the capabilities of informed sub-constituencies to effect tangible agenda-setting change.

In concrete terms, members of intermediary associations might engage in *independent third-party auditing*, an approach that is rapidly gaining traction amongst scholars focused on AI policy (Saward, 2008: 1000–1013; Landemore, 2017: 51–63; Raji et al., 2022: 557–571). Auditing results, as supporters of this approach have argued, ought to be protected from the obfuscating effects of the 'NDA culture' so deeply rooted in Big Tech, and

5 For representative examples of this line of thought, see Carpenter (2023), Mansbridge (2018), and Urbinati (2006). Urbinati's influential account offers important additional reasons why representative models of democracy can be preferable to direct participatory models, on the grounds that representation enforces a reflexive delay between preference aggregation and policy-making, thus enhancing the quality of democratic deliberations. In my view, informed sub-constituencies could play a similar role to elected representatives with respect to the 'reflexive delay' aspect, and thus open up more space for well-reasoned debate about AI policy options before final decisions are made. Urbinati seems skeptical of the idea that non-elected constituency members can fulfil this representative role, but see Landemore (2017) and Saward (2008) for discussion of why opening up the concept of democratic representation would be desirable.

instead be made publicly accessible in auditing result registries. Further, they should, in alignment with (D)'s requirements, be conducted at periodic intervals and embedded in a larger institutional ecosystem tasked with implementing auditing results, such as when it comes to revising technical safety standards (Raji et al., 2022: 566). Important higher-order questions to be addressed as part of auditing, which I borrow from Boyd and Eilish's influential account, include: 'What are the unintended consequences of designing systems at scale on the basis of existing patterns in society? When and how should AI systems prioritize individuals over society and vice versa? When is introducing an AI system the right answer – and when is it not?' (Boyd and Elish, 2018).

In addition, researcher groups can utilize newly emerging agreements between government and industry to grant *privileged access* to newly built tools for the purpose of pre-deployment safety review. The US AI Safety Institute's August 2024 agreement with OpenAI and Anthropic to facilitate such a model points in a promising direction (National Institute of Standards and Technology, 2024). At the same time, when pursuing the 'privileged access' strategy, it is important not to allow a *regulatory-tech industrial complex*, characterized by an undue level of enmeshment of government and industry interests, to take hold. Provided that societies can maintain an appropriate level of independence between industry and government actors, analogous efforts should be scaled up across the entire industry on the grounds that they would enhance informed sub-constituencies' ability to exercise their voice on more equal terms. And of course, it is possible to combine this model with more direct participatory approaches relying less on the opting-in of already-mobilized parts of the constituency, and more on randomly selecting representative samples of regular citizens. On such a model, regulators and experts could facilitate policy-specific *citizen assemblies*, provided with pre-deployment access to some AI tool, to better map relevant political preferences and to foster more informed public deliberation amongst laypeople down the line (Urbinati and Warren, 2008: 387–412; Landemore, 2020).

A third possible counterweight to oligopolistically-driven agenda-setting is the creation of new groups tasked with interrogating the impact of already-deployed AI, particularly at the local level, such as New York City's Algorithmic Decision Systems Task Force, the first of its kind in the US.[6] Closely aligned with my view on the transformative potential of

6 It is worth noting that the task force was plagued by bureaucratic hurdles which prevented its members from obtaining a comprehensive overview over which automated tools the city was using in the most general terms, as public statements by its members and the AI Now Institute's Shadow Report outline (Richardson, 2019).

broadly construed informed sub-constituencies, the task force included not only computer scientists and regulators, but also criminal justice experts (NYC Automated Decision Systems Task Force, n.d.). Initiatives of this kind could be even more impactful if they included participants with more direct lived experiences, such as individuals previously incarcerated on the grounds of a biased algorithmic risk score. As I argued in Chapter 4, risk-sensitive moderate proceduralism implies that people more severely affected by AI-related risk can and should, in many cases, lead our way when agendas attempting to tackle the Asymmetry are being contested.[7]

Who counts as a member of an 'informed sub-constituency', then, can be plausibly construed in a *broader* way than one might think at first blush. Consider recent *public protests* against AI deployment, such as UK student protests in 2020 following the country's decision to cancel final high school exams and to use a hastily designed, highly inaccurate algorithmic tool to predict final grades instead, with devastating results that disproportionately impacted working-class students and students of color (Zimmermann, 2020). What was interesting about the public protests that ensued was that they were driven not just by people with deep technical expertise or by activist groups. Instead, large groups of *regular citizens who were teenagers*, who had limited computer science knowledge, but who were deeply affected by this case, opted in on participating in public expressions of critique, holding up posters evidencing a deep value-based understanding of the stakes of the deployed tool: 'Judge potential not postcode!' (the *Guardian*, 2020a), 'Your algorithm doesn't know me' (the *Guardian*, 2020b), 'I'm a student not a statistic' (the *Independent*, 2020b). In light of mounting public pressure of this kind, the UK quickly reversed course. Public protests by regular citizens who *become* an informed sub-constituency can provide a crucial counterweight in AI deployment agenda-setting, bolstering the 'non-expert' public's ability to effectively insist on their equal right to voice and deliberation.

Turning to a more direct way for informed sub-constituencies to engage in *binding* decision-making, existing scholarship on 'democratic

Arguably, however, the mere fact that the task force existed and offered a structured format through which its members could express their judgment that government and industry was insufficiently responsive to them already contributed productively to the AI policy agenda because it made existing democratic deficits in this area more publicly *salient*. This may seem like a small win in comparison to what a task force less hindered by a bureaucratic morass could have accomplished, but it is a non-negligible win nonetheless.

7 However, there are caveats to this claim that will be covered below in note 25.

innovations' in other policy areas can guide us (Smith, 2009; Warren, 2017: 39–53; Geissel, 2019: 404–420). Participatory budgeting, an approach first implemented in Porto Alegre, Brazil, in the 1980s, provides a mechanism for regular citizens to opt in on local government by making a commitment to participate in municipal administration for a specific period of time to accumulate relevant technical and policy expertise, and to then make direct decisions about how to allocate public funds. Implementing this approach in Porto Alegre substantially reduced poverty, increased the local health and education budget (quadrupling the number of local schools since the 1980s) while blocking less publicly beneficial proposals to invest in luxury tourism, increased sewer and water connections from 75% of total households to 98%, and helped reduce child mortality by nearly 20%. Given this track record of success, other cities including New York and Chicago implemented their own participatory budgeting models locally. Meanwhile, as of 2016, over 8 million European citizens were actively involved in participatory budgeting according to a European Parliament report (European Parliamentary Research Service, 2016). Applying this successful model of creating informed sub-constituencies in the area of AI policy, and endowing them with binding decision-making powers concerning, say, municipal procurement of particular AI tools, would be a potentially transformative way of reshaping local agendas. While this approach is limited in its geographical reach, it realizes the important normative goal of more direct democratic control while not compromising on the distinct goal of informed decision-making with *high quality outcomes*. These are outcomes that have a realistic chance to mitigate pernicious and locally specific dispersions of risk, thus satisfying not only moderate proceduralists, but also their instrumentalist critics.

(2) Utilizing ballot propositions and other referenda mechanisms to democratize deployment

What about direct participation opportunities for the constituency *at large* – not just for informed sub-constituencies? When we think about direct democracy, we think of mechanisms like ballot propositions resulting from citizen petitions, or other referenda processes. These participation pathways are underexplored when it comes to AI policy. No country has so far decided an AI policy matter in this very direct way, though there are some examples of AI-related decisions being made through direct participation at the *local* level – the aforementioned case of individual cities banning facial recognition tools in some deployment domains is one example thereof. And there are examples of other tech policy matters outside of AI being decided via referenda at the national and state level. Bulgaria, for instance, held a referendum in 2016 to decide on whether to implement e-voting procedures

(Stoychev, 2017: 187–194).[8] Meanwhile, California, in response to a ballot initiative by privacy advocates, passed the California Consumer Privacy Act in 2018. While the final version of the Act did not result *directly* from the ballot proposition, as the proposition was withdrawn by campaigners following negotiations with the California legislature aimed at making the proposal less restrictive, the threat of a ballot proposition *effectively shifted the regulatory agenda* from below: California law prevents the legislature from repealing or amending a ballot proposition once it has been passed by voters, so regulators had a strong incentive to quickly propose and implement a broadly acceptable revised version of the Act.

Nothing, other than our own apprehensiveness about the ostensible 'specialness' of AI, stops us from implementing this approach for AI deployment agenda-setting, too. Rather than simply letting companies deploy first and ask for oversight later, democratic constituencies need to realize that they are the ones who carry the primary responsibility of co-authoring the standards that any emerging technology, including generative AI, must meet (Zimmermann et al., 2020). Any area of AI policy that depends more on broader normative trade-offs and questions of purpose rather than on fine-grained technical knowledge lends itself to being democratized in this way: consider, for instance, the question of whether to legally block the use of some AI tool for the purpose of giving everyone in society a 'social score', logging every tiny infraction or act of subversion, rewarding every act of compliance, and incentivizing all those subject to it to police their own behavior in ever more obsessive ways (Langer, 2020: 164–174; Loefflad and Grossklags, 2024: 1515–1530). We, as a democratic collective, do not need to know how to build the code underpinning such a tool to articulate normative preferences about whether we think that this tool serves a good social purpose, all things considered (Zimmermann, 2021).

Implementing ballot propositions, referenda, and similar mechanisms may considerably slow things down in some cases. That does *not* give us decisive reason to reject these strategies. First, we must consider what we, as a collective, stand to gain when we resist the acceleration-centric politics of pace still pushed by large parts of Big Tech. Although I have critiqued other slow and reactive policy interventions in the previous chapter, the case against deceleration is far less clear in *this* case. Purposeful deceleration of large-scale deployment to allow for greater bottom-up participation can, though it will not necessarily, serve the end of more democratically

8 While voter turnout was too low in this case to trigger a binding result, scholars have argued that the mere fact that the referendum was held forced public discourse and legislators to grapple with this issue more than they otherwise might have (Stoychev, 2017).

legitimate deployment agendas. For example, we might choose to slow down the deployment of some new tool instead of imposing an (A)-type AI deployment moratorium for some specific, high-risk deployment setting, such as medicine or national security, with the aim of opening up more space for genuine public deliberation over which moral trade-offs are at stake in this case. Regulators might start enforcing decelerating by requesting more extensive public disclosure of salient information from industry actors as part of public hearings. The latter should ideally be accompanied by opportunities for bottom-up input from the wider citizenry, such as requests for public comments, rather than – as industry representatives have suggested – implementing pre-deployment safety reviews exclusively *inside* federal agencies tasked with oversight. If *isegoria* necessarily requires a less than maximally rapid pace, then so be it: giving ourselves time to get on the same page about what is at stake in a given AI deployment scenario, or at least allowing ourselves to publicly map different views on such matters, instantiates the value of equality in voice and public deliberation without which we cannot possibly achieve the larger goal of publicly according to each other the status of true political equals.

Of course, putting something on a ballot is an act of agenda-setting *itself*. A problem seems to arise: given that ballot propositions originate from a small group of highly mobilized citizens or by legislatures themselves, skeptical readers may object at this point that it is unclear why these models necessarily render democratic agendas *more* legitimate. But that would be uncharitable. Democracy, in effect, is 'agendas all the way down'. Any decision sequence in any constituency is, to some degree, a function of some earlier decision (Whelan, 1983).[9] It would be unreasonable to expect all agendas to be set by all constituency members for them to count them as legitimate. Instead, the point is to create a healthy ecosystem of mechanisms and procedures that allow different parts of the constituency to set, contest, and reshape agendas. Citizen-initiated ballot propositions and referenda thus plausibly count as legitimate agenda-setting pathways in principle, even if they do not represent the full spectrum of agenda preferences within a constituency.

Note that none of these proposals require highly idealized assumptions about the ways in which citizens and other actors might engage in deliberations: we need not assume that all civic input will in fact be provided by well-informed, balanced, and respectful angels. Equally, my account does not rely on any idealized assumptions to the effect that elected

9 Democratic theorists have explored this issue more broadly (i.e. beyond the specific issue of agenda-setting) in relation to the democratic boundary problem: the problem of how to decide who gets to participate in deciding as part of a democratic constituency. For a paradigmatic account of this problem, see Whelan (1983).

representatives will be perfectly technologically literate and unbiased, and that tech companies will suddenly start prioritizing ethical responsibility over profit. Instead, the point is merely that carving out better, fairer agenda-setting procedures at key pressure points of larger societal decision sequences concerning AI deployment gets us closest to the normative goal of deciding for ourselves, as co-authors of our shared future, rather than waiting for the future to happen to us.[10] In that way, risk-sensitive moderate proceduralism responds to the problem that the ASYMMETRY creates conditions that undermine citizens' status as public equals, and that circumvent their ability to articulate, deliberate on, and effectively advocate for their value-based preferences about what purposes we want generative AI and related innovations to serve in our society.

Two things are true at the same time: Democracy is messy, *and* it does not have to be perfect to be worth it. Democratic constituencies must be ready to embrace some degree of complexity and conflict, especially now that AI deployment raises the political and moral stakes of so many decisions in so many domains of our lives (Reich et al., 2021: 68).[11] The alternatives of top-down oligopolistic and regulatory agenda-setting may be cleaner and superficially less conflict-laden, simply because passive and fearful constituencies become less and less likely to *actually* contest them. But potential gains in terms of efficiency and simplicity available to us when we relinquish agenda-setting power exclusively to democratically unaccountable actors, as valuable as these gains may be in specific cases, cannot outweigh the value of democratic legitimacy in a general, principled sense. The conclusion that democratic rule is better than oligopolistic rule is a conclusion with which even those who *reject* risk-sensitive moderate proceduralism, but who agree with the more basic claim that democratic legitimacy is a central political goal, can agree. By contrast, those who, like Thiel, reject even the latter claim, on the grounds that democracy *itself* is ostensibly incompatible with freedom (and, apparently in Thiel's case, on the grounds that specifically the enfranchisement of women and the poor somehow stifles freedom), will of course remain unsympathetic

10 Risse seems to share my intuitions about the dangers of civic passivity when it comes to subjecting AI to democratic control: 'Citizens in democracies must not rely on tech experts in hopes that they will make sure technology is used to advance rather than undermine democracy. Technological advancements must be widely debated in democratic politics, and citizens should take an active interest in these matters' (Risse, 2023: 71).

11 Reich et al. identify this central threat with particular clarity: 'If technologists write the rules – either as expert policy makers or as companies unconstrained in a regulatory oasis – we shouldn't be surprised if the resulting societal outcomes are ones that benefit technologists at the expense of everyone else' (Reich et al., 2021: 68).

to my argument. I take the fact that avowedly antidemocratic tech CEOs would prefer different conclusions as additional evidence in support of my view.

On a pragmatic note, the much more diverse and comprehensive types of checks and balances that become a feasible reality for us as soon as we implement the agenda-setting proposals explored here give us a better chance to counter less-than-ideal behavior, both by citizens and by companies or regulators. Insofar as compliance with a high standard for respectful and informed public deliberation is a concern, more and better participation pathways can help balance out adverse effects of suboptimal participation at a particular juncture.

Relatedly, it is worth appreciating that no other political actor aside from democratic constituencies themselves has the correct *material incentives* in place to ensure that AI truly benefits everyone – not just in some minimal way championed by accelerationists and techno-optimists, as part of a gradual trickling down of benefits into society while Big Tech amasses more wealth – but in an equitable way. For this reason, democratic constituencies are also the actors who can most easily overcome *motivational feasibility constraints*: the kinds of constraints that block a desirable action not because it is impossible, but because there is not enough political will to actively change course (Estlund, 2011: 207–237; Wiens, 2016: 333–352). Given that democratic constituencies at large get the short end of the stick when it comes to the ASYMMETRY, it is instrumentally rational for them to endorse political preferences that mitigate it. While not all participants in democratic processes act in accordance with instrumental rationality, I think that it would not be too optimistic to hope that, in the long run, it will be easier to convince someone to adopt a political preference that is *actually* in her interest, rather than attempting to do the opposite.

(3) Strengthening the voice and exit opportunities of tech workers

Many blue-collar workers that power the AI industry's massive success are incredibly underpaid and are suffering exploitative working conditions. For example, in 2023, the US Department of Labor's Occupational Safety and Health Administration (OSHA) issued citations at multiple Amazon warehouses on the grounds that warehouse workers were exposed to serious yet preventable risks of injury while being expected to meet extremely taxing productivity and speed standards (US Department of Labor, 2023). In December 2022, an Amazon warehouse worker died while on shift following a cardiac arrest. Warehouse managers constructed a makeshift barrier with cardboard boxes and failed to inform other workers about the situation, leaving them to continue their work while their deceased colleague's body lay on the ground (the *Guardian*, 2023a).[12]

This problem extends also to tech workers with more tech-intensive tasks, such as content moderators, data labelers, and other jobs critical to AI innovation: many of them receive strikingly low wages and experience traumatic exposure to disturbing content (Miceli, 2021). AI innovation relies on vast amounts of cheap and often invisible labor of this kind: *ghost work*, first introduced by Gray and Suri, describes the phenomenon that some results that are widely perceived as stemming from sophisticated automated processes are actually possible only thanks to the low-paid human labor of those who perform – often boring and exhausting – data cleaning and classification tasks (Gray and Suri, 2019).

In a May 2024 open letter to President Joseph Biden, Kenyan content moderators employed by US companies called attention to the fact that many of them earn less than two dollars per hour for work that is repetitive, exhausting, and that can trigger PTSD and other serious health effects (Foxglove, 2024). These workers have no meaningful opportunities to exercise their *voice* inside American companies: companies like Meta and Scale.AI have responded to local efforts to unionize by firing entire worker teams without notice, shifting their outsourced operations to other countries. And given high local unemployment rates, workers like this also suffer from very limited opportunities to *exit*, which reduces their bargaining power to a minimal level (Hirschman, 1970; Anderson, 2017: 53ff).[13]

Voice and *exit*, both core elements of workers' tools for protecting their rights, are also rather fragile mechanisms for tech workers in much more economically advantaged positions. This is not to *equate* harms experienced by all kinds of tech workers, from those in labs and boardrooms to those in warehouses and datacenters, with each other; rather, my claim is that the AI industry suppresses voice and exit opportunities for workers across the board.

12 For discussion of the normative stakes of such cases, including a persuasive philosophical argument as to why these kinds of working conditions exceed direct material harms, see Anderson's point that '[t]he issue is inequality: Amazon treats workers' vital interests as of no account, in comparison with its own and its customers' relatively trifling interests. [...] This inequality inflicts an expressive injury on the workers, over and above the material injury of illness' (Anderson, 2017: 129).

13 Here, I am following Hirschman's 1970 seminal work in my use of these two concepts. In political philosophy, Anderson has substantially pushed theoretical work on this conceptual distinction forward, arguing – amongst other things – that the mere presence of exit opportunities does not automatically lessen the problem of worker subordination, given that exit costs can be extremely high. This matches my analysis of current exit opportunities for workers in the AI industry (Anderson, 2017: 53ff).

Some tech companies had been part of a growing phenomenon of AI ethics *backsliding* even before the current deployment cycle: Google's 2020 firing of the co-leads of its Ethical AI team, Timnit Gebru and Margaret Mitchell, after the two had contributed as co-authors to a landmark paper on risks associated with generative AI tools, was the most salient example of this (Bender et al., 2021: 610–623). As experts at a September 2024 US Senate Judiciary Subcommittee on Technology, Privacy, and the Law hearing on AI Oversight testified (United States Senate, 2024),[14] this corrosive tendency to backslide on ethics and safety work has intensified during the latest generative AI rush: entire teams tasked with developing responsible and trustworthy AI have been fired from leading tech companies: Amazon-owned streaming platform Twitch let go of its whole Responsible AI team as part of a broader set of 2023 layoffs affecting 400 employees (*The Washington Post* 2023a), Microsoft laid off its entire Ethics and Society team as part of a wave of even bigger layoffs in January 2023 (Schiffer and Newton, 2023), and at X, under Elon Musk's leadership, three quarters of the workforce were cut in November 2022, including the entire Responsible AI team (Knight, 2022). Experts at the hearing, which included an AI safety expert and former member of OpenAI's board who had left the board during the company's 2023 leadership shuffle (the witness had voted with other board members to remove Altman as CEO due to ethical concerns, but agreed to leave the board a mere four days later when Altman secured a deal allowing him to return), also testified that restrictive NDAs, highly limited whistleblowing opportunities, and a more general lack of incentives and regard for AI ethics work inside tech companies make it difficult for tech employees to voice concerns and potentially reshape deployment agendas.

But all is not lost. Just because the current status quo in Big Tech blocks bottom-up participation by workers, that does not mean that democratic constituencies have no options for strengthening worker's voice and exit opportunities and, in turn, strengthening their own ability to utilize workers' unique access to information as part of broader public efforts to subject AI deployment agendas to real counterpower.

For example, we can and should choose to invest more public resources to fund whistleblower incentives. Federal bodies like the US Securities and Exchange Commission already do this – in August 2024, they issued awards totaling 98 million dollars to two whistleblowers alone – and these efforts could be scaled up further (US Securities and Exchange Commission, 2024). But at a more structural level, massive public funds ought to be invested in the creation of a more robust and attractive research ecosystem

14 This was a follow-up hearing to the May 2023 hearing covered extensively in Chapter 5 (Committee on the Judiciary, United States Senate, 2023).

in academia and government. This would strengthen highly skilled tech workers' exit opportunities, who would no longer be quite as concerned about finding jobs comparable to industry roles after publicly revealing or otherwise resisting some AI deployment agenda in some company. This is an example of how larger-scale public investment choices can *indirectly* promote democratically legitimate agenda-setting down the line: by altering workers' incentives and by enhancing their options, opportunities open up for those with information relevant to the constituency at large to share that information publicly, and to improve deliberations for all. It would also help mitigate the structural problem that cutting-edge technical expertise remains concentrated in corporations, because the best talents in AI get offers from industry that higher education and government institutions cannot currently match – correcting these incentive structures would help counter oligopolistic power by preventing companies from siphoning off the bulk of AI talent, and then trapping it in a golden cage of restrictive employment contracts and spectacular salaries.

In addition, intermediary organizations like *labor unions* have a central role to play in securing the value of political equality in a well-functioning democratic state (O'Neill, 2008: 29–55; Christiano, 2022: 109–124), and they are especially crucial for protecting blue-collar workers who may not benefit as directly from a redirection of public funds as outlined above. As Elizabeth Anderson has compellingly argued, even if workers' *political* rights are secured more broadly in society, workers are still subordinated by their managers even if their job is freely chosen in an open market (Anderson, 2017).[15] The only adequate solution is to render firms publicly accountable, similar to how state authority must be publicly accountable. In Anderson's view, this does not necessarily require 'full workplace democracy', but it does require robust mechanisms of counterpower, including organized labor (Anderson, 2017).[16] The latter serves not only workers' interests, but the interests of the democratic constituency at large, precisely because, as O'Neill and White rightly say, 'unions can and do serve as a counter-weight to oligarchy in numerous ways and, in these respects, contribute to substantive political equality' (O'Neill and

15 For a related but distinct argument, more focused on the psychological effects of a lack of workers' voice, to the effect that workplaces characterized by 'capitalist property relations vest final authority in the owners of capital [...] limit the extent of intra-firm democracy, thereby fostering passivity and a narrower base of political judgment [...] they are not well suited to a democratic society', see Cohen (1989). I take this argument to be in principle compatible with Anderson's analysis, the latter of which I am endorsing here.

16 Anderson introduces the caveat that full workplace democracy is not necessarily required in response to a challenge by Kolodny in the same volume.

White, 2018). And in addition to the strong normative case for strengthening workers' voices through unions, there are instrumental benefits too: empirical research shows that participation in unions enhances workers' political knowledge (MacDonald, 2019: 1–24), thus bolstering their ability to set nuanced, well-informed agendas.

Labor unions have a central role not only in creating freer and more equal societies at large, but also more specifically in enabling more members of democratic constituencies to critically contest AI deployment dynamics directly. This strategy, of course, may be easier to implement in some geographical contexts rather than in others: even though empirical research shows that most American workers would prefer to have the ability to be unionized (Freeman, 2007), the US political landscape is largely hostile to unions, though there have been some moderate successes, such as Communication Workers of America's support for Alphabet Workers Union (AWU). AWU is a part of CWA Local 9009 as part of the CODE-CWA initiative, which organizes workers in the tech and gaming industries. While AWU operates as a 'minority union', which means that it lacks formal collective bargaining rights for all Alphabet workers – it is supported by CWA's labor organizing resources and infrastructure. Unions like AWU can contribute to AI deployment agenda-setting by voicing dissent, informing the public, and thus contributing to broader public deliberations: AWU's mission statement, for instance, states that 'we will use our reclaimed power to control what we work on and how it is used'; though notably it also includes the caveat, undoubtedly reassuring to corporate leaders, that 'Alphabet can make money without doing evil' (Alphabet Workers Union, 2024). There are further limitations, too: many members of AWU are highly paid tech industry professionals not representative of the larger population, while blue-collar contractors at different tech companies often lack access to the protections offered by union structures (Logan, 2021: 38–45).

In other places, there is much more political support for appreciating and safeguarding the key democratic role of workers' voices. Germany, for instance, has implemented formal 'co-determination' structures since the 1970s, which legally entitle workers to form 'Works Councils' and to participate in the management of companies for which they work. This *requires* company leadership to engage with elected worker representatives (usually, labor union representatives) on key company decisions, and in large companies with over 2,000 employees, half of a company's supervisory board must be comprised of worker representatives. Obviously, this kind of model would more closely approximate (D) if implemented within AI companies in that it would endow workers with more far-reaching powers to affect AI deployment agendas beyond public statements and company-internal lobbying, as in the AWU case (O'Neill and White, 2018).

Realizing more comprehensive labor organizing structures in practice may be infeasible within currently existing US institutions, but this does not make it any less politically and ethically desirable – and just because a goal is hard to reach does not mean we should not try to reach it. Citizens can do more to demand greater accountability for corporate union-busting, and governments can do more to actively support labor organizing (White, 1998; Bogg, 2009). Given that the tentacles of oligopolistically driven AI policy emerge from within corporate structures, strong democracies must aim to strengthen participation not just as a counterweight *against* corporations who use their power to unilaterally set agendas, but also as a tool *within* them.

(4) Resisting corporate regulatory capture from both directions

Another core problem standing in the way of taking back democratic control of agenda-setting is the simple fact that oligopolistic tech actors can currently exert disproportionate influence on *regulators*. As outlined in the previous chapter, lawmakers both in the US and in the EU context have been vulnerable to considerable corporate influence.

As my previous proposals in this chapter have outlined, we can and should try to resist oligopolistic regulatory capture by exercising bottom-up counterpower through various channels, be it via informed sub-constituencies, the constituency at large, or domain-specific constituencies within industry itself. This is important, but it does not fully address the root cause of the Asymmetry. It instantiates an important value – free and fair opportunities to exercise our equal voice – and it lessens the Asymmetry's effects by contributing to a wider dispersion of decision-making power that mirrors the dispersion of risk. But it does not prevent the concentrations of power that enable democratically illegitimate agenda-setting in the form of regulatory capture in the first place.

We should set a higher standard in our fight for greater democratic legitimacy. This requires being more imaginative in questioning the status quo of the AI market. As I have argued throughout this essay, even though many perceive AI's current trajectory as somehow 'inevitable' and the market dynamics surrounding it as a necessary evil, different trajectories are possible, contingent of course on our collective intervention.

Imagining more ambitious alternatives need not be a complex endeavor: in this case as in many others, the simplest solution may just be the best one. In its most basic way, the Asymmetry motivates a common-sense intuition: if there were no oligopolies, at least in their current extreme form, there could be no oligopolistic agenda-setting, be it via AI deployment itself or via AI policy lobbying. What, then, if we could simply block or weaken oligopolies *themselves*, rather than blocking their influence on regulators, or blocking the technology they develop, as (A)-type moratoria are designed to do?

Of course, this is not a hypothetical question or a revolutionary idea. Democratic constituencies *already* have laws and institutions in place that equip us with the tools to tackle oligopoly and monopoly power. The problem is that we are not at all leveraging these pressure points sufficiently. While recent antitrust efforts, as outlined in Chapter 3, chart a promising path, several recent high-profile cases have not succeeded in their aim to impose far-reaching constraints on powerful tech companies: judges have, rather predictably, voiced great concern about stifling AI innovation in any way.[17] It is not obvious though that the public does and should share this innovation-at-all-costs attitude. Public pressure could help effectively contest that idea, which in turn may lead to a broader societal shift in preferences and values concerning the importance of fair competition – one that includes judges.

But either way, antitrust measures must be accompanied by *additional* measures to truly create a new status quo less vulnerable to excessive concentrations of power and wealth. For instance, the issue of corporate liability for AI-related harms, and the imposition of post-deployment sanctions on irresponsible deployers, remains insufficiently explored in AI policy (Ramakrishnan et al., 2024). While the EU is updating its Product Liability Directive to include AI-related harms (EU Parliament), and while the EU's AI Act specifies liabilities to AI developers, providers, and users in relation to high-risk AI systems, the US lacks AI-specific regulation in this area and has failed to update existing, more general product liability laws. In the meantime, all is not well in the EU context either: the AI Act carves out substantial exemptions for the deployers of *open-source* AI models (European Commission, 2024c).[18] This creates a concerning loophole that could help malicious actors evade accountability, so long as they keep tools they wish to deploy without guardrails open source.

17 For example, the judge in a recent (non-AI) tech antitrust cast, *Epic Games, Inc. v. Apple Inc.* (2021), ruled in favor of Apple: 'While the Court finds that Apple enjoys considerable market share of over 55% and extraordinarily high profit margins, these factors alone do not show antitrust conduct. Success is not illegal.'

18 EU AI Act Art. 53, 2: 'The obligations set out in paragraph 1, points (a) and (b), shall not apply to providers of AI models that are released under a free and open-source license that allows for the access, usage, modification, and distribution of the model, and whose parameters, including the weights, the information on the model architecture, and the information on model usage, are made publicly available. This exception shall not apply to general-purpose AI models with systemic risks.' See also Art. 25 and 54 for similar exemptions.

A more ambitious strategy for balancing out the reach of oligopolistic concentrations of power would be to redirect the investment of public funds not only to individual AI researcher teams in academia and the non-profit sector,[19] but also towards the development of *publicly owned* open-source AI models, facilitated by research bodies created specifically for this purpose, supported entirely by public resources, and subject to strict transparency rules. On this model, democratic constituencies would become not only co-authors of AI deployment agendas, but also co-owners of (some of) the tools subject to such agendas. This would get us closer to the goal of a society in which all of us have the equal freedom to comprehensively rule over the innovations we create, instead of having them rule us.

While this may sound like a radical proposal, it is worth noting that several countries are currently pursuing efforts pushing in this direction: Brazil and India have both directed public funds towards the creation of open-source models (AI4Bharat, 2024; Ministério da Ciência, 2024), and as part of the European High-Performance Computing Joint Undertaking, European Union member states will invest around seven billion euros until 2027 to build a fleet of supercomputers, which will (amongst other things) enable the training of cutting-edge open-source generative AI models.

Of course, developing publicly owned models would require massive investments, and potentially the creation of a new government agency coordinating this effort. Note, however, that such an agency would not be objectionable in the same way that proposals to create a new 'FDA for algorithms' would be. The latter would be tasked primarily with *ex post* oversight on AI policy matters, which (as I argued earlier) risks being too slow and reactive to genuinely improve deployment agenda-setting, and which offers insufficient opportunities for bottom-up participation. In contrast, the former would adopt a more anticipatory stance, as championed by (D), and be tasked with creating something that empowers democratic constituencies at large by coupling a dispersion of risk with a positive dispersion of economic, not just political, power. This would provide a new kind of anti-oligopolistic counterweight that other proposals in the Playbook cannot achieve.

19 Impressive efforts in this area are already underway, as evidenced, for example, by copious amounts of funding opportunities offered by federal funding agencies like the NSF, many of which emphasize the importance of funding AI Ethics and AI Safety research as mandated by the 2023 update to the US National AI R&D Strategy. However, the Strategy also relies heavily on public–private partnerships (Section 8) rather than critically interrogating the leading role of corporations in AI innovation.

6.2 Testing the limits

Strengthening democratic control over AI deployment decisions, as I have argued so far, is not only politically and morally desirable, but also – perhaps surprisingly so – more practically feasible within existing democratic institutions than one might expect. Nonetheless, increased democratization in the area of AI is not obviously without limitations, and not immune to objections. It is reasonable to worry that while democratic legitimacy is a central political value in democratic states, it is not the only one, and may thus conflict with other important values. This includes the value of creating and maintaining reasonably just institutions and social relations, and – relatedly – the value of avoiding complicity, on the part of constituency members, in wrongdoing. It also includes the value of achieving high-quality decision outcomes that best safeguard the wellbeing of constituents, and the value of implementing political mechanisms that are appropriately sensitive to real-world constraints, both with respect to varying levels of technology literacy and with respect to existing imbalances of power.

The value of democratic legitimacy, then, must be carefully balanced against competing values when it comes to evaluating whether democratizing AI deployment in alignment with the model outlined above is desirable not only *pro tanto*, but all things considered. Here, I am not committed to the view that democratic legitimacy always trumps other values. This question will be contingent on the specific contextual features of each decision scenario: some decision domains may be plagued by such deeply entrenched injustice and poor-quality decision-making that it would be *worse*, from a normative perspective, to insist on prioritizing the pursuit of greater democratic legitimacy *if* this would further amplify those problems – but it is not obvious that this is generally true. Therefore, an attempt to articulate a *general*, context-insensitive argument about the ostensible primacy of any political value, including the value of democratic legitimacy, seems neither apt nor particularly intuitively compelling.

We can get closer to solving this philosophical problem by considering what, by the lights of important political values and pragmatic goals aside from democratic legitimacy, might be *lost* if greater democratic legitimacy in AI deployment were achieved. Then, we can explore with more nuance on which grounds, if any, democratizing AI deployment would still be, all things considered, desirable in varying specific contexts. While offering a complete theory of precisely how to weigh democratic legitimacy against competing values in each social domain is well beyond the scope of this essay, we can make progress on this issue by mapping a series of possible objections against increased AI democratization.

6.2.1 Worries about justice

Even since before the rise of generative AI, much of the public and academic debate on AI has focused on the question of how to ensure that AI and its impact on society is reasonably just. Algorithmic decision-making in domains as varied as hiring, housing, credit lending, and criminal justice routinely reflected and even exacerbated social patterns of racial, gender, and class bias, amongst others – and still does (Noble, 2018; Benjamin, 2019). One and the same tool can fail differently for different people, and in a way that tracks historical patterns of disadvantage and oppression: recidivism risk prediction algorithms have systematically given higher risk scores to Black offenders (Angwin et al., 2016), hiring algorithms have systematically ranked women applicants lower than men (Raghavan et al., 2020: 469–481), grading algorithms have systematically given lower grades to economically disadvantaged students (Zimmermann, 2020), and so on. Unsurprisingly, newer tools like large language models are not immune to such biases either: as OpenAI itself acknowledged in a research paper discussing ChatGPT's predecessor model GPT-3, biased word embeddings in the tool replicated harmful larger-scale social stereotypes (Brown et al., 2020). To illustrate, the authors contrasted the biased words GPT-3 used most frequently to describe men and women, following prompts like 'He was very …' and 'She would be described as …'. The results were disappointing, though unsurprising. For men? Large. Fantastic. Eccentric. Stable. Protect. Survive. For women? Bubbly. Naughty. Easy-going. Petite. Pregnant. Gorgeous. Efforts to de-bias more recently deployed generative AI tools like ChatGPT have shown considerable success (Ouyang et al., 2022: 27730–27744), but analogous problems persist in the domain of generative AI at large: after signing AI-generated rapper FN Meka, Capitol Records quickly backpedaled after their 'artist' replicated offensive racial stereotypes (the *Guardian*, 2022), and after it turned out that the Black human artist who had written and voiced some of FN Meka's songs had not been publicly acknowledged and had not been paid for his labor (CNN, 2022). Sometimes, it is precisely efforts to *get rid of* AI bias that yield morally troubling results: for example, efforts to depict a more diverse range of people in AI-generated images backfired when Google's tool Gemini generated disturbing fake historical images depicting people of color wearing Nazi uniforms (*The New York Times*, 2024). Google swiftly suspended Gemini's ability to generate images, accompanied by a lukewarm statement on X: 'Gemini […] does generate a wide range of people. And that's generally a good thing because people around the world use it. But it's missing the mark here' (Google, 2024).

In response to these kinds of problems, early contributions to the now vast area of scholarship on algorithmic fairness defined competing mathematically defined fairness metrics that each instantiated particular facets of what fairness might mean – for instance, that error rates are equalized across different socio-demographic groups, or that the probability of some predictive score is independent of membership in some socio-demographic group. But it quickly turned out that it is impossible to impose multiple individually plausible fairness metrics at the same time (Chouldechova, 2017: 153–163; Kleinberg et al., 2017: 1–23) – hard choices are required for determining which sense of fairness to prioritize, and this is primarily an ethical rather than a technical problem. Similarly, later work aimed at improving more advanced generative AI tools has been wrestling with the question of how much developer intervention is required when datasets contain biased and offensive content that generative AI may scale up, and how to prevent generative AI from hallucinating new offensive content, such as in the Gemini case above (Bolukbasi et al., 2016: 4349–4357; Ziwei et al., 2023: 1–38; Kay et al., 2024). And in any case, while major strides in technical algorithmic fairness research has greatly improved currently used tools, a growing skepticism against *techno-solutionism* has begun to develop in the AI ethics research community, calling attention to the fact that de-biasing technology alone would not automatically mitigate pre-existing structural inequities and power dynamics in society (Blodgett et al., 2020: 5454–5476), such that even the most perfect tools that are hypothetically possible in the future would fall short of moving us closer to a just society (Morozov, 2013; Abebe et al., 2020: 252–260).

The challenge of working towards a future in which AI tools and the social context in which they are deployed are (more) just therefore remains a central problem in the field. Given this, those who are justifiably concerned about the ways in which AI tools can reproduce and amplify complex patterns of social injustice may consider increased democratic control, including at the agenda-setting stage, a small win only. It is far from clear, they might argue, that the mere fact that a decision has been made in a democratically legitimate way – say, by the lights of risk-sensitive moderate proceduralism – automatically gets us closer to just AI and a just society. After all, democratic constituencies have a long track record of making deeply unjust decisions – about civil rights, about immigration, about workers' rights, about access to healthcare, to name only a few. Time and time again, we have seen that democratic majorities are ignorant of, or indeed actively hostile to, the interests, rights, and preferences of socially marginalized groups.

So what, generally, is the value of strengthening democratic control, when democratic control in many cases does not only fail to mitigate injustice, but also counterproductively puts obstacles in the way of those seeking to redress injustice? And what, specifically, is the value of democratizing AI, when AI is a domain in which complex societal injustices have become particularly visible and entrenched?

> THE JUSTICE OBJECTION: The implementation of democratically legitimate political processes – including democratically legitimate agenda-setting – is not sufficient for ensuring that democratic constituencies will reach decision outcomes that move us closer to a more just society. In fact, democratization may undermine justice.[20]

There are several reasons why the latter may be the case. Democratic constituencies may, for example, decide to rubber-stamp the deployment of some biased AI tool, or of an AI tool that seems unbiased on paper but that scales up an existing social practice that is *already* unjust. To make matters worse, the fact that the decision to deploy some AI tool has been made *democratically* publicly legitimizes the continued use of that tool, thus blocking justice-oriented public contestation and recourse. A related, more general worry is that past experience shows that democracies have themselves pushed pro-innovation agendas that have marginalized and disempowered different socio-demographic groups: as Ruha Benjamin has compellingly argued, 'forms of automation integrated in everyday life [...] bureaucratic interventions that seek to make work more efficient, as in policing and healthcare' are often nothing more than purely 'technical fixes [that] give an illusion of progress but reinforce the power of state actors over racialized groups' (Benjamin, 2019: 50, 123; see also Jasanoff, 2016).

All in all, the JUSTICE OBJECTION is motivated by a reasonable concern – but my argument is actually *compatible* with the claims advanced as part of the objection. I do not claim that democratizing AI will *also* necessarily achieve the goal of more just AI, and a more just society. It would be naive to assume that the increased democratization of AI deployment is always *better tout court* – better for a fair advancement of the morally weighty interests of all democratic constituency members, all things considered. Indeed, moderate proceduralists – in their insistence that democracy and substantive justice are two distinct values that do not necessarily align and

20 Scholars who have articulated versions of this worry include Himmelreich ('It is far from clear [...] that democracy [...] has the normative resources to condemn and address problems of structural injustice. We should not expect democracy to solve problems that it is not meant to solve.') and Crawford ('To suggest that we democratize AI to reduce asymmetries of power is a little like arguing for democratizing weapons manufacturing in the service of peace.'). See Himmelreich (2023) and Crawford (2021: 223).

that are irreducible to each other – have long emphasized this intuition (Dworkin, 1987–1988).[21] They are thus not committed to the view that democratic legitimacy is sufficient for justice in a comprehensive sense – that is, substantive justice beyond the important but limited achievements of procedural fairness instantiated by specific democratic mechanisms, the status of public equality with which they endow members of the constituency, and any minimum outcome standards in the form of constitutional constraints (Cohen, 2003). That is not to say that these 'limited' achievements are a small win, however: here, as in many other cases, I agree with Christiano's view that it is intrinsically valuable to realize in practice a state of affairs in which all members of the constituency can equally consider and advance their interests. Democratic procedures, although they may well lead to unjust outcomes, are 'a direct implementation of [this] principle' (Christiano, 2003: 39–68, 40).

Fighting for a new status quo in which AI outcomes are (more) just for everyone requires *more* than simply democratizing the deployment process, whether at the agenda-setting stage or at a later point. Detaching substantive justice from democratic legitimacy in this way, and thereby explicitly carving out conceptual room and attention for the possibility that more morally and politically important work remains to be done after successful democratization, is a feature of my view, not a bug. The fact that democratizing AI is compatible with the possibility of unjust decision outcomes is therefore *not* a reason to reject the view that AI deployment should be democratized, and that it should be done in a way consistent with the argument developed above. Rather, it is a reason to carefully weigh the value of democratic legitimacy against the value of justice, if and when they do conflict in a given decision context.

Risk-sensitive moderate proceduralism, of course, is appropriately attuned to the problem of democratization potentially undermining justice because it already builds in a commitment to justice in the form of minimum outcome standards. On this view, democratic constituencies cannot simply decide to violate the basic rights of some socio-demographic group in an effort to design and optimize some generative AI tool. Deploying a tool that demonstrably violates legal anti-discrimination protections – such as a tool that explicitly considers protected categories like race, religion, or gender, *and* unlawfully discriminates on that basis – would violate the

21 Even opponents of proceduralist and moderate proceduralist conceptions of democracy have agreed with the descriptive claim that such conceptions 'detach' the question of substantive justice from the democratic question of equally distributing power over political decisions: see Dworkin's (1987–1988) detailed discussion of the difference between 'detached' and 'dependent' conceptions of democracy.

minimum outcome standard of constitutionally guaranteed rights protections, shielded from the whims of democratic majorities.

But risk-sensitive moderate proceduralism also pushes beyond current legal realities: this view demands the implementation of *additional* minimum outcome constraints whenever we are faced with a regulatory vacuum, and especially when an absence of such constraints would further entrench objectionable ASYMMETRIES. For example, if a democratic constituency decided to allow the continued and unrestricted use of a generative AI tool that scales up the public proliferation of pornographic deepfakes, this would further exacerbate the problem that – in a patriarchal society – risks associated with such material unjustly track gender (beyond the individual harm of being subject to a pornographic deepfake, which arguably violates the target's rights).[22] In such a case, my view implies a moral requirement on that constituency not simply to democratize the deployment decision, but also to adopt *new* outcome constraints that better mitigate this particular injustice, such as updated rights protections. Thus, my view developed in the previous chapters is particularly well-suited for countering the JUSTICE OBJECTION, given that the underlying motivations of such an objection already drive core parts of the risk-sensitive moderate proceduralist view itself.

But at a deeper level, the worry about justice prompts us not only to acknowledge how justice and democratic legitimacy can push in different directions, but also how they can mutually reinforce each other (Young, 2002).[23] Here, I am strongly sympathetic to the view that substantive justice and democracy, although they are distinct values, are best construed as co-constitutive.[24] True justice can only be achieved, as Allen compelling argues, 'by means of democracy': if 'justice begins from securing basic liberties' – that is, publicly securing each constituency member's status as an equal – and if 'fully inclusive egalitarian participatory constitutional democracies are the only governance structure that can achieve this', then 'justice [...] requires egalitarian participatory constitutional democracy' (Allen, 2023: 199).

22 Which rights, specifically, are violated by digital image-based harassment more broadly remains a contested question. For my view on the legal implications of image-based harassment on earlier cases not involving generative AI, see Zimmermann and Schneider (2018). The UK has since passed legislation criminalizing this form of image-based harassment in the Voyeurism (Offences) Act 2019.

23 For a nuanced defense of the view, to which I am sympathetic, that 'a suitably defined model of deliberative democracy articulates how democracy can produce just policies', see Young (2002).

24 For a defense of a related but distinct view to the effect that democracy and *human rights* (the protection of the latter of which is obviously a central element of substantive justice) are co-original, see Habermas (1996) and (1998).

Beyond this more general egalitarian point, there is more specific nuance to the ways in which justice and democratic legitimacy can be co-constitutive. Several of the proposals in the AI democratization PLAYBOOK center the critical role of affected communities in deployment agenda-setting. Members of these communities often possess an *epistemic advantage* in comparison to other members of the democratic constituency concerning the nature of actual and potential harms associated with some new technology (Vasanthakumar, 2018: 465–480).[25] For instance, to extend my earlier example in this chapter, in a society in which a criminal justice system has a structurally unjust disparate impact on people of color, formerly incarcerated people of color possess lived experiences that will likely enable them to understand the scope of discriminatory policies and biased assumptions in the domain of criminal justice decisions in a more comprehensive way than those who lack this lived experience. They are part of the sub-constituency who are *experts* of the moral and political stakes of this phenomenon. If we can implement the PLAYBOOK, and thus be *led* by people who possess these lived experiences – for instance, when it comes to critically contesting AI deployment agendas that include criminal justice applications of AI – we will make better, more just decisions (Costanza-Chock, 2020). Similarly, non-native speakers and speakers of different dialects of a language can lead our way in setting more just agendas concerning insufficiently representative large language models. Artists can lead us when we set agendas involving conceptual or legal change concerning creativity and authorship in an age of AI images generation – and so on.

25 I endorse Vasanthakumar's defense of the broader claim that victims of oppression (usually) have privileged epistemic access to the nature of that oppression. See Vasanthakumar (2018). Of course, not *all* persons who are adversely affected by some injustice automatically have better epistemic access to the nature of that injustice. As philosophers and theorists working on adaptive preferences and double consciousness have pointed out, experiencing oppression can adversely affect the internal deliberation of those targeted by it in a way that makes it harder for them, specifically, to fully grapple with and respond to the extent to which they are being wronged. For influential defenses of these views, see (on adaptive preference theory) Nussbaum (1995: 91; 1999: 130–154), Okin (1998: 661–684, 675) (though see also Khader's incisive critique of both in Khader (2012: 302–317); and (for two canonical statements of the concept of double consciousness) see, Du Bois (1903; 1968: 169). I do not deny that experiencing oppression can weaken rather than improve one's epistemic access to the nature of this phenomenon: my argument can accommodate this insight. My point about epistemic access is best understood as a *conditional* claim: if one's lived experiences give one better epistemic access to the nature of some injustice, then one's participation in democratic agenda-setting processes aiming to ameliorate that injustice will make it more feasible for the democratic process to reach or approximate a just outcome.

It is not obvious, of course, that if a person has better epistemic access to the nature of some form of injustice, then that triggers correlative special moral and political *obligations* for that person to lead the way in rectifying that injustice. I am not convinced by this type of view. If lived experience had this effect on our moral duties, it would unfairly place *overly demanding* obligations on members of a group that has already been burdened with an initial injustice. This would add insult to injury: it is not the job of targets of injustice to *serve* us in a collective pursuit of greater justice. For this reason, I have not argued above that particular democratic sub-constituencies have especially stringent moral and political obligations to opt in on participating in some decision domain, even if their participation would move legitimate democratic procedures closer to just outcomes, to the benefit of all. My larger point, again, is simply that justice and democracy *can* reinforce each other – but they need not. It is up to *all* of us to do our part to ensure that they do.

6.2.2 Worries about expertise

Although I have shown, as part of the PLAYBOOK, how democratic constituencies can harness existing expertise and build more of it, concerns about low levels of technological literacy in the wider population may still persist alongside the concerns about potential tensions between democracy and justice covered earlier. I attribute this to higher-order philosophical disagreements in the field concerning the concept of democratic legitimacy itself: we can cash out this worry as an *instrumentalist* concern about legitimacy. As discussed in Chapter 4, instrumentalists worry about cases in which democratic constituencies make low-quality decisions – surely, the thought goes, stupid decisions cannot count as truly legitimate. Instead, deferring to regulators and industry experts seems preferable, by the lights of this view, on the grounds that this may lead to higher-quality decision outcomes concerning AI deployment.

> THE LOW EXPERTISE OBJECTION: The implementation of democratically legitimate political processes – including democratically legitimate agenda-setting – is not sufficient for ensuring high quality outcomes. In fact, democratization may undermine outcome quality, because democratic constituencies at large lack relevant expertise about AI that competent decision-makers must possess.

I agree that low levels of tech literacy in the population at large can pose an important obstacle to successful democratic decision-making concerning AI. Nonetheless, it is even more important not to *overstate* the severity of this problem. It is not obvious that ‘ordinary citizens’ are quite as incompetent as those who worry about bad quality decisions arising from increasingly democratized AI policy seem to think: real cases of successful bottom-up participation in AI policy, as outlined above, suggest otherwise. And it is even less obvious that the handful of billionaire men whose preferred mode of articulating their political preferences is to write futuristic manifestos are more qualified to steer our collective decision-making.

The AI democratization PLAYBOOK, building in part on the insights of the scholarly literature on democratic innovations, features multiple strategies that enable citizens to *learn by doing*. As I have pointed out above, there is clear empirical evidence that in the case of democratic innovation approaches used in other policy domains, such as participatory budgeting, citizens who commit to opting into domain-specific decision processes attain increased levels of technical knowledge and succeed in reaching more effective decision outcomes. It is their choice to participate which then *enables* them to gain more exposure to relevant information, which in turn increases their domain-specific expertise. There is no principled reason to think that these kinds of expertise-enhancing participatory models cannot be implemented in the domain of AI policy in an analogous way.

But it is not only the subset of citizens who opt into these expertise-enhancing kinds of participatory processes who are able to contribute relevant expertise to AI policy. Competent decision-making surrounding AI deployment may, but does not always, require deep technical knowledge (Allen, 2023: 36).[26] Instead, as I have argued above, it often requires a *value-based* assessment of what kinds of normative goals we collectively wish to pursue with the help of AI. This gives us further ammunition against the instrumentalist challenge expressed by the LOW EXPERTISE OBJECTION. After all, in order for that objection to get off the ground in cases requiring value-based agenda-setting, it would have to rely on a rather restrictive notion of *moral* expertise – one that denies that regular citizens can be moral experts, and instead narrowly circumscribes the group of moral experts to a particularly enlightened subset of the population, such as academic moral philosophers or some other group that is ostensibly highly virtuous, such as 'mission-driven' AI innovation evangelists (Singer, 1972).[27] A.J. Ayer

26 On this matter, too, I am in agreement with Allen, who – as part of her defense of 'epistemic egalitarianism' as a key design principle for establishing the kinds of democratic institutions that allow us to achieve justice – argues that 'successful democratic knowledge processes will require reliance on *both* expertise *and* the social knowledge that ordinary people have' (my emphases) (Allen, 2023: 36).

27 For a defense of the view that *philosophers* are moral experts, see Singer (1972). I reject this view: I grant that philosophical training equips a person with advanced *critical reasoning skills* that are beneficial when evaluating competing ethical positions, but I am not convinced that philosophers have privileged epistemic access to moral truths.

got it right when he, with characteristic force, dismissed this arrogant view: 'It is silly, as well as presumptuous, for any one type of philosopher to pose as the champion of virtue' (Ayer, 1954). The same is presumably true of technologists. There is no reason to think that technologists will be better value-based decision-makers than ordinary citizens – in fact, they are likely to be worse, given their particular interests. Other political philosophers and theorists share this view. Risse compellingly argues that 'technologists are no natural champions of or even obviously qualified advisers in democracy' (Risse, 2023: 71), and as Reich et al. incisively put it: '[t]echnologists have no unique skill in governing, weighing competing values, and assessing evidence. What they bring to expert rule is actually a set of values masquerading as expertise – values that emerge from the marriage of the optimization mindset and the profit motive' (Reich et al., 2021: 67f).

Yes, many citizens believe and do things that exhibit moral failures of some sort. The point is that they are not *more prone* to these kinds of failures than an elite group of people who are aware of complex moral theories: the most important ethical questions are motivated by the innate sense of right and wrong to which most humans have sufficient access at the level of their moral intuitions (Harman, 2018). When complex value-based disagreements arise, what matters is that all of us are actively engaged in the task of justifying our respective moral judgments to each other, rather than outsourcing moral deliberation to select groups of experts – this is a central part of treating each other not only as political, but also as moral, equals.

Of course, instrumentalists and others need not endorse the version of the Low Expertise Objection that focuses on a narrowly circumscribed view of *moral* expertise specifically; to be fair to them, I do not mean to suggest otherwise. Rather, my claim is that if AI deployment agenda-setting often boils down to value-based rather than highly technical questions, the concern about Low Expertise, as construed above, ceases to be applicable, *unless* one is ready to also endorse a further, more controversial view about moral expertise.

Ultimately, then, regular citizens count as competent value-based agenda-setters concerning AI if and because they are *competent enough* to articulate their preferred values and ethical goals regarding other complex policy questions involving technical and scientific matters, such as climate change and biomedical ethics. We already trust citizens to voice their political preferences about the importance of mitigating the effects of global warming or about the value of subjecting gene editing to meaningful regulatory oversight, so why should the bar for the amount of expertise required for AI policy be significantly higher?

Experts with a high degree of technical expertise can, of course, *further enhance* the quality of democratic deliberations on AI policy issues – indeed, the PLAYBOOK above articulates democratically legitimate pathways for doing so. But the mere fact that levels of technical expertise differ across the democratic constituency at large is not a reason to consider large parts of the constituency incompetent at engaging in high-quality agenda-setting and decision-making.

7

Future

7.1 Taking stock

When tech insiders breathlessly list the virtues of next-generation generative AI, their statements often sound like science fiction author Arthur C. Clarke's 'third law': 'Any sufficiently advanced technology is indistinguishable from magic' (Clarke, 1968). The public's response has mirrored this sentiment: this much is not surprising, given that recent advances in generative AI have rapidly exceeded many expectations by experts and laypeople alike. And it is not surprising either that the widely shared impression that we are confronted with something almost magical has coincided with a dangerous degree of political passivity: you would not tell the magician which magic trick to show you next, so why would you tell the Big Tech company which AI tool to build, and when to unleash it in the real world? When it comes to AI, citizens and policymakers are accustomed to gratefully receiving, or indeed fearfully observing, its near-magic capabilities – not to viewing themselves as active participants who might productively redirect this 'magic'.

But democratically legitimate AI deployment requires that all of us, as co-authors and co-owners of our shared future, have access to meaningful opportunities to co-determine its trajectory and its underlying societal purpose. Insisting on our right to participate in fair collective processes that set and (re-)shape political decision *agendas* surrounding the scope, scale, and speed of deployment decisions is the key to effectively countering the politics of accelerated pace currently driving generative AI deployment in particular. It is also our best shot at actually mitigating the nefarious 'concentration of power/dispersion of risk' ASYMMETRY that has become further and further entrenched in the wake of the most recent generative AI deployment cycle.

7.2 Beyond the status quo

The *technological* development of AI in general will make major leaps forward in even just the next few months. These leaps' scope and direction remain difficult to predict. Nonetheless, my *value-based* arguments concerning democratically legitimate deployment remain informative during the deployment cycles yet to come. Strong democracies need a stable conception of what kinds of decision processes count as legitimate in principle. That conception ought not to be highly dependent on the technological changes *du jour*. Yes, technological specifics can – and often do – make a moral and political difference for any view about how democratic constituencies ought to respond to the emergence of a given new tool. And yes, it is therefore reasonable to expect that modifications of my argument may be in order in light of coming technological advancements. Nonetheless, my core normative arguments are sufficiently general so as to guide *future* strategies aiming to democratize AI deployment beyond the current moment.

To illustrate one bigger-picture implication of my view, consider my analysis of market power in the tech industry. Any future form of a 'concentration of power/dispersion of risk' ASYMMETRY at the scale seen throughout the latest generative AI deployment cycle – or worse – will raise *normative* problems structurally *similar* to those addressed in this essay. Of course, whether the particular ASYMMETRY as I have framed it will remain in effect or indeed intensify is not obvious. The recent wave of antitrust lawsuits in the US and the European AI Act are just two examples of how different regulators have pursued ambitious (though still limited) efforts to curtail Big Tech's power. The EU AI Act imposes rigorous requirements on tech companies with respect to AI tools classified as 'high risk', such as those used in biometric identification, critical infrastructure, and hiring. And it articulates comprehensive consumer transparency and disclosure obligations for AI deployers, thereby targeting opaque business practices helping tech companies retain outsized market power. On the other side of the pond, the FTC's recent legal actions against tech giants like Google and Apple could, if successful, diminish these companies' oligopolistic power, thus lessening the current ASYMMETRY.

These developments suggest that future AI deployment may unfold in less unconstrained and unpredictable ways. However, antitrust efforts and any other policy targeting oligopolistic actors directly – though much-needed and potentially transformative – are but a *complement* for genuine democratic control over deployment decisions, not a *substitute* thereof. True democratic legitimacy requires opportunities for each constituency member to participate in collective decisions in a 'THICK' sense, that is, in a way that goes beyond mere electoral participation and that includes, crucially, opportunities to participate in agenda-setting. By contrast, mobilizing antitrust regulation to decrease the oligopolistic or monopolistic power of companies, and thus achieving desirable *outcomes* that are broadly in the interest of citizens getting the short end of the stick in a given ASYMMETRY, is insufficient for democratic legitimacy, although federal bodies like the FTC plausibly count as indirectly democratically authorized agents. Given this, my argument implies that – in this AI deployment cycle and in future ones – no matter how well-positioned some governmental agency or policy is to mitigate some ASYMMETRY, something important is lost if we fail to democratize AI in the THICK sense.

Relatedly, my analysis of the ASYMMETRY has emphasized that democratizing AI will require careful thought about which economic and political arrangements best enable constituency members to exercise mechanisms of *equal voice* and *exit*. This remains a bigger-picture concern beyond the current AI deployment cycle, and beyond the AI industry as such. As I have argued, current market structures and property rights frameworks often prioritize business interests, blocking citizens from effectively demanding transparency concerning AI products, and meaningful recourse for AI-related harms. Further, citizens lack opportunities to effectively contest how their own data is being extracted and used to develop profitable technologies that manipulate and surveil them, while public ownership models for innovative technologies remain underexplored.[1] In addition, specific subsets of the democratic constituency remain particularly vulnerable to the ways in which societies choose (or fail) to intervene upon markets. For instance, tech workers' moral rights to express their value-based views about the purpose of the products they develop, to blow the whistle on potential risks, to organize themselves, and to assert and defend their interests under exploitative labor conditions, are insufficiently protected and enforced as comprehensive legal rights in many democratic constituencies. This is true even when their political participation rights *qua* citizens are secured. Inside corporations, structures of subordination can persist nevertheless, and companies have used their political influence to stifle efforts to strengthen workers' rights inside and outside of the firm.

1 In this essay, I have focused particularly on approaches that aim to constrain the power of oligopolistic actors by protecting fair market competition and innovation, rather than on approaches that seek to transfer oligopolistic power directly into state institutions (and ostensibly into the hands of the people by extension – as supporters of this approach tend to argue), for instance by *nationalizing* tech companies. I am less optimistic about the latter approach, given that it would not necessarily solve the problem of asymmetrical concentrations of power, but rather simply *shift* these concentrations of power towards governmental actors, who may well – similar to industry actors – make unilateral decisions that evade public accountability.

In sum, current dynamics of AI deployment underscore the urgency of resulting ASYMMETRIES, emphasizing the need to utilize various participation pathways as set out in the PLAYBOOK to reshape societal distributions of power and wealth enabled by emerging technologies.

In addition, how much democratic decision-makers need to *know* to be able to decide *well* points to a larger philosophical and practical issue. Is the 'THICK' democratization of complex policy domains like, but not limited to, AI deployment possible if and when levels of domain-specific technical expertise remain low in the democratic constituency at large? I have acknowledged that low technological literacy levels pose an important potential obstacle to successful democratization. At the same time, based on concrete examples of successful political mobilization surrounding AI policy issues in different political contexts, I have argued that many commentators have overstated the extent to which 'ordinary' citizens currently lack technological literacy, and seriously underestimated their capacity to acquire a better level of understanding of AI. In future waves of AI deployment, too, democratic constituency members may be less doomed with a low level of expertise than one may suppose. A lack of detailed technological understanding was never the core problem blocking successful democratization – a lack of *value-based political participation and mobilization* is. Inspired by the 'democratic innovations' literature in political philosophy and democratic theory, I have shown that participation and mobilization themselves can powerfully enhance citizens' expertise on a given policy matter: political mechanisms that make 'THICKER' democratic participation regarding AI deployment possible may ultimately also increase tech literacy.

Similarly, though more broadly, as I have observed in this essay, conceptual and normative work on *agenda-setting* has long been considered one of the most influential foundations of the field of contemporary democratic theory, yet recent scholarship in this field has paid comparatively less attention to this important line of inquiry. Despite this lack of recent attention, I have argued that effectively democratizing any given policy domain, including AI deployment, necessarily requires engaging in iterative, anticipatory processes of democratically legitimate agenda-setting, rather than relying on other – more familiar, but less impactful – political participation mechanisms. Utilizing pressure points at the AI agenda-setting stage is our best available defense against morally and politically objectionable ASYMMETRIES. I expect this claim to generalize usefully to other domains of interest to political philosophers: democratizing AI in the way I have suggested could function as an instructive case study for other innovative democratization efforts outside of the AI space. Reviving this somewhat neglected field of research, then, promises to yield productive normative insights into how we should protect collective decision processes against nefarious influences operating in markets and states characterized by vast asymmetries of power and wealth.

7.3 Pushing further

A number of complex political and philosophical questions invite further reflection, both from the reader and from my interlocutors in this volume.

I anticipate the possibility of deeper skepticism about the comparative desirability and feasibility of increased democratization in the first place. Whether further democratizing *any* decision domain will necessarily improve the social order established in that domain is notoriously controversial. After all, democratization by itself does not guarantee that the outcomes of collective decisions will be just, or that they will be of high quality in comparison to the kinds of decisions we might achieve when outsourcing decision-making power exclusively to experts, or that they will achieve some other desirable goal (see Chapter 6). Indeed, there may be cases in which the goal of democratization and other important goals pull us in opposite directions. If this were the case, the key question warranting further scrutiny would be whether AI democratization is *uniquely* objectionable in this way, and on those grounds, or whether instead AI democratization is objectionable for the same reasons that increased democratization *in general* – if and when it can be pursued only at the expense of competing desirable goals – is objectionable.

Interestingly, my arguments in this essay imply that the further question of whether democratizing AI will (and should) align with a more or less *techno-skeptical response* to AI deployment remains an entirely *contingent* one. Under current AI deployment dynamics, increased democratization will ideally seek to *constrain and contest* unilateral deployment decisions by tech oligopolies, and thus to tackle the democratic legitimacy deficit currently prevalent in the AI space. However, this may change in the future: the current AI gold rush, much like previous ones, may be succeeded by yet another 'AI winter' – a period of low private sector enthusiasm for, and low public sector investment in, AI technologies, such as in the late 1970s and throughout the 1990s (Crevier, 1993: 203ff; Russell and Norvig, 2009: 24). During a renewed AI winter, democratic constituencies may well provide an agenda-setting counterweight in the other direction, pushing for *increased* investment into AI research and development. This, too, could be a productive way of resisting corporate and top-down regulatory agenda-setting. Ultimately, this view suggests that the goal of democratizing AI is not necessarily linked to any particular evaluative view about whether further technological innovation in this area is all-things-considered *desirable*: the latter plausibly depends, in part, on the specific values and preferences of the democratic constituencies directly affected by AI.

There is another remaining, and more general, question about the distinctiveness of problems arising in the context of AI, and especially generative AI. What *kind* of philosophical problem does generative AI pose? Either generative AI deployment raises genuinely *new* philosophical questions. Or there are important similarities between – currently largely unregulated – generative AI deployment and deployment dynamics involving existing technologies for which there does exist strong democratically authorized regulation, such that generative AI does not pose any genuinely new philosophical problems.

I have sought to reconcile these intuitions: on the one hand, it is true that rapid, large-scale generative AI deployment risks undermining democratic legitimacy in a way that resembles other, less mysterious threats to this core political value. Advances in nuclear technology, for instance, were initiated by government and industry actors, circumventing bottom-up democratic control. This initially hindered citizens' ability to fully exercise their rights to participate in co-determining the future trajectories of decisions related to nuclear energy and nuclear defense policy. But public contestation of these issues ended up reshaping agendas and showed that adopting effective regulation for complex policy problems became more feasible when greater public awareness and deliberation allowed ordinary citizens to articulate value-based preferences in this area, often boosted by advocacy efforts by scientific experts and activists. Complex AI policy questions *could* follow a similar path – that is, if we can resist *AI exceptionalism*, the depoliticizing view that AI is fundamentally unlike any other policy domain and therefore cannot possibly be understood by the wider public. Subjecting AI deployment to effective democratic control would then be a matter of *actually implementing* existing participatory strategies within existing or newly created democratic institutions, rather than adopting an attitude of learned helplessness premised on the assumption that AI is simply too unique, too novel, too complicated for us to try to grasp and direct.

But on the other hand, generative AI deployment in particular illuminates the familiar problem of a democratic legitimacy deficit with *unprecedented* urgency, thus rendering a well-understood problem space at the same time more salient *and* less straightforwardly feasible to intervene upon. As political philosophers have long argued, when the nature of feasibility constraints evolves, turning hard goals into (near-)impossible goals (Gilabert and Lawford-Smith, 2012: 809–825), so do the normative goals subject to them: after all, there is widespread philosophical agreement that we cannot be morally required to do what we cannot possibly do (Kant, 1998: 540).

In this sense, generative AI deployment does pose a genuinely new kind of problem for democratic legitimacy. The facts pertaining to the technology itself – its domain-unspecific nature, and its rapidly accelerating capabilities – are qualitatively different from the previous status quo featuring less sophisticated forms of AI focused on classification tasks in pre-defined decision domains. So are facts pertaining to the social context in which this new technology is deployed – a context in which a further emboldened oligopoly is willing to make their products freely available at a scale not seen before, and in which the barrier for entry has been especially low for the AI consumer base.

Finally, the question of *how* best to democratize AI harbors the potential of constructive controversy. When faced with cases of undemocratic agenda-setting via the mere act of large-scale deployment, which concrete participation pathways are politically and morally preferable? In the PLAYBOOK, I have argued that *informed sub-constituencies*, including groups of people experiencing more direct AI-related risk exposure than others, have a central role to play, as do regular citizens engaged in bottom-up *value-based* practices of contestation, as well as *workers* inside tech companies; and I have emphasized the need to couple participatory agenda-setting along those lines with *larger-scale* institutional and procedural safeguards against oligopolistic power as such, beyond the AI market. Could the concrete strategic alternative (D) developed in this essay, under which all four of these components fall, be usefully modified? Which additional pressure points not covered here might be conducive to more democratically legitimate AI deployment?

7.4 Co-authors and co-owners of our shared future

These open questions, and possibly others, remain. Their lasting presence underlines the complex ambiguities with respect to the normative stakes of technological progress. The insight that these questions resist an uncontroversial, one-size-fits-all solution – although I have made the case in this essay for an overarching set of value-based goalposts well-positioned to guide our collective evaluation of AI independent of the specific nature of evolving technological characteristics (§7.2) – illuminates, yet again, the fact that the future trajectory of AI is fundamentally open. It is open in the same way in which the path of scientific discovery and technological innovation is always subject to uncertainty and as such difficult to predict comprehensively. Whether the next path-breaking AI innovator will resemble Fleming more than Oppenheimer is equally unclear. And further, AI's trajectory remains open in the sense that its positive or negative impact on society will be a function of real human choices, which are neither predetermined nor immune to contestation. It is up to all of us to shape the future instead of merely waiting for it to happen. We can *choose* the extent to which we want to relinquish decision-making power to corporations, lobbyists, and experts. We can *choose* which risks we are willing to accept, and to which AI-enabled benefits we want to aspire. This may not always be apparent, given that AI deployers often publicly present specific technological trajectories as inevitable. Despite – and indeed because – of that, I take the fact that all of these are open questions in principle to provide further support of my view that *democratically legitimate* AI deployment will always require active intervention by the many affected by it, rather than the few holding the power to initiate rapid deployment decisions that undercut our collective ability to freely co-author and to equitably co-own our shared future.

Our collective imagination of technological progress has always been susceptible to a hype-or-doomsday logic oscillating between unduly deferential magical thinking and unhelpfully distracting fearmongering. What gets lost when we give into this discursive dynamic, focused on passively (yet often somewhat hysterically) observing how technology might affect our society, is our ability to pay due attention to the real ways in which we as a society can actively take charge of technology. In 1937, Aldous Huxley warned that 'technological advance is rapid. [But] technological progress has merely provided us with more efficient means for going backwards' (Huxley, 2017: 9). The context of Huxley's claim was, of course, historically specific. It is hard to imagine that Huxley's thought was not to some degree colored by the looming threat of war in Europe and, in particular, the rise of a reactionary modernism that prompted fascist movements to embrace and mythologize the power of technological progress while at the same time rejecting socially progressive ideas rooted in a commitment to liberalism and democracy.

Yet despite its location in a very particular moment in time, Huxley's diagnosis remains applicable today: technological progress *can* provide the powerful with tools to further cement their disproportionate wealth and influence. It *can* also, alongside those technological capabilities, provide economic and social elites with dangerous rhetorical ammunition as to why greater inequalities and lesser freedoms are not just in their benefit, but ostensibly in all of ours.

At the same time, as I have emphasized in this essay, it is important not to allow a view like Huxley's – as accurately as it captures a present and potential future threat to the ideal of a society of free equals – to collapse into unduly deterministic pessimism. Huxley's claim, then, is best understood as a warning rather than a prediction. The pursuit of technological progress may very well push against the pursuit of social progress; but it need not. Instead, democratic constituencies can and should make deliberate choices that shape technological progress so as to render it compatible with the goal of social progress – and the earlier they do so, the better. Realizing that powerful potential is what democratizing AI deployment is all about.

References

Abebe, R. Barocas, S., Kleinberg, J. et al. (2020), Roles for computing in social change. *Proceedings of the 2020 Conference on Fairness, Accountability, and Transparency*. Association for Computing Machinery, New York: 252–260.

Acemoglu, D. and Johnson, D. (2023), *Power and Progress: Our Thousand-Year Struggle Over Technology and Prosperity*. Hachette.

AI4Bharat (2024), *Research lab at IIT Madras*. Available online at: https://ai4bharat.iitm.ac.in/ (last accessed November 30, 2025).

Allen, D. (2023), *Justice by Means of Democracy*. University of Chicago Press.

Allen, D. and Weyl, E.G. (2024), The real dangers of generative AI. *Journal of Democracy* 35, no. 1: 147–162.

Alphabet Workers Union (2024), Why we organize. Available online at https://www.alphabetworkersunion.org/about-us (last accessed October 30, 2024).

Amazon Blog (2020), We are implementing a one-year moratorium on police use of Recognition. Available online at: https://www.aboutamazon.com/news/policy-news-views/we-are-implementing-a-one-year-moratorium-on-police-use-of-rekognition (last accessed November 30, 2025).

Amodei, D. (2023), 'C.E.O. of Anthropic, on the paradoxes of A.I. safety and Netflix's "Deep Fake Love".' Hard Fork podcast, *The New York Times* (7/21/2023). Available online at: https://www.nytimes.com/2023/07/21/podcasts/dario-amodei-ceo-of-anthropic-on-the-paradoxes-of-ai-safety-and-netflixs-deep-fake-love.html?showTranscript=1 (last accessed November 30, 2025).

Amodei, D. (2024), Machines of loving grace. Available online at: https://darioamodei.com/machines-of-loving-grace#1-biology-and-health (last accessed November 30, 2025).

Anderson, E. (2017), *Private Government: How Employers Rule Our Lives (and Why We Don't Talk about It)*. Princeton University Press.

Andreessen, M. (2023), The techno-optimist manifesto. Available online (October 16, 2023) at: https://a16z.com/the-techno-optimist-manifesto/ (last accessed November 30, 2025).

Angwin, J., Larson, J., Mattu, S., and Kirchner, L. (2016), Machine bias. *ProPublica*. Available online at: https://www.propublica.org/article/machine-bias-risk-assessments-in-criminal-sentencing (last accessed November 30, 2025).

Anthropic (2023), Collective constitutional AI: Aligning a language model with public input. Available online at: https://www.anthropic.com/news/collective-constitutional-ai-aligning-a-language-model-with-public-input (last accessed November 30, 2025).

Arneson, R.J. (2003), Defending the purely instrumental account of democratic legitimacy. *Journal of Political Philosophy* 11, no. 1: 122–132.

Ars Technica (2022), New Meta AI demo writes racist and inaccurate scientific literature, gets pulled. Available online at: https://arstechnica.com/

information-technology/2022/11/after-controversy-meta-pulls-demo-of-ai-model-that-writes-scientific-papers/ (last accessed November 30, 2025).

Ayer, A.J. (1954), *On the Analysis of Moral Judgments. Philosophical Essays.* Palgrave Macmillan.

Aytac, U. (2024), Big Tech, algorithmic power, democratic control. *The Journal of Politics* 86, no. 4: 1431–1445.

Bachrach, P. and Baratz, M.S. (1961), Two faces of power. *American Political Science Review* 56, no. 4: 947–952.

Barbrook, R. and Cameron, A. (1995), The Californian ideology. *Mute* 1, no. 3. Available online at: https://www.metamute.org/editorial/articles/californian-ideology (last accessed November 30, 2025).

Barlow, J.P. (2019), Declaration of the independence of cyberspace. *Duke Law and Technology Review* 18, no. 1: 5–7.

Barry, B. (1965), *Political Argument.* Routledge and Kegan Paul.

BBC Newsnight (2024), X Post on 5/17/2024, @BBCNewsnight. https://x.com/BBCNewsnight/status/1791587541721780400 (last accessed November 30, 2025).

Bender, E., Gebru, T., McMillan-Major, A., et al. (2021), On the dangers of stochastic parrots: Can language models be too big? 🦜. *Proceedings of the 2021 ACM Conference on Fairness, Accountability, and Transparency* (FAccT '21). Association for Computing Machinery: 610–623.

Benjamin, R. (2019), *Race After Technology: Abolitionist Tools for the New Jim Code.* John Wiley and Sons.

Birhane, A. and Van Dijk, J. (2020), Robot rights? Let's talk about human welfare instead. *Proceedings of the AAAI/ACM Conference on AI, Ethics, and Society* (AIES '20) (2020): 207–213.

Blodgett, S.L. Barocas, S., Daumé III H., and Wallach, H. (2020), Language (technology) is power: A critical survey of 'bias' in NLP. *Proceedings of the 58th Annual Meeting of the Association for Computation Linguistics.* Association for Computational Linguistics: 5454–5476.

Bloomberg (2024a), OpenAI discusses giving Altman 7% stake in for-profit shift. Available online at: https://www.bloomberg.com/news/articles/2024-09-25/openai-cto-mira-murati-says-she-will-leave-the-company (last accessed November 30, 2025).

Bloomberg (2024b), OpenAI's Altman concentrates power on path to $157 billion valuation. Available online at: https://www.bloomberg.com/features/2024-openai-executives/ (last accessed November 30, 2025).

Blue Origin (n.d.), About Blue. https://www.blueorigin.com/about-blue (last accessed November 30, 2025).

Blumenthal, R. and Hawley, J. (2023), Bipartisan Framework for U.S. AI Act. U.S. Senate Subcommittee on Privacy, Technology, and the Law, September 7, 2023. Available online at: https://www.blumenthal.senate.gov/imo/media/doc/09072023bipartisanaiframework.pdf (last accessed: November 30, 2025).

Bogg, A. (2009), *The Democratic Aspects of Trade Union Recognition.* Hart Publishing.

Bolukbasi, T., Chang, K-W., Zou, J., et al. (2016), Man is to computer programmer as woman is to homemaker? Debiasing word embeddings. *Neural Information Processing Systems* (NeurIPS): 4349–4357.

Bostrom, N. (2009), The future of humanity. In: *New Waves in Philosophy of Technology*, eds. Jan Kyrre Berg Olsen, Evan Selinger, Soren Riis. Palgrave McMillan: 186–215.

Bostrom, N. (2014), *Superintelligence: Paths, Dangers, Strategies*. Oxford University Press.

Boyd, D. and Elish, M.C. (2018), Don't believe every AI you see. *New America*. Available online at: https://www.newamerica.org/pit/blog/dont-believe-every-ai-you-see/ (last accessed November 30, 2025).

Brennan, J. (2016), *Against Democracy*. Princeton University Press.

Broockman, D.E., Ferenstein, G., and Malhotra, N. (2019), Predispositions and the political behavior of American economic elites: Evidence from technology entrepreneurs. *American Journal of Political Science* 63, no. 1: 212–233.

Brown, T.B., Mann, B., Ryder, N., et al. (2020), Language models are few-shot learners. arXiv:2005.14165v4 [cs.CL].

Bud, R. (2007), *Penicillin: Triumph and Tragedy*. Oxford University Press.

Buolamwini, J. and Gebru, T. (2018), Gender shades: Intersectional accuracy disparities in commercial gender classification. *Proceedings of Machine Learning Research* 81: 77–91.

Calo, R. and Citron, D.K. (2021), The automated administrative state: A crisis of legitimacy. *Emory Law Journal* 70: 797–846,

Carpenter, D. (2023), Agenda democracy. *Annual Review of Political Science* 26, no. 1: 193–212.

Carpenter, D. and Ezell, C. (2024), An FDA for AI? Pitfalls and plausibility of approval regulation for frontier artificial intelligence. *Proceedings of the AAAI/ACM Conference on AI, Ethics, and Society* (AIES '24) 7, no. 1: 239–254.

Center for AI Safety (2023), Statement on AI risk. Available online at: https://www.safe.ai/work/statement-on-ai-risk (last accessed November 30, 2025).

Chalmers, D. (2010), The singularity: A philosophical analysis. *Journal of Consciousness Studies* 17: 7–65.

Chalmers, D. (2023), Could a large language model be conscious? *Boston Review*. Available online at: https://www.bostonreview.net/articles/could-a-large-language-model-be-conscious/ (last accessed November 30, 2025).

Chouldechova, A. (2017), Fair prediction with disparate impact: a study of bias in recidivism prediction instruments. *Big Data* 5, no. 2: 153–163.

Christiano, T. (2003), An argument for democratic equality. In: *Philosophy and Democracy: An Anthology*. Oxford University Press: 39–68.

Christiano, T. (2004), The authority of democracy. *Journal of Political Philosophy* 12, no. 3: 266–290.

Christiano, T. (2008), *The Constitution of Equality: Democratic Authority and Its Limits*. Oxford University Press.

Christiano, T. (2022), Algorithms, manipulation, and democracy. *Canadian Journal of Philosophy* 52, no. 1: 109–124.

City and County of San Francisco Board of Supervisors (2019), Ordinance no. 103–19 (Stop Secret Surveillance Ordinance).

Clarke, A.C. (1968), Clarke's Third Law on UFOs. *Science* 159, no. 3812: 255.

CNBC (2023), Google, Amazon, Nvidia and other tech giants invest in AI startup Hugging Face, sending its valuation to $4.5 billion. Available online at: https://www.cnbc.com/2023/08/24/google-amazon-nvidia-amd-other-tech-giants-invest-in-hugging-face.html (last accessed November 30, 2025).

CNBC (2024), Sam Altman tells OpenAI staff there's no plan for him to receive a 'giant equity stake' in company. Available online at: https://www.cnbc.com/2024/09/26/openais-sam-altman-tells-employees-he-didnt-get-giant-equity-stake.html (last accessed November 30, 2025).

CNN (2022), The rise and fall of a virtual rapper reignites old questions about art – with a new twist. Available online at: https://www.cnn.com/2022/09/11/entertainment/fn-meka-ai-virtual-artists-music-cec/index.html (last accessed November 30, 2025).

Coeckelbergh, M. (2024), *Why AI Undermines Democracy and What to Do About It*. Polity.

Cofone, I.N. (2023), *The Privacy Fallacy: Harm and Power in the Information Economy*. Cambridge University Press.

Cohen, J. (1989), The economic basis of deliberative democracy. *Social Philosophy and Policy* 6, no. 2: 25–50.

Cohen, J. (2003), Procedure and substance in deliberative democracy. In: *Philosophy and Democracy: An Anthology*, ed. T. Christiano. Oxford University Press: 17–38.

Committee on the Judiciary, United States Senate (2023), Oversight of A.I.: Rules for Artificial Intelligence. Hearing before the Subcommittee on Privacy, Technology, and the Law. Available online at: https://www.govinfo.gov/content/pkg/CHRG-118shrg52706/pdf/CHRG-118shrg52706.pdf (last accessed November 30, 2025).

Computer History Museum (2004), Bill Gates, Chairman and Chief Software Architect of Microsoft, in Conversation with John Hennessy. Available online at https://www.youtube.com/watch?v=6dpSy8nklsQ. (last accessed November 30, 2025).

Computer Weekly (2024), Amazon defends facial-recognition tech sale to FBI despite moratorium. Available online at: https://www.computerweekly.com/news/366569552/Amazon-defends-facial-recognition-tech-sale-to-FBI-despite-moratorium (last accessed November 30, 2025).

Conyon, M. Ellman, M., Pitelis, C.N., et al. (2022), Big Tech oligopolies, Keith Cowling, and monopoly capitalism. *Cambridge Journal of Economics* 46, no. 6: 1205–1224.

Costanza-Chock, S. (2020), *Design Justice: Community-Led Practices to Build the Worlds We Need*. MIT Press.

Crawford, K. (2021), *The Atlas of AI: Power, Politics, and the Planetary Costs of Artificial Intelligence*. Yale University Press.

Crevier, D. (1993), *AI: The Tumultuous Search for Artificial Intelligence*. Basic Books.

Dahl, R.A. (1961), *Who Governs? Democracy and Power in an American City*. Yale University Press.

Douglas, H.E. (2009), *Science, Policy, and the Value-Free Ideal*. University of Pittsburgh Press.

Du Bois, W.E.B. (1903), *The Souls of Black Folk*. A.C. McClurg and Co. [(1997) Eds. David W. Blight and Robert Gooding-Williams, Bedford Books].

Du Bois, W.E.B. (1968), *The Autobiography of W.E.B. Du Bois: A Soliloquy on Viewing My Life from the Last Decade of Its First Century*, H. Aptheker (ed.). International Publishers.

Dworkin, R. (1987–1988), What is equality - Part 4: Political equality. *University of San Francisco Law Review* 22: 1.

Dworkin, R. (1996), *Freedom's Law: The Moral Reading of the American Constitution*. Harvard University Press.

Estlund, D. (2008), *Democratic Authority: A Philosophical Framework*. Princeton University Press.

Estlund, D. (2011), Human nature and the limits (if any) of political philosophy. *Philosophy and Public Affairs* 39: 207–237

Eubanks, V. (2018), *Automating Inequality: How High-Tech Tools Profile, Police, and Punish the Poor*. St. Martin's Press.

European Commission (2024a), AI Act: Have your say on trustworthy general-purpose AI. Available online at: https://digital-strategy.ec.europa.eu/en/consultations/ai-act-have-your-say-trustworthy-general-purpose-ai (last accessed November 30, 2025).

European Commission (2024b), AI Pact. Available online at: https://digital-strategy.ec.europa.eu/en/policies/ai-pact (last accessed November 30, 2025).

European Union (2024c), Regulation (EU) 2024/1689 of the European Parliament and of the Council of 13 June 2024 laying down harmonised rules on artificial intelligence (Artificial Intelligence Act). *Official Journal of the European Union* L 2024/1689: 1–144.

European Parliamentary Research Service (2016), Briefing: Participatory budgeting: An innovative approach. Available online at: https://www.europarl.europa.eu/RegData/etudes/BRIE/2016/573894/EPRS_BRI(2016)573894_EN.pdf (last accessed November 30, 2025).

Federal Trade Commission (2023), FTC sues Amazon for illegally maintaining monopoly power. Available online at: https://www.ftc.gov/news-events/news/press-releases/2023/09/ftc-sues-amazon-illegally-maintaining-monopoly-power (last accessed November 30, 2025).

Feinberg, J. (1989), Voluntariness and assumptions of risk. In: *The Moral Limits of the Criminal Law Volume 3: Harm to Self*. Oxford University Press: 98–142.

Finkelstein, C.O. (2003), Is risk a harm? *University of Pennsylvania Law Review* 151: 963–1001.

Forbes (2024a), A year in review of IBM's ambitious AI strategy. Available online at: https://www.forbes.com/sites/patrickmoorhead/2024/02/01/a-year-in-review-of-ibms-ambitious-ai-strategy/ (last accessed November 30, 2025).

Forbes (2024b), The real-time billionaires list. Available online at: https://www.forbes.com/real-time-billionaires/ (last accessed November 30, 2025).

Foreign Policy (2023), OpenAI's CEO goes on a diplomatic charm offensive. Available online at: https://foreignpolicy.com/2023/06/20/openai-ceo-diplomacy-artificial-intelligence/ (last accessed November 30, 2025).

Foxglove (2024), Open letter to President Biden from tech workers in Kenya. Available online at: https://www.foxglove.org.uk/open-letter-to-president-biden-from-tech-workers-in-kenya/ (last accessed November 30, 2025).

Freeman, R. (2007), *America Works: Thoughts on an Exceptional US Labor Market*. Russell Sage Foundation.

Fung, A. and Cohen, J. (2021), Democracy and the digital public sphere. In: *Digital Technology and Democratic Theory*, eds. Lucy Bernholz, Hélène Landemore, and Rob Reich. University of Chicago Press: 23–61.

Future of Life Institute (2023), Pause giant AI experiments: An open letter. Available online at: https://futureoflife.org/open-letter/pause-giant-ai-experiments/ (last accessed November 30, 2025).

Galbraith, J.K. (1952), *American Capitalism: The Concept of Countervailing Power*. Houghton Mifflin.

Gebru, T. and Torres, E.P. (2024), The TESCREAL bundle: Eugenics and the promise of utopia through artificial general intelligence. *First Monday* 29, no. 4.

Geek Wire (2018), Transcript: 'Chief slowdown officer' Jeff Bezos shares Amazon management tips. Available online at: https://www.*Geek Wire*.com/2018/full-transcript-chief-slowdown-officer-jeff-bezos-shares-amazon-management-wisdom/ (last accessed November 30, 2025).

Geissel, B. (2019), Democratic innovations in Europe. In: *Handbook of Democratic Innovation and Governance*, eds. Stephen Elstub and Oliver Escobar. Edward Elgar Publishing: 404–420.

Gilabert, P. and Lawford-Smith, H. (2012), Political feasibility: A conceptual exploration. *Political Studies* 60, no. 4: 809–825.

Gizmodo (2018), Google removes 'Don't Be Evil' clause from its code of conduct. Available online at: https://gizmodo.com/google-removes-nearly-all-mentions-of-dont-be-evil-from-1826153393 (last accessed November 30, 2025).

Goodin, R.E. (2007), Enfranchising all affected interests, and its alternatives. *Philosophy and Public Affairs* 35, no. 1: 40–68.

Google (2024), @NewsFromGoogle Post on X. (2/21/2024). Available online at: https://x.com/NewsFromGoogle/status/1760354549481546035 (last accessed November 30, 2025).

Gray, M.L. and Suri, S. (2019), *Ghost Work: How to Stop Silicon Valley from Building a New Global Underclass*. Houghton Mifflin Harcourt.

Habermas, J. (1996), *Between Facts and Norms: Contributions to a Discourse Theory of Law and Democracy*. MIT Press.

Habermas, J. (1998), Remarks on legitimation through human rights. *Philosophy and Social Criticism* 24, no. 2–3: 157–171.

Harman, E. (2018), Is it reasonable to 'rely on intuitions' in ethics? In: *The Norton Introduction to Philosophy*, Second Edition, eds. Gideon Rosen, Alex Byrne, Joshua Cohen, Elizabeth Harman, and Seana Shiffrin. W. W. Norton and Company: 895–903.

Himmelreich, J. (2023), Against democratizing AI. *AI and Society* 38: 1333–1346.

Hirschman, A.O. (1970), *Exit, Voice and Loyalty: Responses to Decline in Firms, Organizations and States*. Harvard University Press.

Honig, B. (2011), *Emergency Politics: Paradox, Law, Democracy*. Princeton University Press. https://www.europarl.europa.eu/RegData/etudes/BRIE/2023/739342/EPRS_BRI(2023)739342_EN.pdf

Hua, S. and Belfield. H. (2023), Effective enforceability of EU competition law under ai development scenarios: A framework for anticipatory governance. *Proceedings of the 2023 AAAI/ACM Conference on AI, Ethics, and Society*. Association for Computing Machinery: 596–605.

Huxley, A. (2017), *Ends and Means: An Inquiry into the Nature of Ideals*. Routledge.

IBM (2020), IBM CEO's letter to Congress on racial justice reform. Available online at: https://web.archive.org/web/20200609031426/https:/www.ibm.com/blogs/policy/facial-recognition-susset-racial-justice-reforms/ (last accessed November 30, 2025).

IBM Newsroom (2023), AI alliance launches as an international community of leading technology developers, researchers, and adopters collaborating together to advance open, safe, responsible AI. Available online at: https://newsroom.ibm.com/AI-Alliance-Launches-as-an-International-Community-of-Leading-Technology-Developers,-Researchers,-and-Adopters-Collaborating-Together-to-Advance-Open,-Safe,-Responsible-AI (last accessed November 30, 2025).

Jasanoff, S. (2016), *The Ethics of Invention: Technology and the Human Future*. W.W. Norton and Company.
Kant, Immanuel (1998), Critique of pure reason. In: *The Cambridge Edition of the Works of Immanuel Kant*, eds. Paul Guyer and Allen W. Wood. Cambridge University Press, A548/B576, 540.
Karp, A. (2023), Our Oppenheimer moment: The creation of A.I. weapons. *The New York Times*. Available online at: https://www.nytimes.com/2023/07/25/opinion/karp-palantir-artificial-intelligence.html (last accessed November 30, 2025).
Kay, J., Kasirzadeh, A., and Mohamed, S. (2024), Epistemic injustice in generative AI. *arXiv:2408.11441 [cs.AI]*.
Khader, S.J. (2012), Must theorising about adaptive preferences deny women's agency? *Journal of Applied Philosophy* 29, no. 4: 302–317.
Kleinberg, J.M., Mullainathan, S., and Raghavan, M. (2017), Inherent trade-offs in the fair determination of risk scores. In: *8th Innovations in Theoretical Computer Science Conference, ITCS 2017*, January 9–11, 2017, Berkeley, CA, USA (LIPIcs, Vol. 67): 1–23.
Knight, W. (2022), Elon Musk has fired Twitter's 'Ethical AI' team. *Wired*. Available online at: https://www.wired.com/story/twitter-ethical-ai-team/ (last accessed November 30, 2025).
Kolodny, N. (2014), Rule over none I: What justifies democracy? *Philosophy and Public Affairs* 42, no. 3: 195–229.
Landemore, H. (2013), *Democratic Reason: Politics, Collective Intelligence, and the Rule of the Many*. Princeton University Press.
Landemore, H. (2017), Deliberative democracy as open, not (just) representative democracy. *Daedalus* 146, no. 3: 51–63.
Landemore, H. (2020), *Open Democracy: Reinventing Popular Rule for the Twenty-first Century*. Princeton University Press.
Langer, P.F. (2020), Lessons from China – The formation of a social credit system: Profiling, reputation scoring, social engineering. In: *The 21st Annual International Conference on Digital Government Research*, eds. Seok-Jin Eom and Joohoo Lee. The Association for Computing Machinery: 164–174.
Lazar, S. (2024), Power and AI. In: *The Oxford Handbook of AI Governance*, eds. Justin B. Bullock, Yu-Che Chen, Johannes Himmelreich, et al. Oxford University Press: 198.
Liao, M. (2020), The moral status and rights of artificial intelligence. In: *Ethics of Artificial Intelligence*, ed. S. Matthew Liao. Oxford University Press: 480–504.
List, C. and Goodin, R.E. (2001), Epistemic democracy: generalizing the condorcet jury theorem. *Journal of Political Philosophy* 9, no. 3: 277–306.
Loefflad, C. and Grossklags, J. (2024), How the types of consequences in social scoring systems shape people's perceptions and behavioral reactions. In: *Proceedings of the 2024 ACM Conference on Fairness, Accountability, and Transparency*, Association for Computing Machinery: 1515–1530.
Logan, J. (2021), Crushing unions, by any means necessary: how Amazon's blistering anti-union campaign won in Bessemer, Alabama. *New Labor Forum* 30, no. 3: 38–45.
Longino, H, (2004), How values can be good for science. In: *Science, Values, and Objectivity*, eds. Peter K. Machamer and Gereon Wolters. University of Pittsburgh Press: 127–142.

Luccioni, S., Yacine, J., and Strubell, E. (2024), Hungry processing: Watts driving the cost of AI deployment? *Proceedings of the 2024 ACM Conference on Fairness, Accountability, and Transparency* (FAccT '24). Association for Computing Machinery: 85–99.

MacAskill, W. (2022), *What We Owe the Future*. Basic.

MacDonald, D. (2019), How labor unions increase political knowledge: evidence from the United States. *Political Behavior* 43: 1–24.

Mansbridge, J. (2018), Recursive representation. In: *Creating Political Presence: The New Politics of Democratic Representation*, eds. D Castiglione and J Pollak. University of Chicago Press: 298–338.

Marcus, G. (2024), OpenAI's Sam Altman is becoming one of the most powerful people on Earth. We should be very afraid. *The Guardian*. Available online at: https://www.theguardian.com/technology/article/2024/aug/03/open-ai-sam-altman-chatgpt-gary-marcus-taming-silicon-valley (last accessed November 30, 2025).

Marinetti, F.T. (1909), *Manifesto del Futurismo*. Rassegna Internazionale Poesia. Poligrafia Italiana.

Miceli, M. (2021), Data Workers Inquiry [research project]. Available online at: https://data-workers.org/ (last accessed November 30, 2025).

Microsoft Bing Blogs (2023), The new Bing and Edge – Learning from our first week. Available online at: https://blogs.bing.com/search/february-2023/The-new-Bing-Edge-Learning-from-our-first-week (last accessed November 30, 2025).

Ministério da Ciência, Tecnologia e Inovação (2024), IA para o Bem de Todos: Proposta de Plano Brasileiro de Inteligencia Artificial 2024-2028. Available online at: https://www.gov.br/mcti/pt-br/acompanhe-o-mcti/cct/legislacao/arquivos/IA_para_o_Bem_de_Todos.pdf (last accessed November 30, 2025).

MIT Technology Review (2016), Why Microsoft accidentally unleashed a neo-Nazi sexbot. Available online at: https://www.technologyreview.com/2016/03/24/161424/why-microsoft-accidentally-unleashed-a-neo-nazi-sexbot/ (last accessed November 30, 2025).

Moment of Zen Podcast (2023), Balaji on the tribal lens, America's blunder, and his plan to save San Francisco. Available online at: https://www.youtube.com/watch?v=mIJLW_Rc6Rg (last accessed November 30, 2025).

Morozov, E. (2013), *To Save Everything, Click Here: The Folly of Technological Solutionism*. Public Affairs.

Narayanan, A. and Kapoor, S. (2024), *AI Snake Oil: What Artificial Intelligence Can Do, What It Can't, and How to Tell the Difference*. Princeton University Press.

National Institute of Standards and Technology (2024), U.S. AI safety institute signs agreements regarding AI safety research, testing and evaluation with Anthropic and OpenAI. Available online at: https://www.nist.gov/news-events/news/2024/08/us-ai-safety-institute-signs-agreements-regarding-ai-safety-research (last accessed November 30, 2025).

Noble, S.U. (2018), *Algorithms of Oppression: How Search Engines Reinforce Racism*. NYU Press.

Nussbaum, M. (1995), Human capabilities: female human beings. In: *Women, Culture, and Development*, eds. Martha Nussbaum and Jonathon Glover. Clarendon Press: 61–104.

Nussbaum, M. (1999), *Sex and Social Justice*. Oxford University Press.

Nvidia Newsroom (2024), Microsoft and NVIDIA announce major integrations to accelerate generative AI for enterprises everywhere. Available online at: https://nvidianews.nvidia.com/news/microsoft-nvidia-generative-ai-enterprises (last accessed November 30, 2025).

NYC Automated Decision Systems Task Force (n.d.). *Members*. Available online at https://www.nyc.gov/site/adstaskforce/members/members.page (last accessed November 30, 2025).

Okin, S. (1998), Feminism and multiculturalism: some tensions. *Ethics* 108, no. 4: 661–684.

O'Neill, M. (2008), Three Rawlsian routes towards economic democracy. *Revue de Philosophie Economique* 8, no. 2: 29–55.

O'Neill, M. and White, S. (2018), Trade unions and political equality. In: *Philosophical Foundations of Labour Law*, eds. Hugh Collins, Gillian Lester, Gillian, and Virginia Mantouvalou. Oxford University Press: 229–252.

Oberdiek, J. (2017), *Imposing Risk: A Normative Framework*. Oxford University Press.

Office of Public Affairs, Department of Justice (2024), Press Release: Justice department sues Apple for monopolizing smartphone markets. Available online at: https://www.justice.gov/opa/pr/justice-department-sues-apple-monopolizing-smartphone-markets (last accessed November 30, 2025).

Office of Science and Technology Policy (2023a), Request for information: national priorities for artificial intelligence. Available online at: https://www.whitehouse.gov/wp-content/uploads/2023/05/OSTP-Request-for-Information-National-Priorities-for-Artificial-Intelligence.pdf (last accessed October 30, 2024).

Office of Science and Technology Policy (2023b), Trade Regulation Rule on Commercial Surveillance and Data Security: Advance notice of proposed rule-making; request for public comment; public forum. *Federal Register* 87, no. 161 (2022): 51273–51299.

OpenAI (2023a), Democratic inputs to AI. Available online at: https://openai.com/index/democratic-inputs-to-ai/ (last accessed November 30, 2025).

OpenAI (2023b), How Should AI systems behave, and who should decide? Available online at: https://openai.com/index/how-should-ai-systems-behave/ (last accessed November 30, 2025).

OpenAI (n.d.), Our structure. Available online at: https://openai.com/our-structure/ (last accessed November 30, 2025).

Ouyang, L. Wu, J., Jiang, X., et al. (2022), Training language models to follow instructions with human feedback. *Advances in Neural Information Processing Systems* 35: 27730–27744.

Palantir Technologies Inc (2024), Q1 2024 Earnings Webcast. Available online at: https://www.youtube.com/watch?v=KcG1TBPw1V8. (last accessed November 30, 2025).

Pasquale, F. (2019), Rethinking the knowledge problem in an era of corporate gigantism. In: *The Democratization of Artificial Intelligence: Net Politics in the Era of Learning Algorithms*, ed. Andreas Sudmann. Transcript: 285–296.

Peng, K. (2020), Facial recognition datasets are being widely used despite being taken down due to ethical concerns. Here's how. *Freedom to Tinker*. Available online at: https://freedom-to-tinker.com/2020/10/21/facial-recognition-datasets-are-being-widely-used-despite-being-taken-down-due-to-ethical-concerns-heres-how/ (last accessed November 30, 2025).

Perrigo, B. (2023), Exclusive: OpenAI lobbied the E.U. to water down AI regulation. *Time Magazine*. Available online at: https://time.com/6288245/openai-eu-lobbying-ai-act/ (last accessed November 30, 2025).
Pettit, P. (2012), *On the People's Terms: A Republican Theory and Model of Democracy*. New York: Cambridge University Press.
Praxis Citizen Pledge (n.d.), https://drive.google.com/file/d/1zN-Rd2tkWJim4kOTzjbl6m7ehZxT0m9U/preview Available online at: https://www.praxisnation.com/ (last accessed November 30, 2025).
Raghavan, M., Barocas, S., Kleinberg, J., and Levy, K. (2020), Mitigating bias in algorithmic hiring: Evaluating claims and practices. *Proceedings of the 2020 Conference on Fairness, Accountability, and Transparency*. Association for Computing Machinery: 469–481.
Raji, I.D., Xu, P., Honigsberg, C., and Ho, D. (2022), Outsider oversight: Designing a third party audit ecosystem for ai governance. *Proceedings of the 2022 AAAI/ACM Conference on AI, Ethics, and Society*. Association for Computing Machinery: 557–571.
Ramakrishnan, K., Smith, G., and Downey, C. (2024), *US Tort Liability for Large-Scale Artificial Intelligence Damages*. Rand Corporation.
Raz, J. (1986), *The Morality of Freedom*. Oxford University Press.
Reich, R., Sahami, M., and Weinstein, J. (2021), *System Error: Where Big Tech Went Wrong and How We Can Reboot*. HarperCollins.
Reuters (2023), ChatGPT-maker OpenAI says it has no plans to leave Europe. Available online at: https://www.reuters.com/technology/openai-has-no-plans-leave-europe-ceo-2023-05-26/ (last accessed November 30, 2025).
Richardson, R. ed. (2019), Confronting black boxes: A shadow report of the New York City Automated Decision System Task Force. *AI Now Institute*. Available online at: https://ainowinstitute.org/ads-shadowreport-2019.html (last accessed November 30, 2025).
Risse, M. (2023), *Political Theory of the Digital Age: Where Artificial Intelligence Might Take Us*. Cambridge University Press.
Robertson, A. (2023), ChatGPT returns to Italy after ban. *The Verge*. Available online at https://www.theverge.com/2023/4/28/23702883/chatgpt-italy-ban-lifted-gpdp-data-protection-age-verification (last accessed November 30, 2025).
Romer, T. and Rosenthal, H. (1978), Political resource allocation, controlled agendas, and the status quo. *Public Choice* 33: 27–43.
Roose, K. (2023), How ChatGPT kicked off an A.I. arms race. *The New York Times*. Available online at: https://www.nytimes.com/2023/02/03/technology/chatgpt-openai-artificial-intelligence.html (last accessed November 30, 2025).
Rosenvallon, P. (2006), *La Contre-Démocratie: La Politique à l'Âge de la Défiance*. Seuil.
Russell, S.J. and Norvig, P. (2009), *Artificial Intelligence: A Modern Approach*. Third edn. Pearson.
Sadowski, J., Viljoen, S., and Whittaker, M. (2021), Everyone should decide how their digital data are used – not just tech companies. *Nature* 595:169–171.
Saward, M. (2008), Representation and democracy: revisions and possibilities. *Sociology Compass* 2: 1000–1013.
Schattschneider, E.E. (1960), *The Semisovereign People: A Realist's View of Democracy in America*. Harcourt Brace Jovanovich.

Schiffer, Z. and Newton, C. (2023), Microsoft lays off team that taught employees how to make AI tools responsibly. *The Verge*. Available online at : https://www.theverge.com/2023/3/13/23638823/microsoft-ethics-society-team-responsible-ai-layoffs (last accessed November 30, 2025).

Schmidt, E. (2024), Fireside. *AI+Energy Summit, Special Competitive Studies Project*. Available online at: https://www.youtube.com/watch?v=oC46CzxT750. (last accessed November 30, 2025).

Schyns, C. (2023), The lobbying ghost in the machine: Big Tech's covert defanging of Europe's AI Act. *Corporate Europe Observatory*. Available online at: https://corporateeurope.org/sites/default/files/2023-03/The%20Lobbying%20Ghost%20in%20the%20Machine.pdf (last accessed November 30, 2025).

Simons, J. (2023), *Algorithms for the People: Democracy in the Age of AI*. Princeton University Press.

Singer, P. (1972), Moral experts. *Analysis 3*,. no. 4: 115–117.

Sitaraman, G. and Narechania, T.N. (2024), An antimonopoly approach to governing artificial intelligence. *Yale Law and Policy Review* 43, no.1: 95–170.

Sloane, M., Moss, E., Awomolo, O., and Forlano, L. (2022), Participation is not a design fix for machine learning. *Proceedings of the 2nd ACM Conference on Equity and Access in Algorithms, Mechanisms, and Optimization* (EAAMO '22). Association for Computing Machinery: 1–6.

Smith, G. (2009), *Democratic Innovations: Designing Institutions for Citizen Participation*. Cambridge University Press.

Song, S. (2012), The boundary problem in democratic theory: why the demos should be bounded by the state. *International Theory* 4, no. 1: 39–68.

Srinivasan, A. (2015), *Stop the Robot Apocalypse*. London Review of Books 37, no. 18. Available online: at https://www.lrb.co.uk/the-paper/v37/n18/amia-srinivasan/stop-the-robot-apocalypse (last accessed November 30, 2025).

Srinivasan, B. (2022), *The Network State: How To Start a New Country*. Available online at: https://thenetworkstate.com/ (last accessed November 30, 2025).

Stein, C. and Fegert, J. (2024), Bridging realities: Exploring enablement factors for XR participatory urban planning. *ECIS 2024 Proceedings* 31: https://aisel.aisnet.org/ecis2024/track17_greenis/track17_greenis/31

Stoychev, S.P. (2017), The 2016 referendum in Bulgaria. *East European Quarterly* 45, no. 3–4: 187–194.

The *Guardian* (2020a), Ofqual ignored exams warning a month ago amid ministers' pressure. Available online at: https://www.theguardian.com/politics/2020/aug/19/ofqual-was-warned-a-month-ago-that-exams-algorithm-was-volatile (last accessed November 30, 2025).

The *Guardian* (2020b), England exams row timeline: was Ofqual warned of algorithm bias? Available online at: https://www.theguardian.com/education/2020/aug/20/england-exams-row-timeline-was-ofqual-warned-of-algorithm-bias (last accessed November 30, 2025).

The *Guardian* (2022), Capitol Records drops 'offensive' AI rapper FN Meka after outcry over racial stereotyping. Available online at: https://www.theguardian.com/music/2022/aug/24/major-record-label-drops-offensive-ai-rapper-after-outcry-over-racial-stereotyping (last accessed November 30, 2025).

The *Guardian* (2023a), 'Lack of respect': outcry over Amazon employee's death on warehouse floor. Available online at: https://www.theguardian.com/technology/2023/jan/09/amazon-employee-death-warehouse-floor-colorado (last accessed November 30, 2025).

The *Guardian* (2023b), 'It's pillage': thirsty Uruguayans decry Google's plan to exploit water supply. Available online at: https://www.theguardian.com/world/2023/jul/11/uruguay-drought-water-google-data-center (last accessed November 30, 2025).

The *Independent* (2020a), Microsoft gets exclusive access to AI deemed 'too dangerous to release'. Available online at: https://www.independent.co.uk/tech/microsoft-openai-gpt3-exclusive-b550673.html (last accessed November 30, 2025).

The *Independent* (2020b), 'Ridiculous', 'unfair' and 'an absolute shambles': GCSE students await their results following Ofqual U-turn. Available online at: https://www.independent.co.uk/life-style/gcse-results-exam-grades-appeal-a-levels-ofqual-a9677136.html (last accessed November 30, 2025).

The New York Times (2023), The Silicon Valley elite who want to build a city from scratch. Available online at: https://www.nytimes.com/2023/08/25/business/land-purchases-solano-county.html (last accessed November 30, 2025).

The New York Times (2024), Google chatbot's A.I. images put people of color in Nazi-Era uniforms. Available online at: https://www.nytimes.com/2024/02/22/technology/google-gemini-german-uniforms.html (last accessed November 30, 2025).

The Software Alliance (2023), BSA Recommendations on the EU Artificial Intelligence Act. Available online at: https://www.bsa.org/files/policy-filings/08062021aiactreccpospaper.pdf (last accessed November 30, 2025).

The Washington Post (2022), The Google engineer who thinks the company's AI has come to life. Available online at: https://www.washingtonpost.com/technology/2022/06/11/google-ai-lamda-blake-lemoine/ (last accessed November 30, 2025).

The Washington Post (2023a), As AI booms, tech companies cut AI ethicists. Available online at: https://www.washingtonpost.com/technology/2023/03/30/tech-companies-cut-ai-ethics/ (last accessed November 30, 2025).

The Washington Post (2023b), Top tech firms sign White House pledge to identify AI-generated images. Available online at: https://www.washingtonpost.com/technology/2023/07/21/ai-white-house-pledge-openai-google-meta/ (last accessed November 30, 2025).

The Washington Post (2024), Elon Musk gives $75M to his own America PAC in push to elect Trump. Available online at: https://www.washingtonpost.com/politics/2024/10/16/elon-musk-trump-support-america-pac/ (last accessed November 30, 2025).

The White House (2021), National AI Advisory Committee: Meetings. Available online at https://ai.gov/naiac/ (last accessed November 30, 2025).

The White House (2023), FACT SHEET: Biden-Harris administration secures voluntary commitments from leading artificial intelligence companies to manage the risks posed by AI. Available online at: https://www.whitehouse.gov/briefing-room/statements-releases/2023/07/21/fact-sheet-biden-harris-administration-secures-voluntary-commitments-from-leading-artificial-intelligence-companies-to-manage-the-risks-posed-by-ai/ (last accessed November 30, 2025).

Thiel, P. (2007), The Straussian moment. In: *Politics and Apocalypse* (Studies in Violence, Mimesis and Culture), ed. Robert Hamerton-Kelly. Michigan State University Press: 189–218.

Thiel, P. (2009), The education of a libertarian. *Cato Unbound: A Journal of Debate*. Available online at: https://www.cato-unbound.org/2009/04/13/peter-thiel/education-libertarian/ (last accessed November 30, 2025).
Thomson, J.J. (1986), *Rights, Restitution, and Risk: Essays in Moral Theory*. Harvard University Press.
TIME Magazine (2023), TIME100 Most Influential People in AI 2023: Sam Altman. Available online at: https://time.com/collection/time100-ai/6309022/sam-altman-ai/ (last accessed November 30, 2025).
United States Senate (2023), Bipartisan Framework for U.S. AI Act. Available online at: https://www.blumenthal.senate.gov/imo/media/doc/09072023bipartisanaiframework.pdf (last accessed November 30, 2025).
United States Senate (2024), Oversight of A.I.: Insiders' Perspectives. *Hearing before the Subcommittee on Privacy, Technology, and the Law,* Committee on the Judiciary, United States Senate (9/17/2024). Available online at: https://www.judiciary.senate.gov/committee-activity/hearings/oversight-of-ai-insiders-perspectives (last accessed October 30, 2024).
Urbinati, N. (2006), *Representative Democracy: Principles and Genealogy*. University of Chicago Press.
Urbinati, N. and Warren, M.E. (2008), The concept of representation in contemporary democratic theory. *Annual Review of Political Science* 11, no. 1: 387–412.
UK Home Office (2023), Contract Notice: Home Office Biometrics Matcher Platform and associated Services.' Notice reference: 2023/S 000-021422. Available online at: https://www.find-tender.service.gov.uk/Notice/021422-2023?origin=SearchResultsandp=1 (last accessed November 30, 2025).
US Department of Labor (2023), Press Release: US Department of Labor finds Amazon exposed workers to unsafe conditions, ergonomic hazards at three more warehouses in Colorado, Idaho, New York. Available online at: https://www.dol.gov/newsroom/releases/osha/osha20230201-0 (last accessed November 30, 2025).
US Securities and Exchange Commission (2024), Press release: SEC Issues awards totaling $98 million to two whistleblowers. Available online at: https://www.sec.gov/newsroom/press-releases/2024-103 (last accessed November 30, 2025).
Vallor, S. (2024), *The AI Mirror: How to Reclaim Our Humanity in an Age of Machine Thinking*. Oxford University Press.
Vasanthakumar, A. (2018), Epistemic privilege and victims' duties to resist their oppression. *Journal of Applied Philosophy* 35, no. 3: 465–480.
VentureBeat (2024), Dell Technologies building AI Factory with Nvidia, growing AI efforts with Hugging Face, Meta and Microsoft. Available online at: https://venturebeat.com/ai/dell-technologies-builds-ai-factory-with-nvidia-and-grows-enterprise-ai-efforts-with-hugging-face-meta-and-microsoft/ (last accessed November 30, 2025).
Viljoen, S., Goldenfein, J., and McGuigan, L. (2021), Design choices: mechanism design and platform capitalism. *Big Data and Society* 8, no. 2: 1–13.
Waldron, J. (1999), *Law and Disagreement*. Clarendon Press.
Warren, M.E. (2017), A problem-based approach to democratic theory. *American Political Science Review* 111, no. 1: 39–53.
Weyl, E.G. and Tang, A. (2024), Augmented deliberation. In: *Plurality: The Future of Collaborative Technology and Democracy*. Independently published: 276–290.

Whelan, F.G. (1983), Democratic theory and the boundary problem. In: *Nomos XXV: Liberal Democracy*, ed. J. R. Pennock and J.W. Chapman. New York University Press.

White, S. (1998), Trade unionism in a liberal state. In: *Freedom of Association*, ed. Amy Gutmann. Princeton University Press: 330–356.

Wiens, D. (2016), Motivational limitations on the demands of justice. *European Journal of Political Theory* 15, no. 3: 333–352.

Winner, L. (1980), Do artifacts have politics? *Daedalus* 109, no. 1: 121–136.

Wired (2023), Inside Mark Zuckerberg's top-secret Hawaii compound. Available online at : https://www.wired.com/story/mark-zuckerberg-inside-hawaii-compound/ (last accessed November 30, 2025).

Worsnip, A. (2017), Cryptonormative judgments. *European Journal of Philosophy* 25, no. 1: 3–24.

Young, I.M. (2002), *Democracy and Justice. Inclusion and Democracy*. Oxford University Press.

Zerilli, J. (2021), *A Citizen's Guide to Artificial Intelligence*. MIT Press.

Zimmermann, A. (2020), The A-level injustice shows why algorithms are never neutral. *The New Statesman*. Available online at: https://www.newstatesman.com/politics/2020/08/the-a-level-results-injustice-shows-why-algorithms-are-never-neutral (last accessed November 30, 2025).

Zimmermann, A. (2021), The power of choosing not to build: justice, non-deployment, and the purpose of AI optimization. Discussion Paper, Carr Center for Human Rights Policy, Harvard Kennedy School.

Zimmermann, A. and Schneider, A. (2018), Written evidence: Voyeurism (Offences) (No.2) Bill. UK Parliament: Public Bills Committee. Available online at: https://publications.parliament.uk/pa/cm201719/cmpublic/Voyeurism/memo/VOB09.htm (last accessed November 30, 2025).

Zimmermann, A., Di Rosa, E., and Kim, H. (2020), Technology can't fix algorithmic injustice. *Boston Review*. Available online (January 9, 2020) at: https://www.bostonreview.net/articles/annette-zimmermann-algorithmic-political/ (last accessed November 30, 2025).

Ziwei, Ji. Lee, N., Frieske, R., et al. (2023), Survey of hallucination in natural language generation. *ACM Computing Surveys* 55, 12, Article 248: 1–38.

Zuboff, S. (2018), *The Age of Surveillance Capitalism: The Fight for a Human Future at the New Frontier of Power*. Public Affairs.

Zuckerberg, M. (2021), Connect Keynote. Available online at: https://www.youtube.com/watch?v=Uvufun6xer8 (last accessed November 30, 2025).

Part II

Responses

8

AI, democracy, and the problem of collective disempowerment

Chiara Cordelli

Introduction

Debates about the ethics of AI have tended to predominately focus on questions of fairness and on the quality of outcomes. Many have pointed out how search engines reproduce social stereotypes (Noble, 2018). Try, for instance, to search for 'school girl' and sexualized images of women will likely appear on your screen, whereas if you type 'school boy' the engine will respond with smiling and well-behaved students in school uniforms. Others have condemned the lack of transparency, as well as the biased and discriminatory character of AI tools, especially when used to make crucial determinations, such as the identification of potential criminals (Barabas, 2020: 83–111). These debates are certainly important. However, they neglect a further concern raised by the current AI regime, which is its compatibility with the demands of democracy and democratic legitimacy. Such concern is largely separable from questions of fairness and substantive justice, since decisions which are made fairly and have desirable outcomes can still be democratically illegitimate, as the often-mentioned examples of enlightened dictators and benevolent colonial powers demonstrate.

In *Democratizing AI*, Annette Zimmermann provides a poignant account of the problem that AI poses for democratic legitimacy. Zimmermann argues that the current AI regime effectively grants to AI deployers – who are private, unauthorized, and unaccountable corporate actors – agenda-setting power, that is, the power 'to set regulatory agendas merely by making AI tools publicly available, which in turn forces an *ex post* regulatory response' (Zimmermann, 2026). By unilaterally deciding which AI tools to deploy, private actors 'set technology regulation and technology ethics agendas ... while simultaneously offloading responsibilities for *ex post* harm mitigation onto government actors and democratic constituencies' (Zimmermann, 2026). The moral problem the system of private deployment generates, Zimmermann rightly points out, is not just one of domination – the fact that some are subject to the arbitrary and unilateral will of a few corporate actors – but rather one of collective autonomy or political self-determination. In Zimmermann's own words 'democracy … promises to deliver a society in which all of us are the co-authors of our joint future' (Zimmermann, 2026). However, by accepting the current AI regime, which deprives citizens of agenda-setting power when it comes to the deployment of AI tools, and which relegates the role of the democratic state to one of *ex post* regulator, citizens 'relinquish an essential feature of democracy itself: the right to exercise free and equal control over the nature and scope of decisions shaping their shared future' (Zimmermann, 2026). In order to fulfill democracy's promise, Zimmermann concludes, citizens should play a much more proactive role in making agenda-setting decisions as to which AI tools ought to be deployed in the first place, and for which ends.

Although Zimmermann's democratic vision is appealing, her call for democratization is ultimately insufficient to realize democracy's promise, or so I will suggest. Beyond a brief appeal to the value of public equality, Zimmermann does not tell us much about the ground of our democratic right to collectively shape the future. I will thus start by arguing that the value of public equality is insufficient to support a case for a right to collective self-rule. The right to collectively shape the future can only be justified by appealing to a more fundamental interest – the interest in relating to one's own sociopolitical world in a non-alienated way. We relate to the social world in a non-alienated way when we can be reasonably expected to understand and affirm this world as our own; that is, as (i) the product of our collective doing and valuing, rather than as the result of alien and uncontrollable forces, and as (ii) expressing our joint aims.[1]

From this alienation-centered account of the grounds of democratic rule, I will then draw two implications concerning the insufficiency of Zimmermann's democratizing solution. The first implication is that, once we ground the demands of democracy in an interest to relate to our socio-political world in a non-alienated way, it becomes clear that the problem AI poses for democracy is much deeper than citizens' loss of *ex ante* control over agenda-setting deployment decisions. This is because certain AI tools could progressively lead to the disempowerment of humanity, even if democratically deployed. What if democratic constituencies, now endowed with

1 I briefly defend this argument in Cordelli (2025): 1–16. Anna Stilz also argues that non-alienation is a ground of political self-determination: see Stilz (2015). However, the conceptual account of alienation I endorse differs from Stilz' in important respects, and so does the argument for regarding non-alienation as a grounding value of political self-determination, as well as the range of decisions political self-determination should be about.

full agenda-setting power, authorize the deployment of a superintelligent AI who ends up ruling over us? Call this *the problem of collective disempowerment by AI*. The resulting regime of 'rule by AI' or 'rule of none', I will argue, would not violate public equality, as everyone would be equally subject to AI's impersonal ruling, and yet it would be incompatible with the very grounds of the right to collective self-rule, for the world that would result from it would not be a world we could be reasonably expected to understand and affirm as our own. My argument will thus support a *pro tanto* case, grounded on the value of democracy itself, for constitutional limits on AI deployment specifically aimed at preventing the problem of collective disempowerment by AI, and thus of 'rule of none', above and beyond the substantive limits concerning the asymmetrical distribution of risks, or the protection of minorities, that Zimmermann rightly defends. The second implication concerns the fact that the privatization of AI deployment is just one instance of a much larger problem of citizens' loss of collective control over their future, and thus of alienation, under capitalism. Capitalism structurally disempowers citizens, by privatizing control over economic decisions that fundamentally shape the future of their societies, investment *in primis* (Cordelli, 2025). This is *the problem of collective disempowerment, beyond AI*. Once this problem is taken into account, it becomes clear that giving citizens agenda-setting power over AI is insufficient to fulfill the promise of democracy, and the demand of non-alienation, unless the democratization of AI is accompanied by a much broader democratization of the economy.

The grounds of democratic rule

Democracy promises us to be the joint, and equal, authors of our society's future. It promises us a system where we can all actively contribute, on equal footing, to the making of political decisions. It promises us 'rule of all'.

But, what grounds democracy, so understood? Why is it important that people are granted the opportunity to collectively participate in the making of laws and of fundamental decisions determining the structure and future of their society?

Zimmermann's answer is that 'the reason why we should make decisions democratically rather than in some other way is that doing so fairly treats each citizen as a public equal, in voice and in deliberation, which is intrinsically valuable' (Zimmermann, 2026). But, of course, this begs the question: what does it mean to treat someone as a public equal? And, does an appeal to public equality suffice to ground a claim to democracy as rule of all?

If public equality is understood, following an influential view, in relational terms as the absence of inequalities of status, authority, or consideration, then we have insufficient grounds for democracy as rule of all (Kolodny, 2014: 195–229). This is because relational equality can be in principle secured through 'rule of none', a purely impersonal system of ruling, whereby laws and policies are made by robots or by an artificial intelligence. In other words, public equality *qua* relational equality is indifferent between rule of all and rule of none.

Perhaps, then, public equality should be understood differently, as respect for people as equal normative authorities. Respecting people in this way means to respect their ability to judge for themselves what decisions should be implemented. Along these lines, Waldron argues that what ultimately grounds the case for democracy is the fact that, given the existence of reasonable and irreducible disagreement about justice, we are respected as having the status of equal normative agents only if we are placed in the position to exercise our capacity to judge what rights we have and which decisions we ought to be subject to (Waldron, 2001).[2] This argument may exclude a system where we are passively ruled by robots, because such a system would bypass our capacity to judge. However, it does not seem sufficient to ground a positive case for democracy either. To see why, imagine a robustly motivated, yet unelected pollster dictator who before making any relevant political decisions, regularly polls or surveys his subjects' views and then reliably makes decisions accordingly (Enoch, 2021: 143–165). Arguably the subjects would be shown equal respect for their capacity to judge what decisions are best, and yet the pollster dictator is far from counting as a democratic ruler.

One could rebut that the pollster dictator would fail to respect its subjects as public equals because he would ultimately subject them to his arbitrary, unchecked will. Indeed, even if well-motivated the pollster could decide at whim not to follow his subjects' judgment. This rebuttal reframes the problem as one of non-domination. Then perhaps what grounds a claim to democracy as rule of all is a claim not to be dominated by an arbitrary will (Pettit, 2013). But, while a concern about domination may rule out the pollster dictator, it does not suffice to rule out 'rule of none'. Purely impersonal rule would arguably not be dominating, as it would subject no one to the arbitrary will of anyone one else in particular.

And, yet, I take it that many would find a system of impersonal ruling unappealing, however just, egalitarian, and non-dominating, and this is precisely because we think that there is something valuable about people

2 I defend a similar account in Cordelli (2020: Ch.2). Although in that context I do not introduce the interest in non-alienation as a ground of democratic self-rule, I do argue for the insufficiency of both non-domination and equal respect as grounds of democracy, and defend the need for a pluralist account.

being, collectively, the authors of the rules to which they are subject. But, the question, again, is why is this form of collective authorship valuable?

If an appeal to public equality or non-domination cannot provide the whole answer, then maybe an appeal to individual autonomy can supplement them. Indeed, some have recently tried to revive an autonomy-based account of the grounds of democracy. According to James Wilson, who has in my view developed the most sophisticated version of this account, the same interest in self-direction that gives us 'first-order' autonomy claims against others that they refrain from interfering in certain choices of ours, also gives us 'second-order' autonomy claims that others give appropriate consideration to our judgments, along with the judgments of others, about decisions that determine how our contexts of choice are shaped (Wilson, 2021: 194–226). The idea here is not that democracy gives individuals full self-direction over how their context of choice is shaped, since their judgment is just a drop in a bucket already full with the judgments of many others. The idea is rather that democracy is the only way of 'respecting' people's interest in self-direction. As Wilson puts it, there would be 'an untenable tension between demanding respect on grounds of self-direction in the first-order case but denying the need for such respect in the second'. Even if insightful, this view is subject to a *futility problem.* How can something be a way of 'respecting' a person's interest in self-direction if this something is a futile means of fulfilling such interest? Insofar as shared, even equally shared, political authority or control is futile for individual self-direction – since, in a democracy, an individual vote does not have a determinant causal influence on the outcome – it remains mysterious how an interest in the latter can ground a claim to the former.

It seems, then, that we need a value that simultaneously (1) picks rule of all over rule of none *and* that (2) can ground a positive case for (equally) shared control rights, by showing that such rights are not futile for the realization of the value in question.

Lovett and Zuehl have, to my knowledge, proposed the most plausible account of such value (Lovett and Zuehl, 2022: 467–498). They have argued that what grounds the case for democracy as rule of all, beyond equality or non-domination, is the value of 'joint authorship'. Joint authorship amounts to having one's joint intentions expressed in the world. A commitment to joint authorship simply means that political decisions must express the joint intentions of individual citizens (individuals' joint intentions). Democracy is a form of collective action – something we do together – through which citizens get to express, through policies made directly or through elected representatives, their joint intentions about what the world should be like. The advantage of joint authorship compared to autonomy as self-direction is that having shared, even if not final, influence or control over outcomes is sufficient, and thus not futile, for the realization of joint authorship. In other words, the realization of the value of joint authorship does not depend on individual control. As Lovett and Zuehl put it:

> How much one enjoys the value of joint authorship in relation to something is not directly proportional to how much causal influence you individually had to that thing. What matters is how much your joint intentions causally contribute to the policy. The more widely shared the intention is the more its overall causal influence. When a joint intention causes something, the individual intentions of which it is made each causally contribute to the policy (Lovett and Zuehl, 2022: 467–498).

In sum, democracy is valuable, and superior to rule of none, because it makes us joint authors of important decisions, thereby enabling us to express our joint intentions in the world. And, importantly, democracy is not a futile means to fulfill our interest in being joint authors of those decisions, because joint authorship does not depend on individual control or determinant individual causal influence.

Despite its plausibility, the joint authorship account suffers from two limitations. First, Lovett and Zuehl do not tell us why joint authorship is valuable. To be precise, they say that to enjoy joint authorship means to enjoy 'a distinctively collective kind of autonomy' (Lovett and Zuehl, 2022: 467–498). But they don't tell us why collective autonomy is valuable. What is valuable about having one's joint intentions expressed in the world? Joint authorship cannot answer this question and thus cannot serve as the end of the justificatory chain.

The second problem is that, if what matters is to have our joint intentions expressed in the world, joint authorship is not *necessary* to achieve it. This is because, as the pollster dictator example shows, citizens could in principle have their joint intentions expressed in the world – say intentions formed through a deliberative process – without having any power to author the decisions through which those intentions are expressed. The dictator pollster could bring about a world that expresses the citizens' joint intentions, even when the citizens have no decisional power, and thus are not the authors of those decisions. So, the fact that the world expresses your joint intentions together with the fact that your intentions causally contribute to the policy do not seem sufficient to explain the value of joint authorship because we can have both without you having any authorship at all.

We then need a value that can explain both why we want *our joint intentions to be expressed in the world*, and why we want them to be expressed *through our joint authorship*. I believe the answer points towards a more fundamental interest in wanting to relate to the world in a particular way. More precisely, we want the world to express our joint intentions because we want to relate to the world as something we can affirm or identify with rather than as something *alien* to us. Further, we want our intentions to shape the world directly through our own choices and actions because we want to relate to the world in an agential capacity, as something we have contributed to bring about and shape, rather than in a passive capacity, as an external, *alien* imposition. In brief, we want joint authorship because we want to relate to the world in a non-alienated way.

An interest in non-alienation is thus what grounds (beyond equality or non-domination) the case for joint authorship and thus for democracy as rule of all. Non-alienation in turn requires both affirmation and agency. A non-alienated relation to the world is obtained when we can be reasonably expected to understand and affirm the world as something that expresses our joint aims, and as something we have collectively brought about.

My account of alienation builds on Rahel Jaeggi's understanding of alienation as *a relation of failed appropriation*. According to this relational account, a social form of life is alienated when individuals cannot make it 'their own' – they cannot affirm it as the product of their own actions and as an expression of their agency. Unlike Jaeggi, however, I'm not concerned with a relation of alienation between an individual and her own life or self, but rather with *social alienation*: a relation of alienation between citizens and their sociopolitical order (Jaeggi, 2014). A relation of failed appropriation, and thus of alienation between citizens and their sociopolitical order, I take it, occurs when citizens cannot be reasonably expected to understand and affirm the basic structure of their society, and its course (i) as the result of their collective valuing and doing – that is to say, as the product of their own collective activity, and (ii) as reflecting their own considered judgments and priorities (Stilz, 2015). These two elements are analytically separable, even if closely connected in practice, for in principle citizens could understand themselves as being the effective agential cause of something, e.g. their own society, and still be alienated from it, if they cannot understand it as an object 'fit' to be affirmed, whether because the resulting world systematically fails to reflect their considered judgments and priorities, or because it is too irrational to be worthy of their affirmation.

Once we agree that non-alienation grounds a case for democracy it becomes clear why Zimmermann is right that democracy is centrally about having shared control over the future. Only citizens who can understand their sociopolitical word as a result of their collective agency – something that they together contributed to bring about, rather than the product of uncontrolled or externally imposed forces – can relate to the resulting world as their own, rather than as an alien imposition. Further, only citizens who can understand the sociopolitical world as expressing their joint intentions, rather than the intentions of a robot or of a dictator – can affirm it as their own, rather than relating to it as something alien to them (Cordelli, 2025).

Importantly, the interest in non-alienation also explains what is wrong with being ruled by an impersonal machine, or being subject to 'rule of none' even if such ruling does not, by assumption, subject us to anyone else's particular will, or create objectionable relational inequalities between rulers and ruled (Cordelli, 2025). In the case of rule of none, alienation derives from the fact that citizens are passively subject to rules they have, *de facto*, played no part in shaping and cannot control, or help transform. Further, such rules cannot be reasonably regarded as reflecting the citizens' priorities, even if they happen, coincidentally, to converge with those priorities. Citizens cannot therefore be reasonably expected to regard the sociopolitical world that results from impersonal ruling as a result and expression of their shared agency, and they lack the conditions of shared control and involvement necessary to make such a system their own – to come to relate to it in an agential capacity rather than as merely passive recipients. The phenomenological manifestations of alienation in this context would likely be a pervasive sense of powerlessness and a radical detachment or indifference from one's political and social reality, not necessarily a sense of inferiority or subordination.

In sum, if a commitment to either non-domination or public equality overdetermines the choice between 'rule of all' and 'rule of none', non-alienation provides us with powerful reasons to prefer the former over the latter, since under the rule of none it will be unreasonable to expect citizens to relate to their sociopolitical order in a non-alienated way.

Why does this matter for Zimmermann's treatment of AI as a democratic problem? *In primis*, it matters because it helps clarify the nature of Zimmermann's concern about citizens losing control over their future, by losing control over transformative decisions concerning AI deployment. The problem at stake is not just one of political inequality – the fact that only a few AI deployers enjoy agenda-setting power – as Zimmermann would seem to argue, for loss of control would generate a moral problem even if citizens were all equally disempowered by, say, a super AI capable of ruling in their place. The problem of loss of control is also, and more fundamentally, a problem of alienation – the fact that having lost control over transformative decisions that significantly shape their future, citizens cannot relate to the resulting world as to something they have collectively authored, and as expressing their jointly established priorities. They can only relate to it as something alien to them.

In what follows I will draw two further implications of my analysis for Zimmermann's case in favor of democratizing AI. The first implication is that *granting citizens agenda-setting power* over AI deployment may not be sufficient to overcome the problem that AI poses for democracy, for the fundamental problem with collective loss of control could remain, and indeed get worse, even after a more egalitarian distribution of agenda-setting power among citizens is achieved. The second implication is that granting citizens agenda-setting power *over AI* would not be sufficient to solve the more fundamental problem of democratic loss of control over the future, and thus of alienation. Here the concern is that, beyond decisions to deploy AI, there are many, equally transformative decisions that the contemporary organization of society, and in particular our capitalist economy, removes from citizens' joint authorship and control. In order to fulfill democracy's promise, the democratization of AI would then need to be accompanied by a much broader democratization of the economy. Given space constraints, I will only be able to provide a brief treatment of both points. But, hopefully, what I will say will be sufficient to pave the way for future discussion.

Why *democratizing* AI is not enough: the case for constitutional limits

Recently, scholars and scientists have voiced concerns about the possibility of AI ultimately disempowering humanity and independently governing us. Philosopher Toby Ord, for example, has claimed that 'the most plausible existential risk from AI' consists of a state of affairs where 'humanity would have permanently ceded its control over the future' (Ord, 2020: 148). Similarly, computer scientists Jan Leike and Ilya Sutskever have claimed that 'the vast power of superintelligence could … lead to the disempowerment of humanity' (Leike and Sutskever, 2023). I am not in a position to ascertain the likelihood of such a threat materializing. But, if the above scholars are right that the threat of collective disempowerment by an AI superintelligence is real, and that *ex post* regulatory tools would be insufficient to prevent it once certain AI tools have been deployed, it follows that the problem of loss of control over the future Zimmermann identifies would remain even once the democratization of agenda-setting power is complete, and all AI deployment decisions are in democratic hands. This is because democratic constituencies could in principle democratically decide to deploy AI tools which would then lead to the disempowerment of humanity, and thus ultimately to a form of 'rule by none' (i.e. rule by AI itself). Now, what grounds a case *for* democracy – an interest in non-alienation – is also what grounds a case *against* impersonal rule. For, as we saw, even if rule by AI turned out to be fair, just, egalitarian, and non-dominating (as it would not subject citizens to the will of anyone in particular, nor to the power of someone with superior moral standing), it would still be alienating.

It would still deliver a world that we could not reasonably be expected to regard and affirm as our own – as something we can relate to as agential structuring forces, rather than as merely passive recipients.

If this is correct, then, democracy itself should justify, in light of its own grounding value, constitutional constraints on what kind of AI tools can be democratically deployed, above and beyond the substantive constraints concerning the asymmetrical imposition and distribution of risks that Zimmermann defends. This opens up the difficult question of what exactly should be constitutionally constrained, and of whether these constraints should follow qualitative (concerning the kind of AI tools deployed) and/or quantitative (concerning the overall amount of AI tools deployed) criteria, since the disempowerment of humanity by AI could arguably result from the aggregation of many deployment decisions that, if individually taken, may be fairly innocuous. However, as I have argued in a different context, constitutional constraints can at times be justified and designed to prevent aggregative harms, and aggregative rationales are sometimes used by Constitutional Courts themselves to impose bans on otherwise permissible actions.[3] For the purpose of this response, it will be enough to show that some constitutional constraints on AI deployment may be necessary to fulfill democracy's promise, above and beyond the solutions, otherwise compelling, proposed by Zimmermann.

Why democratizing *AI* is not enough: the case for economic democracy

Suppose that agenda-setting power concerning AI deployment has been returned to citizens, there is a democratic state capable of effectively regulating AI, and appropriate constitutional constraints to avoid humanity disempowerment by AI are in place. Would democracy's promise, as defined by Zimmermann, be fulfilled? Not if much of capitalism is still in place. This is because the problem of loss of collective control over the future, rightly identified by Zimmermann as a central democratic problem, is generated not only by loss of control over AI deployment, but also and

3 The US Supreme Court, for example, has argued that limits to private financial contributions to political campaigns can be justified by a compelling government interest in preserving the integrity of the electoral interest, integrity that would not be undermined by a few isolated donations but that would be compromised by the corrosive effects of private donations, considered in aggregation. I have made a similar argument in defense of constitutional limits to the privatization of public services in Cordelli (2020: Ch. 4, p. 154).

more broadly, by loss of political control over transformative economic decisions – decisions capable of determining the material, social, and cultural structure of our future societies. Such loss of control is, as I have argued elsewhere, structural to capitalism, and in particular to its mode of investment (Cordelli, 2025). This is a consequence of two distinctive features of capitalism.

First, capitalism, definitionally, leaves most investment decisions to private markets. This means that it depoliticizes or privatizes transformative decisions that determine the future course of a society (Beckert, 2016). By 'investment decisions' I mean decisions concerning the overall rate of investment, which in turn greatly influences the rate of growth, as well as decisions concerning the financing of enterprises and credit allocation, which in tun shape the kind, extent, direction, and distribution of overall production. Such decisions largely determine how many and which jobs will exist, what objects will be produced, what innovation will be supported, whether a society will be able to fulfill its environmental commitments, as well the shape of cities and inhabited spaces (consider, for example, how the architecture of cities such as London and NYC changed as a consequence of foreign private investments). No set of decisions could be more crucial for shaping the material, social, and cultural constitution of a society; for its sustainability over time; and for a society's ability to exercise its freedom to create new trajectories. The privatization of investment under capitalism thus effectively deprives citizens of the capacity to democratically control the future course of their society, precisely like the privatization of AI deployment decisions.

Second, under capitalism, production is determined by largely uncoordinated investment markets – the logic of which requires, as stressed by economists such as Keynes, that investors act not on the basis of what they reflectively believe is valuable or useful, let alone on deliberatively established priorities, but rather on their guesses concerning other investors' expectations of future profit, under conditions of radical uncertainty (Keynes, 1936). Such markets are thus structurally prone to deliver wasteful and irrational outcomes – what Marxists refer to as the 'anarchy of production'.

The privatization of investment under capitalism matters morally because it fails to provide the conditions – conditions of collective control, participatory involvement, and deliberation – that would make it reasonable for citizens to understand the resulting society as the product of their collective doing and valuing, rather than as the result of largely uncontrollable and impersonal market forces. The feature of anarchy also matters because it prevents citizens from relating to their society – a society that largely results from past investment decisions – as an object worthy of their affirmation, both because the resulting economic and social structure cannot reflect their deliberatively endorsed priorities, and also because it lacks sufficient rationality to be worthy of being affirmed.

All this means that capitalism structurally generates a morally defective, because alienated, relation between citizens and their society. Citizens stand in an alienated relation to their society because, due to the depoliticization of transformative economic decisions, they cannot understand and affirm their society as the result of their collective agency; and, because of anarchy, citizens cannot relate to it in an affirmative way. A pervasive sense of both powerlessness and detachment, not a sense of ingratiation or subordination, are the most common phenomenological expressions of such alienated relation.

If my analysis is correct, then, there is no way of fulfilling the promise of democracy – 'a society in which all of us are the co-authors of our joint future' – and of realizing its grounding values, including non-alienation, without a broader democratization of the economy. Zimmermann's call for the democratization of AI's deployment decisions is a welcome step in the right direction. But without the simultaneous democratization of major economic decisions, including investment and credit allocation, citizens' loss of collective control over the future will remain largely untouched, and so will be democracy's promise.

References

Barabas, C. (2020), Beyond bias: re-imagining the terms of 'ethical AI' in criminal law. *The Georgetown Journal of Law and Modern Critical Race. Perspectives* 19: 83–111.

Beckert, J. (2016), *Imagined Futures: Fictional Expectations and Capitalist Dynamics*. Princeton University Press.

Cordelli, C. (2020), *The Privatized State*. Princeton University Press.

Cordelli, C. (2025), *What Is the Wrong of Capitalism?* Cambridge University Press.

Enoch, D. (2021), Autonomy as non-alienation, autonomy as sovereignty, and politics. *Journal of Political Philosophy* 30, no. 2: 143–165.

Jaeggi, R. (2014), *Alienation*. Columbia University Press.

Keynes, J.M. (1936), *The General Theory of Employment, Interest and Money*. Macmillan.

Kolodny, N. (2014), Rule over none I: What justifies democracy? *Philosophy and Public Affairs* 42, no. 3: 195–229.

Leike, J. and Sutskever, I. (2023), Introducing superalignment. OpenAI Blog (July 5, 2023). Available online at: https://openai.com/index/introducing-superalignment/ (last accessed March 15, 2026).

Lovett, A. and Zuehl, J. (2022), The possibility of democratic autonomy. *Philosophy and Public Affairs* 50, no. 4: 467–498.

Noble, S.U. (2018), *Algorithms of Oppression: How Search Engines Reinforce Racism*. New York University Press.

Ord, T. (2020), *The Precipice: Existential Risk and the Future of Humanity*. Hachette Books.
Pettit, P, (2013), *On the People's Terms*. Cambridge University Press.
Stilz, A. (2015), *Decolonization and Self-Determination*. Cambridge University Press.
Waldron, J. (2001), *Law and Disagreement*. Cambridge University Press.
Wilson, J. (2021), An autonomy-based argument for democracy. *Oxford Studies in Political Philosophy* 7: 194–226.
Zimmermann, A. (2026), *Democratizing AI*. Manchester: Manchester University Press.

9

Representative democracy and the harms of AI

Ritwik Agrawal and Thomas Christiano

Introduction

The key conceptual move at the heart of Annette Zimmermann's bold and original argument is the idea that deployment of an AI tool is at the same time a kind of setting of the agenda for collective decision-making. The structure of the argument starts from the major premise A that: if some action involves the setting of an agenda for decision-making then it ought to be controlled democratically; (B) deployment of an AI tool does involve setting the agenda in an area of critical concern for collective decision-making; therefore (C) the deployment of an AI tool ought to be decided democratically. The premise A is accepted by many democratic theorists. The second premise needs to be unpacked. First, we need to know what 'deployment' means. It is not formally defined in Zimmermann's essay, but it seems to mean that one puts some object on the market for sale. Or in some cases, an item may be put out on the web (such as ChatGPT) with the idea that enough users will purchase more sophisticated versions for a price. Deployment occurs after a significant amount of research has gone into creating and training AI models. All of this is based on more fundamental research usually conducted in universities and research institutes, sometimes (and indeed in the case of Generative AI) decades before prototypes are ready for deployment in the wider marketplace.

The second premise asserts that deployment implies the setting of an agenda for collective decision-making for a society. Here the idea seems to be that once an AI system has been deployed, the society must take account of its widespread use if it has any success. The society must then decide how it will respond once people have had access to an AI tool and used it. The widespread use will have large-scale effects on society. As Zimmermann says, it will impose large-scale risks on persons. But she also says that deployment has other large-scale effects on the society, such as the distribution of income and wealth, the distribution of market power, and the effects on workers who are working in the AI industry and beyond.

All of these effects and hence the agenda-setting that follows are produced by a small number of firms in the market. This is the most basic instance of the ASYMMETRY Zimmermann is worried about. It involves a deep inequality in the abilities of individuals to influence the larger society. She claims that this effect of AI is distinctive of AI. But we are not sure about this. The making of industrial factories created widespread pollution, which in some ways is analogous to the risks AI imposes. There are broad and serious risks of many technological developments, including, for example, research on viruses and other biological agents. We don't mean to suggest that safeguards used in some sectors with broad and serious risks necessarily apply to AI, but it is a possibility that needs to be examined. Asserting that AI poses unique risks can foreclose learning from a serious examination of existing regulatory regimes in sectors as diverse as pharmaceuticals, biological and chemical research, deployment of nuclear energy, and so on.

The first context we would need to study to assess AI deployment would be an economic analysis of the markets in AI. The basic idea would be to study the nature of markets in AI products and determine where the idea of a collective effect can be found. Initially, one might think that the exchange of AI products would be a matter for individuals to decide. Certainly, in the context of highly competitive markets, one would think that this is all that matters. If that is true, then the concern for agenda-setting, which is inherently associated with democratic decision-making, would not arise.

However, in the case of AI products, we are not dealing with perfectly competitive markets, by hypothesis. First, we are dealing with markets in which there is a great deal of missing information. This is brought out by the fact that innovation is the principal generator of new AI products. There is a traditional problem in this kind of market, which is that it takes a lot of research to develop new products, but once they are developed, they are often easily replicated. One main cost of production in this context is the research and development that ensures innovation. Producers would then have little incentive to invest in the research since they would not benefit from the actual production. This implies that for such markets to work, either producers are not moved by the usual incentives or some kind of system of monopoly patent rights over the character of their inventions has to be developed to enable the producers to profit from their innovations. This has been the traditional route for encouraging innovation in the United States and Europe. The problem with this is that it generates a distortion in the market and tends to favor large producers.

This leads to the first set of problems Zimmermann emphasizes in her discussion of AI deployment. The tendency in the United States has been the development of firms with a massive amount of market power. They have two kinds of market power that particularly concern her. First, they have market power in that there are very few firms that sell or offer AI products, and these firms can coordinate with each other in certain circumstances. We have the problem of monopolistic markets. In this case, the firms can artificially keep up prices and restrict supply. But they also have another kind of market power, they have the ability to have very large-scale effects on the society in which they operate. Second, by virtue of their size they are monopsonistic employers so that there are only a small number of firms and a large number of workers. Hence, they can, by cartelization or specialization, suppress wages and provide poor working conditions. As a result, they contribute to increasing inequality in the society, an important large-scale effect.

These two problems are not unique to AI technology. The problem of monopolistic markets due to the high cost of innovation or other significant barriers to entry is common to many industries in the United States and the problem of monopsony is a problem that is quite general in the US (Manning, 2021: 3–26).

But there is another set of problems that Zimmermann focuses on that may also suggest the need for collective choice. These are problems that can also be understood as defects in competitive markets. It would be useful to catalog these problems in the traditional terms of economics: externalities, asymmetries of information, and public bads. These are all problems that complicate the simple picture of mutual advantage that undergirds economic theories of exchange.

Externalities occur when costs or benefits are given to persons in a market that they have not contracted for. The clearest cases of these in AI are the cases of hallucinations, the spreading of malware, the spreading of biases, privacy invasion, and copyright violations. To the extent that these things happen, they are not merely one-off events but can be spread throughout the internet. The cases of hallucinations and the spread of bias, and some cases of the spreading of malware, are largely accidental externalities. In the cases of malware, much invasion of privacy, and copyright violations, there are often external effects that are imposed by some people on very large groups of persons. These problems are not so much distinctive of AI, but they can be imposed quickly on very large numbers of persons.

Asymmetries of information are pervasive on the internet and the capacity to amplify them is greatly increased with AI. Deepfakes, plagiarism, and luring the vulnerable are all instances of this. Here there are exchanges but one side doesn't know what is being exchanged. There is a peculiar kind of problem that arises from misuse of AI, which is plagiarism. Young people in schools are often attracted to simply generating materials through generative AI instead of doing the hard work of writing their assignments. These young people think they are benefiting from this procedure but in fact they are missing out on the fundamental good of developing their own abilities to think and write clearly and critically and their abilities to try to understand the complex ideas of others. Here is a case where they are deceiving others, but they are also doing damage to themselves. And the effect of this could be very large, diminishing the quality of education for a large number of people and thus diminishing the level of education present in the society. This could eventually affect almost every aspect of society, including its ability to retain a democratic character.

This suggests the third major problem, which is that of public bads. The case of the possible decline in educational standards discussed in further detail below is a possible case of a public bad because each person would prefer to contribute to the production of the public bad and wouldn't see much incentive in doing their part in reducing it. There are other possible public bads that can arise from the use of AI products. One is the powerful effect that it can have on the siloing of political opinions and interests and the consequent effect of these on the polarization of society with regard to politics. This is a phenomenon which is already attracting much concern from political scientists and philosophers in the United States and it could significantly worsen with the advent of generative AI (Kreps and Kriner, 2023: 122–131).

What is it to democratize deployment?

Zimmermann suggests that these problems give rise to the need to democratize the deployment of AI. She says that AI producers set the agenda for societies in two ways: First, they have an outsized influence on political decision-makers through campaign finance and lobbying. Second, and most important, firms are setting the agenda for subsequent democratic decision-making when they deploy technology (Zimmermann, 2026: 40). We can see this kind of agenda-setting in the conquest of land by one country. The taking of land creates 'facts on the ground', which are very hard to change and so set the agenda for subsequent negotiations. Zimmermann insists that this kind of agenda-setting is distinctive of AI. We are not so sure, as indeed our conquest example demonstrates.

What is the justification for the claim of agenda-setting by AI producers? The idea must be that they create a set of facts by deploying technology, which facts are such that a democratic society must respond to them. They create the problems to which a democratic society must be providing the solutions. The agenda-setting character is determined by the specificity of the facts that are created, and that the democratic response must be properly attuned to the facts that have been produced.

But there are a number of problems with this claim. First, it is hard to see why we stop with deployment. Why not start with the development of models and the training of models? These are facts as well that may or may not determine a set of appropriate responses and rule out other responses. We might go even further back by discussing the fundamental research that makes the creation of the models possible and say that this fundamental research is determining the limited set of possible responses. There must be some sense in which human actions, when they aggregate, create an agenda because the aggregate must rule out certain solutions as possible and rule in certain other ones as possible. Do we want to say that all these things ought to be thought of as agenda-setting and that they ought to be democratically decided in advance? This seems like an excessively demanding conception of democracy because it looks like the behaviors of persons generally involve agenda-setting. Second, there is another sense in which it is not clear that these things constitute an agenda. The view seems to be that once a technology is deployed one has let the genie out of the bottle, and it cannot be put back in (Zimmermann, 2026: 5). Admittedly, once a technology has been released into the market it will take more effort and planning to fundamentally change that market – say, by banning the product – but it is by no means impossible. It has been done many times. Many societies have permitted guns to be sold on the market for many years and then banned guns or at least their general use. Many societies have permitted pollutants to be put in the air or water and then banned or regulated the use of those pollutants. It is true that more actions were necessary to withdraw the pollutants or guns, but there is no sense that the agenda could not include all the alternatives that were present before the pollutants were introduced.

So, the claim that the deployment of AI technology amounts to setting the agenda for a society's decision-making is not very plausible. In addition, there are costs to accepting this claim, such as possibly slowing down innovation, progress, and even creativity in the development of algorithms by over- or mis-regulating a nascent industry.[1]

Nevertheless, the idea that democratic decision-making should play a role is a plausible one. But we need to consider the idea of democratic control in the case of each of the kinds of harm and risks of harm.

1 For an illustrative example of blanket regulation seriously impeding innovation, consider the ban on flying supersonic aircraft due to the disturbing effects of the sonic boom typically associated with such aircraft. Since the ban applied to all supersonic aircraft, it impeded the development and testing of innovative supersonic aircraft without the ill effects of sonic booms. For an overview, see Dourado and Hammond (2016).

Harms posed by AI

If we go from the catalog of harms we described above, there are some harms that don't seem to be properly dealt with through democracy. For example, the deep fakes seem to be better dealt with through tort law. Nor do some of the other harms, such as hallucinations, seem primarily to be the job of democracy.

There are clear cut tortfeasors in these cases and offenders ought to be held liable for their wrongs. Hallucinations seem also to be harms that are best dealt with through the law of torts and to some degree in markets. A hallucination is after all a clear defect in the product and the source of the harm can be attributed to the product. This can be a clear case of a tort. Furthermore, producers have incentives to improve the products so as to avoid hallucinations as much as possible, so a well-organized market should help do away with these. Another case of this kind of tort is the spreading of malware and viruses. There is already a developing cyber tort law on these issues. To be sure, a democratic society must play a role in structuring this law, though a lot of it will be structured through the common law.

The problems of copyright infringement and intrusion of privacy will eventually require serious democratic intervention. Copyright infringement cases such as *New York Times vs. OpenAI* can be dealt with by the courts through tort law. But there are issues in the above case that will need to be resolved at the democratic level, such as the relative importance of copyright and technological innovation. Another problem here concerns how to define the appropriate sphere of privacy and what the relative value of privacy is compared to the values that are advanced by the developing technology. This will play an important role in determining how much protection of privacy is required. These problems will require serious democratic deliberation and negotiation to delimit as has already been done to some degree in European Union law.

Public bads

There are a number of public bads that are already arising from generative AI. A prominent case concerns plagiarism in schools and universities. The problem with rampant plagiarism using AI is that quality of education will dramatically decrease. This has the structure of a public bad. To be clear, one major part of the problem is that students are increasingly thinking of their education in purely instrumental terms as a way of getting access to a credential that is meant to increase their lifetime incomes dramatically. AI can help them do this without them having to do the necessary work (which the credential is meant to signal) or having to risk a very low grade on an assignment thereby disabling them from acquiring the credential. Of course, if students were interested in learning for its own sake, as many are, they would not take this route. But that seems increasingly less prevalent. The net effect could be a less well-educated society. The effects of this are a less productive society, a society less well able to engage in the give and take of democratic debate and discussion, and a society less able to appreciate the more sophisticated and nuanced goods in life. In short, it is a serious problem for society. It is a public bad because any student who appreciates the problem but still wants to guarantee doing well enough on assignments, is likely not to have a reason to do their assignments without AI. This is because they can see that their individual actions of studying for an assignment and doing it without AI are not going to make a significant difference to the overall level of education in society. Unless they value the activity intrinsically, they will not act honestly. And this brings another dimension to the problem. This is the problem of information. Education is meant to give people information in the broadest sense. If they do not pursue their education honestly but only for the sake of the credential, they will not know the intrinsic benefits of education and will miss out on those benefits. Hence there are two distinct mechanisms by which a market fails in this case: lack of knowledge of the benefits of being educated and the public bad of having an uneducated society.

Another public bad, which Zimmermann notes briefly in her essay, is that of pollution caused by the dramatic energy requirements of data centers, which are slowing down or even reversing progress in transitioning to green energy sources (Volcovici and Kearney, 2024). By their nature, public bads often require democratic intervention since individual actors do not have adequate incentives to act upon them, though it is important to note that this may not always be true, partly because public bads are rarely purely public bads. The plagiarism issue in schools is being partly dealt with by many instructors by simply reverting to handwritten assignments in class. This solution is not perfect and does not apply to online classes and other learning situations. Still, we agree with Zimmermann that a democratic playbook is often needed to respond to these challenges, though we have concerns about the specifics of her approach that we discuss below.

Market power

As Zimmermann notes, the current landscape of generative AI is dominated by a few market players with very deep pockets. This has partly to do with the frontier nature of the technology (thus requiring rare and hence very expensive talent) and partly with the enormous capital expenditure involved in massive data centers running extremely expensive chips. These data centers also incur large ongoing costs. All this means that only a few market players currently enjoy asymmetric power in critical decisions regarding development and deployment of AI technology.

Given these realities, any democratic intervention has to balance incentives for private investment in frontier research with social objectives. In some ways, the challenges are similar to those encountered in the pharmaceuticals sector. Drug development is complex, risky (from a return on investments point of view), and very costly. A strong patents regime is supposed to provide incentives for private players to invest time, effort, and money into developing new drugs. Companies developing generative AI claim ownership over critical deployment decisions partly on account of the risks they have undertaken in developing the technology. A feasible democratic playbook needs to find ways to adequately incentivize investments that spur innovation while safeguarding the needs of democratic constituents.

An emerging consideration is whether trade barriers are acceptable in this area. Recently, a Chinese company released DeepSeek, a powerful generative AI model that performs comparably to the top US-developed models like ChatGPT and Claude, but at much lower computing costs to train the model (Wang and Kanrarcioglu, 2025). On the one hand, competitors like DeepSeek help customers by driving costs down in a well-functioning market (for example, OpenAI responded to DeepSeek by introducing more powerful models and more configuration options for users that pay higher subscription fees). On the other hand, there is a concern that new entrants to the market may be piggybacking on the risks undertaken by early movers like OpenAI, which, in the absence of a protection regime, can drive down the incentives for continued innovation. The tapestry here is complex, as the history of software tells us that sometimes the most far-reaching innovations have happened through open-source projects, which repudiate patent regimes and other protectionist measures (Von Hippel, 2005: 267–278; West and Gallagher, 2006: 82–106). Briefly put, there are multiple channels through which innovation has proceeded in the software space, and we have no reason to think that things will be any different with generative AI. Any regulatory structure must have enough flexibility to allow for this multiplicity of approaches.

Large-scale injustices

One of the most significant harms that can arise from the large-scale deployment of generative AI is mass unemployment. Since AI is good and getting better at systematic tasks such as generating reports, writing legal briefs, quickly analyzing a mass of data, and coding, there is the worry that masses of white-collar workers, who make good money in a variety of knowledge industries including IT, accountancy, law, consulting, etc., could be rendered unemployed in a few years. Apart from the direct immiseration of these workers and their families, this puts at risk various support jobs, in establishments such as cafes, restaurants, cleaning services, and the like. There are also the associated social risks of rising unemployment, including higher crime rates, higher alcoholism, and drug-use, etc., to consider. There is, in addition, a global justice dimension in that a large proportion of good jobs in emerging economies like India, the Philippines, Indonesia, Turkey, Brazil, etc. are in IT and related knowledge sectors, which seem most at risk from the large-scale deployment of generative AI. If a mass of such jobs were to vanish in these countries, they would be hard pressed to continue on a path of sustained economic growth. This will have ramifications for reduction of poverty and realization of the United Nations' Sustainable Development Goals, which depend upon developing countries, particularly those with large populations, growing steadily and using the fruits of economic growth to build physical and social infrastructure to improve the lives of their citizens.

Tackling these potential harms clearly requires democratic intervention, at the national and multilateral levels. A mass change in employment patterns will have cascading effects of various kinds, which will affect entire countries and, in some cases, the relationships between countries. For example, it is plausible that slowing economic growth in developing countries will worsen the challenges of migration for developed countries. This suggests that any democratic playbook to tackle the potential harms of generative AI needs to have an international vision and capacities to work with various stakeholders in the international system.

Democratic playbook: mobilizing democracy through informed sub-constituencies

One of Zimmermann's main innovations is that democratic councils (what she calls informed sub-constituencies), with adequate representations of experts among their membership, should have a key oversight role in AI deployment. Zimmermann believes that this is necessary to bridge the core problem of ASYMMETRY in agenda-setting power that is currently loaded in the favor of the large corporations that are developing and deploying generative AI technology, while the risks of these technologies are distributed across society. Zimmermann argues that these democratic councils can bridge the gap between purely top-down regulation and purely bottom-up people's movements; her proposal therefore is to develop a mixed approach which utilizes the democratic potential of people's movements as well as the power of the regulatory state, with the mix aiming at both AI safety and potential for continued innovation in this sector.

While we agree with Zimmermann's mixed approach, we believe that the design of informed sub-constituencies places her in a difficult dilemma. Briefly stated, the dilemma is that democratic councils can either play a largely advisory role and be ineffective (apart from possibly duplicating other existing institutional arrangements) or their decisions can be binding and thus not very democratic. To tackle the latter horn of the dilemma first: if the democratic councils are empowered, presumably by legislative action, to make binding decisions, it is difficult to see them as bottom-up democratic rather than another federal agency, perhaps on the lines of the FTC. This diffuses Zimmermann's mixed approach to something quite similar to the status quo, with the possible addition of a federal commission for AI safety to gather regulations in this area under one head. Over a period of time, even the best intentioned informed sub-constituencies are likely to turn into captured bureaucracies unless informed by radical design choices aimed at preventing such an outcome. We invite Zimmermann to say more about institutional design in this context.

On the other hand, if informed sub-constituencies play a largely advisory role, then it is unclear how they can generate the countervailing power necessary to tackle the Asymmetry problem, since there are large vested interests at play to keep agenda-setting power in the hands of powerful corporations. Either way, it is not obvious how democratic councils can effectively (and in a sustained manner) play the ambitious role that Zimmermann envisages for them.

There are some other elements in Zimmermann's democratic playbook, such as the use of referenda, unionization of technology workers, and generating countervailing economic power. We will briefly examine these in turn.

Recent experiences with referenda to constrain the actions of powerful corporations have not been encouraging. We are thinking, for example, of Proposition 22 in California, where voters upheld the freedom of companies like Uber and Lyft to continue treating their drivers as independent contractors, thus not being constrained to provide benefits that would be due to employees (Sumagasay, 2024). In the prevailing electoral system, where big money rules, especially after the 2008 Citizens United verdict of the US Supreme Court, it is likely that important referenda would be captured by big money interests. This means that they can hardly play the role of countering Asymmetry in agenda-setting power that Zimmermann wants them to.

On the other hand, we agree with Zimmermann that increasing penetration of unions, especially in the technology space, can help generate desirable countervailing power. As she notes, a vast majority of technology workers are not unionized, and are thus unable to either collectively bargain for their rights or respond in one voice to matters of critical public concern, such as the safety of generative AI systems deployed at scale. As experts closest to the development of these systems, it seems necessary that these workers have an organized voice and exit options, as Zimmermann argues for. We also note that unions are sometimes resource rich and can spend the amounts necessary to win important electoral victories in a money-dominated electoral system. These factors suggest that increased unionization is quite an important part of any plausible democratic playbook to tackle ASYMMETRY.

An alternative approach

Our inclination is to put more resources into representative government. Representative government has the capacity to bring together ordinary citizens and expertise in a way that makes the latter intelligible and accountable to the former. The whole system – including representatives, political parties, and interest groups – is structured in such a way to make the expert knowledge intelligible to ordinary citizens (Christiano, 2012). Moreover, representative institutions already have democratic structures and they enjoy legitimacy within our societies. Representative government also has the power in the modern world to exact conditions from the most powerful economic actors. For example, the European Union was able to require Apple to make its phones accessible to standard charging ports (i.e., USB Type-C), instead of continuing to use proprietary charging ports (Ashworth, 2022). These latter made it difficult or impossible for users to connect their existing peripherals with Apple phones, unless they were already compatible with Apple's proprietary charging port. More generally, we also saw the EU pass the General Data Protection Regulations (GDPR) which are designed to limit the data that web surfers share with websites without their knowledge (Europa, n.d.).

We recommend three proposals and would like to hear Zimmermann's opinion on these. First, we recommend strengthening antitrust law to diminish the market power of tech companies. This would have the effect of striking at the asymmetry directly and diminishing the power of any particular economic agent as well as probably enhancing the efficiency of the market. An important aspect of strengthening antitrust law and regulations concerns restrictions on media cross-ownership; that is, the control of different forms of media by the same individual or entity (Baker, 2006). Increasingly, large tech companies have come to acquire direct power in shaping media narratives, often by owning powerful media entities. Restricting their ability to do so by strengthening media ownership regulations would directly address their undue agenda-setting power that Zimmermann identifies as a key worry.

Second, we recommend very strong campaign finance mechanisms to loosen the hold of powerful economic agents over politicians. This would strike directly at the concerns of regulatory capture, whether of existing democratic institutions, or indeed of any new ones like the informed sub-constituencies recommended by Zimmermann. Third, we support, with Zimmermann, more forceful unionization efforts regarding workers in the technology industry. This will strengthen alternative sources of information about technology and improve the ability of ordinary workers to organize and become informed politically so as to serve as a counterweight to the powerful influence of technology corporations (Christiano, 2019). We realize that these proposals are not very feasible in the near term in the United States. But the proposals Zimmermann suggests that are different from our own – such as national referenda or mini publics making decisions over tech deployment – are no more feasible. Whenever there is some wherewithal for implementation, our proposals, if implemented, are better suited to deal with the harms and risks of AI deployment in a sustained manner by drawing upon the resources available to representative democracy.

References

Ashworth, B. (2022), A new EU law would force iPhones to adopt USB-C charging. *Wired*. Available online at: https://www.wired.com/story/eu-law-usb-c-iphones-lightning/ (last accessed March 15, 2026).

Baker, E.C. (2006), Media Concentration and Democracy: Why Ownership Matters. Cambridge University Press.

Christiano, T. (2012), Rational deliberation among experts and citizens. In: *Deliberative Systems*, ed. J. Mansbridge and J. Parkinson. Cambridge University Press: 27–51.

Christiano T (2019), Democracy, participation and information: Complementarity between political and economic institutions. *San Diego Law Review* 56: 4.

Dourado E. and Hammond S. (2016), Make America boom again: how to bring back supersonic transport. *Mercatus Research* (2016). Available online at: https://www.mercatus.org/system/files/mercatus-dourado-supersonic-transport-v1.pdf (last accessed March 15, 2026).

Europa (n.d.), Data protection under GDPR. Available online at: https://europa.eu/youreurope/business/dealing-with-customers/data-protection/data-protection-gdpr/index_en.htm (last accessed March 15, 2026).

Kreps, S. and Kriner, D. (2023), How AI threatens democracy. *Journal of Democracy* 34, no. 4: 122–131.
Manning, A. (2021), Monopsony in labor markets: A review. *ILR Review* 74, no. 1: 3–26.
Sumagasay, L. (2024), California companies wrote their own gig worker law. Now no one is enforcing it. *Cal Matters*. Available online at: https://calmatters.org/economy/2024/09/gig-work-california-prop-22-enforcement/ (last accessed March 15, 2026).
Volcovici, V. and Kearney, L. (2024), Data-center reliance on fossil fuels may delay clean-energy transition. *Reuters*. Available online at: https://www.reuters.com/technology/artificial-intelligence/how-ai-cloud-computing-may-delay-transition-clean-energy-2024-11-21/ (last accessed March 15, 2026).
Von Hippel, E. (2005), Open source software projects as user innovation networks. In: *Perspectives On Free and Open Source Software*, eds. Joseph Feller, Brian Fitzgerald, Scott A. Hissam, and Karim R. Lakhani. MIT Press: 267–278.
Wang, C. and Kantarcioglu, M. (2025), A review of DeepSeek models' key innovative techniques. *arXiv preprint*. arXiv:2503.11486.
West, J. and Gallagher, S. (2006), Patterns of open innovation in open source software. *Open Innovation: Researching a New Paradigm* 235, no. 11: 82–106.
Zimmermann, A. (2026), Democratizing AI. Manchester University Press.

10

'After the revolution'? On Annette Zimmermann's idea to democratize the AI agenda-setting

Nadia Urbinati

The 'California ideology'

In my early research, I became interested in the philosophical visions that, in the first decades of the nineteenth century, paved the way for the myth of American exceptionalism: attributing experimental value to life, thinking of the future as a horizon of moral choice, believing in the 'natural' disposition to freedom. The first chapter of Annette Zimmermann's excellent manuscript brings to mind that old myth, which pragmatism then translated into the maxim 'thinking in the making' that shaped what Alexis de Tocqueville identified as the religion of progress: faith in science's power to solve all human problems, provided that no obstacle blocks the experimental drive. This adrenaline-generating mentality can inspire both destructive plans and uplifting beliefs. It marks the spirit of the exceptionalism of AI, a combination of libertarian ideology and the 'magic' of technology, the 'glory of human ambition and achievement' (Andreessen 2023, cited in Zimmermann, 2026), something between Prometheus and Mephistopheles. 'California ideology' mimics that of transcendental communities, which George Kateb defined as 'democratic individualism' (Kateb, 1992: 240–266).

Nonetheless, old and new exceptionalism and individualism are different. Whereas the former grew at the beginning of democratization and infused American society with powerful ideals of self-reliance and equal respect, the latter has grown within an established and worn-out democracy, and its futurist faith longs for evasion from democracy. Silicon Valley's innovators are not convinced that political deliberation involving the incompetent many should have the right to subject their experimental technology to the public interest. Furthermore, they have no qualms about defending oligarchy as a legitimate status gained through nerdy entrepreneurship.

Techno-utopianism challenges democratic equality at the bottom. Some oligarchs dream of an Übermensch who will break the democratic rules that lift the incompetent many and humiliate the gifted few. 'We believe in the natural human drive to make things, to gain territory, to explore the unknown [...] we are conquerors' (Andreessen, 2023). 'Californian ideology' sponsors a split and clear-cut dualism between liberty and equality and questions the moral legitimacy of democratic rules (Thiel, 2009; cf. Bobbio, 1994). Furthermore, it makes the massive concentration of money with technology a legitimate justification to control the development of AI. Essentially, it claims that decisions on the direction and speed of technological innovation must be the responsibility of Silicon Valley leaders alone.

The challenge of our time

Managing AI innovation is the challenge facing contemporary democracy. Zimmermann's proposal to subject the modeling of the AI agenda to democratic procedures is convincing because it identifies the locus of power where the priorities of research and investment for the future are decided.

> current dynamics of AI deployment pose a distinct and philosophically interesting democratic problem, given that industry-based deployers are usually neither directly nor indirectly democratically *authorized*, and given that they *de facto* have largely *uncontested* agenda-setting power: AI deployment is currently a highly anti-competitive agenda-setting environment. (Zimmermann, 2026: 12).

Worth noting are Zimmermann's choice of keywords, 'authorization', 'contestation', and 'competition', as the normative and procedural pillars of modern democracy that regulate informal deliberation in society and decision-making in institutions. Zimmermann's criterion is consistent with a diarchic conception of democracy, whereby the principles of political equality (*isonomia* or one person, one vote) and of an equal right of influence (*isēgoria* or power of voice) are the Cartesian axes of a system of 'fair and participatory procedures' that can (must) democratically govern the implementation of AI, counteracting the effects that the asymmetry of power has on decisions in the field of experimentation and implementation (ibid.). The place of agenda-setting in representative democracy has been emphasized by key theorists, among them Robert Dahl (who stressed the role of the 'agenda of matters that are to be decided by means of the democratic process': Dahl, 1988: 113) and Elmer E. Schattschneider (who thought that the agenda-setting defines the scope of conflict: Schattschneider, 1975). The AI agenda-setting should follow the same logic of public accountability as all other intermediations and agenda-settings operating in a democratic society.

Below, I will examine the two domains that Zimmermann claims should be democratically governed – the length of the experimental temporality and the distribution of risks and benefits – and then discuss her proceduralist strategy with an attentive eye on the role of the AI 'technical experts', the intellectuals of our times. Finally, I will offer some critical reflections or raise doubts on the political strength of her proposal. My doubts do not pertain to her strategy's normative argument and meaning; they are political and rely upon Zimmermann's very analysis of the AI world. Examining those two domains should help us see that her 'moderate' strategy of interfering with the AI agenda-setting via procedures may look almost utopian. Although normatively consistent, Zimmermann's moderate strategy does not stress enough the radical nature of the conflict opposing oligarchy to democracy, which reveals an unprecedented tension between individual liberty and political equality in existing democratic societies. Mariana Mazzucato reminds us that AI is not 'just another sector' and is going to shape all domains of the economy; it is 'not a neutral technology', and although it can develop freely, 'it would need to be powered and deployed, which requires access to the gatekeeper's cloud computing platforms – such as Amazon Web Services, Microsoft Azure, and Google Cloud' (Mazzucato, 2025).

Whatever these giants seek to do (i.e., overcome the state and 'reboot medievalism as a model of justice', Slobodian, 2023: 122), to be contained and controlled they would need a more muscular democratic state. This leads me to surmise that Zimmermann's moderate proceduralist proposal falls into a conundrum since the process of deliberation that should support it is heavily dependent upon and exposed to a techno-economic power of persuasion and decision-making that is firmly in the hands of a Mandarin class of oligarchs. Can democratic procedures operate in a patrimonial structure of power?

Time, risks, and benefits

> AI users, who are usually corporate actors not subject to direct democratic authorization and accountability, are currently able to unilaterally set the regulation of technology and the ethical agenda of technology simply by developing tools and granting public access to them while simultaneously offloading responsibility for *ex-post* harm mitigation to government actors and democratic constituencies (Zimmermann, 2026: 11).

Disagreement about the length of experimental temporality is disagreement about the fundamental power to establish the criteria for the distribution of risks and benefits. We can illustrate this through the two concepts around which the question of duration revolves: *harm principle* and *negative freedom*.

We may detect two approaches to the harm principle in the question of duration: 'short-term' and 'long-term'. The first requires *ex ante* control of possible harm, and the second *ex post* control of harm suffered. 'Short-term' suggests adopting not only a reactive approach to a given fact (or innovation) but also exercising control over the dynamics of innovation before embracing or adopting it on a large scale: the goal is to put the public (our interest) first and research second. 'The long term', on the other hand, assumes that innovation must have complete freedom to show its potential; stopping a process to test its predictable harm would compromise the innovation; in sum, the technological process is self-correcting, much like our freedom of choice. Zimmermann argues that the long-term vision

> ranks the normative goals of freedom and wellbeing higher than the value of equality This entrenches social relations that are at odds with democratic equality [...] Rather than embracing the idea that all of us have the right to shape the direction of technological innovations that affect all of us, these views stipulate that tech elites [...] have not only the right but also a duty to chart our collective path for the benefit of the cluelesss masses. This is the case of libertarianism and accelerationism (Zimmermann, 2026: 25).

Short-term collides with negative freedom when it asks political authority to interfere with the agent's choice. Long-term claims that the state should not interfere with AI's research agenda to protect some hypothetical harm or spare people from suffering. The latter embodies negative liberty, the former political freedom. Recalling Isaiah Berlin, we would say that the long-term would be a quest for freedom as non-interference, while the short-term would elect a goal other than individual liberty.

Negative liberty presumes a narrow conception of harm, which people must experience, not just fear or hypothetically anticipate, to claim justified interference. An agent's freedom is violated when her choice is interrupted by an external authority to protect another good, not freedom (equality, the wellbeing of many, justice). This is the core of libertarian philosophy. Peter Thiel writes that the task is 'to find an escape from politics in all its forms, also democracy' (Thiel, 2009). Mimicking the assault on the social welfare state in the aftermath of World War II, libertarians oppose any regulatory authorities and want to protect 'their' AI industry. In Milton Freedman's words: '[T]here is evidence that a democratic society, once established, destroys a free economy' (Brimelow, 1988: 176). Along the same line, Robert Nozick argued that the problem with state interference in social choices for reasons of just distribution is that its interference with individual decisions can never be stopped because liberty always generates always new inequality.

To contest the long-term vision, Zimmermann argues that the new course of AI demands regulatory intervention because generative AI differs from earlier forms of AI and 'machine learning as algorithmic decision-making'. Those forms were 'narrow' as they were programmed for specific predefined fields, such as healthcare, criminal justice, insurance, transportation, etc. However, generative AI is a process that does not have any particular domain and its breadth of application – and, more importantly, evolution – is challenging to control and difficult to stop; moreover, it is so fast in learning that it makes existing rules old right away; finally, decisions to deploy powerful technology are not always easily reversible.[1] Therefore, since companies can make decisions that harm society, democratic constituencies have the right and, indeed, the duty to 'exercise active, *ex ante* control about which policy options and choices require democratic deliberation and contestation' (Zimmermann, 2026: 11). Interfering with generative AI scientific programs is to protect a fundamental good: citizens' equal dignity and political power.

As a risk factor, 'acceleration' is the bone of contention, as the European Union claimed in challenging Silicon Valley's risk-friendly ideology. Conversely, the Silicon Valley people claim that a wait-and-see approach should be endorsed as improvement is the goal. 'The only way to improve a product like this, where the user experience is so much different than anything anyone has seen before, is to have people like you using the product and doing exactly what you all are doing' (Microsoft's Bing Blog cited in Zimmermann, 2026: 9). To AI generative, the public is like a laboratory, and humans are its guinea pigs; stopping the process would be tantamount to stopping an experiment before allowing it to evolve. On the other hand, not stopping it would be tantamount to allowing risks to flow without the people having any power to protect themselves from their results.

The conflict over time length is radical because it concerns two liberties and, therefore, who has the right to decide to interfere. Within this context, compromise is difficult. In all Western democracies, compromise has been practiced constantly between social classes or parts holding diverging interests, and valuable results have been obtained in welfare and rights

1 'Consider the example of Duke MTMC, a dataset of two million video frames recorded in public spaces on Duke University's campus and released publicly without proper privacy protections for people featured in the videos. In the aftermath, controversial research on computer vision-based surveillance technology utilized this data, and following public backlash, it was taken down in June 2019. Nonetheless, within the following year, at least 135 research papers utilized that dataset – and others derived from it – after it had been taken down' (p. 5).

policies. However, this case is different because generative AI companies enjoy monopolistic power, which puts compromise out of place (as we saw, Thiel thinks it is time for freedom to drop democracy).

We are faced here with a binary logic, which derives from the radical asymmetry between the interests of the oligarchs/professionals and those of the democratic community. The former tolerate minimal controls at their discretion; the latter believe that controls are necessary when the risks outweigh the benefits to the public. The nature of the two interests reveals the existence of two incommensurable goods: financial power and political power. In sum, the two interpretations of 'temporality' embody opposite claims to sovereignty: money and politics. And since sovereignty is an exclusive good, compromise seems hardly conceivable.

Furthermore, AI innovators back up their claims with the rhetorical aura of the good of science: the research method demands that the chain of hypotheses, tests, and innovations be left to run indefinitely. Interrupting experimentation 'to exercise active ex-ante control' and waiting for its effects to be verified (thinking about the present rather than the future and slowing down the process rather than accelerating it) would violate moral and research liberty. The logic of scientific research and individual liberty overlap in the telos of progress, which carries on two primary goods to be protected. People can wait or be sacrificed, but science and liberty cannot.

When Zimmermann challenges the ideology of an extended temporality, she proposes to apply democratic rules to a realm that libertarians have traditionally kept out of the political domain: individual freedom and research. This move makes her strategy radical, even if she presents it as 'moderate proceduralism' or a fair democratic process, thanks to which citizens could participate equally in deciding the rules and goals of agenda-setting. 'Rather than uncritically accepting AI exceptionalism, that is, the idea that AI is a highly unusual policy area that cannot be subjected to democratic contestation and control, we – as democratic constituencies – must identify ways to take control of it, drawing inspiration from how other complex policy areas have been democratized' (Zimmermann, 2026: 11).

Considering the binary logic mentioned above, democratizing agenda-setting can hardly be a moderate strategy. It is not the logic of research that radicalizes it but the monopoly–money–technology nexus. This knot of 'absolutes' makes AI different from the many other complex arenas democratized in past decades.

A similar scheme returns in the asymmetrical power relationships in decisions about risks and benefits. In current generative AI, the risks do not 'perfectly correspond' to the benefits because the long-term vision is structurally predisposed to solutions that create more sacrifices for everyone except for the professionals and the oligarchs. A democratic government must challenge the asymmetrical relationships that the monopolistic system generates, which makes risks dispersed among the many and benefits concentrated among the few. Democratic equality rejects the logic of the zero-sum game (no compromise) with which the AI oligarchs regulate the risk/benefit ratio in their favor. *Democracy is not risk averse but asymmetry of power averse*. All of this looks like the script of a movie we have already seen in the past, but with a significant difference.

Old and new struggles

Since the beginning of the nineteenth century, capitalist relations have been more or less successfully subjected to the will of political communities, thanks also to the conquest of suffrage and, therefore, the acquisition of greater contractual power by the weaker parts of society. The laborer classes could obtain a less unequal distribution of risks and benefits through trade unions and affiliated parties and their ability to influence public opinion and political decisions. Asymmetry of power between parts and interests is also a problem in high-tech oligopolistic global capitalism. What has changed today are the actors involved and, in fact, the form of capitalism.

First, there are no longer organized masses capable of limiting the power of the capitalists through political conflicts under the rule of law. Second, the object of contention is not made of tangible things, such as salary or the length of the working day – things that people immediately perceive, see, and understand (although Zimmermann dispels the idea that low wages are no longer a problem in the high-tech industry; on the contrary, she shows how manual workers in Silicon Valley are poorly paid and not unionized). The subjects of this new conflict are also immaterial, such as the complex techniques and protocols of the AI research agenda. Of course, old social conflicts, too, aimed at rewriting the rules and obtaining new legislation. However, those rules directly translated into better living conditions for the claimants. Conversely, the new regulations on how to govern AI agenda-setting have no direct impact on people's lives and imagination, making the issue less likely to stir the general public. The topic of this new conflict is more symbolic than material and more likely to attract an educated public or expert audience than the general public at large.

Furthermore, millions of people enthusiastically welcome AI products and do not perhaps perceive acceleration as a problem: those very people that democracy would like to protect from the exploitation that the asymmetrical distribution of risks and benefits generates. This immateriality confirms that now, more than ever, the object of contention is democracy. The question is that today, democracy seems to be a too-distant good for many people to appreciate, given the lack of power ordinary citizens have and feel to have in influencing politicians and institutions (the literature on the crisis of democracy is abundant).

And what about the other part, the capitalists? Is the oligopolistic capitalism that owns AI generative well disposed toward its democratic deployment? Probably not. However, Zimmermann does not pay sufficient attention to the consent fabrication, which germinated from the structural relations of power and poisons deliberation at the start. This choice is understandable, considering that her argument is normative and oriented to justify the argument for procedural intervention. However, it is necessary to address the power symmetry deficit that underlies the asymmetry in the distribution of risks and benefits to make the procedural strategy not a simple panacea: the political problem of AI control stems from an upstream problem involving the inequality of power of social forces. Zimmermann is aware (and, rightly, not too worried) that this fight for proceduralism will not mobilize the masses; that will be a struggle for only a tiny minority that grasps its importance and considers it relevant. 'Given that ballot propositions originate from a small group of highly mobilized citizens or by legislatures themselves, skeptical readers may object at this point that it is unclear why these models necessarily render democratic agendas more legitimate. But that would be uncharitable. Democracy, in effect, is "agendas all the way down" (Zimmermann, 2026: 44). Any decision sequence in any constituency is, to some degree, a function of some earlier decision'. Zimmermann is right that we should not be purists on this 'minority' constituency. Many times in the past, minorities have initiated democratic struggles. The problem lies elsewhere, however.

The procedural strategy

The global nature of the AI sector and tools seems to suggest that the best strategy for governing it democratically is to resort to regulations and governance, to rely on the courts and the autonomy of justice from political power, and to shift the focus beyond elections and traditional political games. 'The future trajectory of current oligopolies will be in part a function of regulatory and democratic interventions into the AI deployment landscape'; therefore, the question is to elaborate 'an analysis of what kinds of democratic agenda-setting interventions are available and what their respective future consequences might be for democratic constituencies' ability to keep oligopolies in check' (Zimmermann, 2026: 10 footnote 5). Furthermore, since the dynamics of AI deployment substantially impact global societies, regulatory power may be a more suitable tool if concerted among various state actors. Whereas it is unrealistic to hope for a democratic global government, aiming for cooperation among states in regulation seems realistic. The European Union is the best example of how sovereigns can challenge transnational powers (for example, in fiscal matters).

Not having imperial national sovereignty like China and the United States, the European Union has developed new and extensive forms of regulatory power. The empire of regulation has proven capable of correcting one of the causes of the weakness of sovereignty, thus compensating, even if in a limited way, for the absence of a sovereign continental political government. Just as Al Capone was imprisoned thanks to a legal loophole (he was arrested for tax fraud, not for the murders he had committed and for which he was still being prosecuted), global capitalism can be contained with indirect weapons. Of course, the mafia remained undefeated, but some essential victories against its adepts were scored. The EU fits well into this paradigm of indirect governance; it stands as a model of incremental sovereignty that can influence and regulate new forms of capitalism, correct imbalances between states, and limit the agenda-setting of multinational corporations and generative AI. The weapon of rights, rules, and norms makes the European Union an agent representing the interests of its citizens and the public worldwide. This model gives hope that the struggle between democrats and oligarchs, although it cannot be resolved once and for all, can be fought effectively and in the service of democratic communities and citizens.

To be sure, Zimmermann is not content with regulations and the rule of law. As we have seen, she argues that issues relating to the priorities of the AI agenda raise questions that directly impact democratic values and government. So, the purpose of her book is not just practical problem-solving; it is not just about governance and rules. Its aim is also to introduce readers to various normative and theoretical issues related to beliefs and ideologies (for example, libertarian or social) that influence opinion formation. The point is that AI is not an industry like any other, as its impact on voters and governments is enormous and complex to identify, control, and tame. Because of this complexity and the radical nature of the logic of agenda-setting and the effects its products have on our minds, Zimmermann rightly believes that self-regulation is not a convincing path. Democratic states must intervene.

The democratic process is complex and involves decisions and opinions. It can intervene from the bottom-up and the top-down, from outside and inside state institutions. Zimmermann proposes the joint use of these strategies. This broad constellation of practices combines with a convincing and essential conceptualization of democracy. Zimmermann best shows the limits of the minimalist theory of democracy: the AI persuasion system forces us to go beyond elections as the central institutions of democracy, not because we wish to diminish their role, but because we are aware of their centrality in democracy and their power to change political scenarios.

Zimmermann suggests, convincingly, correcting the minimalist conception with a richer proceduralism that is attentive to extra-state forms of participation, associations, and movements that make democracy a government in which political equality (*isonomia*) is intertwined with equal freedom of speech and the power of voice (*isēgoria*).

> [...] *a binding decision* at some juncture of a process forces other political actors to grapple with a new status quo, which makes it a more impactful tool for setting future agendas. Similarly, having the ability to provide not only input, but also to *audit and critique* the deployment choices of other actors, means having the ability to hold others publicly accountable, which is crucial for determining how future agendas should be redirected: democratic constituencies need first to have tools to uncover what might have gone wrong in a given case of AI deployment before they can identify publicly beneficial AI policy issues that no other political actor – such as industry leaders – is incentivized to feature on agendas.
>
> In my view, we can best achieve these stronger forms of democratically legitimate agenda-setting power if we do not rely exclusively on democratic constituencies as a whole, and instead focus on harnessing the power of *informed sub-constituencies* (Zimmermann, 2026: 70–71).

Thus advancing a virtuous interaction between experts and citizens. Intermediation is the central theme of Zimmermann's procedural approach. It is also central to the broader project of defending democracy. In recent decades, political scientists have studied the transformation (and decline) of parties and the media in their ability to represent and give value to citizens' demands and movements. They have identified the self-referential political class that cartelized post-mass parties produce as a factor in the decline of participation and trust in democracy. We have learned from the experience of populism the need democracies have to rebuild intermediary bodies. The authoritarian turn that populism has facilitated in all democratic countries demonstrates how crucial and democratically valuable social and political intermediation is: to counter the concentration of power, articulate demands, and give a representative voice to the many. Intermediary bodies limit power by giving power (Urbinati, 2025: 1–12). They are vehicles for civic culture, social solidarity, and citizens' empowerment.

Zimmermann identifies three intermediate functions in the implementation of AI: *binding decision* (like the joints that fix the conditions for the research process to continue), *re-examining and criticizing* (like the controllers of the entire elaboration to see what goes wrong), and *technical competence* (expertise as an aid to democratic constituencies). The last one is an original proposal by Zimmermann. It consists of the cooperation of episteme with the lay public. Intermediate democratic actors, such as advocacy groups and third-party experts, would have the auxiliary support of 'informed sub-constituents', consisting of experts who can assist democratic citizens with their specialized knowledge (p. 69). For this cooperation to be realized, the class of 'technical experts' would be expected to be divided between those working in the private AI sector and those working for the general public. Whereas in the past, social forces competed to attract to their side the intellectuals functional to their aspirations, today, this is primed to happen with the new intellectuals who are, in fact, organic to the AI world. This looks like an interesting reformulation of Antonio Gramsci's reflection on the role of the intellectuals in the struggle for emancipation or, on the contrary, for domination. It is, therefore, *an invitation to democratic theorists to open a new chapter of research on the civic/democratic education of technical experts.* These experts are not purely 'technical' as AI agenda-setting is not purely neutral; their expertise is permeated with ideological views, such as those criticized by Zimmermann (acceleration and the not 'neutral' question of the distribution of risks and benefits between AI companies and the public). If technical experts are to be 'utilized' as auxiliaries in the service of democratic intermediation, their formation and training is a topic that should not be left to private corporations where AI is created. This is also because, today, the values and principles of democracy are not spontaneously born in society, where citizenship is reduced to voting every few years and, in the meantime, consists at most of reactive attention to stimuli created on purpose by social media and measured in surveys.

Focusing on intermediation is thus timely and unavoidable also because our democracies depend heavily on the nature of hi-tech innovations, which steer opposing movements: on the one hand, they make it more difficult to form stable associations and tend to disjoint society; on the other hand, they offer citizens invaluable means of communication and information that can help form movements and make claims. We rightly complain about social isolation, disassociation, and individualistic anomie, but technology also allows us to reach distant people and build representative platforms even at a supranational level. Therefore, the intermediate democracy Zimmermann wittily proposes is fundamental to setting the agenda in all policy sectors and, indeed, in AI; it is a resource that cannot be denied or underestimated. However, unlike the old social and political intermediation, which relied on leaders, movements, and well-defined parties, it is not yet clear how AI can guarantee the same pluralism and the same planning autonomy and not instead promote self-referential groups and intolerant niches that disintegrate and fragment citizenship while deepening the power of the few.

Conclusion

I can, therefore, come to the 'skeptical' point. First, however, I must emphasize that skepticism about procedural reformism is not intended to inspire pessimism about the effectiveness of democratic regulatory intervention. On the contrary, it aims to train a positive and vigilant attitude towards democratizing AI deployment.

As we have seen, the interpretation of freedom is controversial when we evaluate AI's role and its impact on political and social life. Zimmermann prioritizes democratic accountability. Of course, the oligarchs are not accountable to the public for how they rule their companies. Zimmermann believes democratic constituencies are entirely legitimate in holding generative AI agenda-setting accountable. This polarization takes us back to the roots of democratic power.

As mentioned above, the socioeconomic sources of the asymmetry of risks and benefits distribution in the AI agenda-setting is a task that transcends 'procedural minimalism' as it entails a challenge over sovereignty. Let's remember that sovereignty is the political structure allowing the state to govern the entire society. So, although Zimmermann presents her proposal as 'minimal' and 'modest' because it asks the actors to play the democratic game according to its rules, the character of her proposal is, in effect, utopian and, in this sense, radical: not because it plans to overturn the unequal structure of social power – democracy seems to have to coexist with oligarchy – but because it presumes possible compromise between monopolistic power and democratic regulation.

> Even if oligopolistic industry actors successfully capture agendas with respect to one particular deployment domain or procedure, other participation pathways may still offer opportunities for citizens to exercise agenda-setting counterpower. For this reason, the interventions identified here target different types of decision sequences using different participatory mechanisms and centering different types of actors while paying special attention to the value of agenda-setting contributions by specific *sub-constituencies* and *intermediary actors* (Zimmerman, 2026: 69).

Bolstering agenda-setting 'creates healthier democratic institutions overall, in which democratically illegitimate influences in one or some participation pathways need not spell disaster for the larger goal of democratically legitimate agenda-setting more generally' (p. 69).

We live in what scholars call 'a democracy of the public' or audience democracy. Zimmermann seems to believe that this kind of democracy, which so profoundly relies on social media replacing parties, can curb the will of the oligarchs. We saw how the clash between negative liberty and democratic freedom cannot find a terrain of agreement because oligarchs own the technology industry; they do not simply employ it. The question is that when the owners claim that the criteria of the agenda-setting must be decided by those who design it, they claim their discretionary power in a domain that directly impacts democratic opinion and will formation – that can (as we saw with recent US elections) deeply condition and even determine electoral results.

There must be no polar environment to contemplate a reformist approach capable of regulating the compromise between the parts involved. We have seen that compromise is *de facto* out of place in the monopolistic environment of AI production and deployment. It is, therefore, fatal for a reformist strategy to stop at the door of such a radical conflict. It doesn't have the teeth to face it. In this context, the predictable condition for a reformist strategy to remain in play is accepting a level of inequality beyond discussion. Of course, the democratic norm must presuppose social equality and equal consideration, even if it does not need to presuppose total substantive or communist equality. However, we must accept that economic and social inequalities are not beyond our amending proposals and are not so deep as to make asymmetry a factual blackmail that ordinary citizens cannot escape. Overcoming inequality is a future horizon for a democratic ideal to shape politics. Any reform must consider this premise, as Zimmermann also makes clear.

However, this means that proceduralism risks being ineffective since it would be utopian to think that procedures have the strength to correct the structural asymmetry of power, which underlies the distribution of risks and benefits in AI deployment. The egalitarian premise cannot be circumvented and, today, inequality is a boulder that hinders any reformist proposal. This naked fact is under our eyes, as we see with the oligarchic assault on the American state and the EU regulatory model. Before it is too late, democratic states must react with extraordinary and concerted measures. AI governance is a global issue; only cooperation between sovereign democracies could hope to subject AI companies to democratic will and rules. To paraphrase the title of a book by Robert Dahl, Zimmermann's procedural reform seems suitable for 'after the revolution'.

References

Andreessen, M. (2023), The Techno-Optimist Manifesto. Available online (October 16, 2023) at: https://a16z.com/the-techno-optimist-manifesto/ (last accessed March 15, 2026).

Bobbio, N. (1994), *Right and Left: The Significance of a Political Distinction*, trans. Allan Cameron. The University of Chicago Press.

Brimelow, P. (1988), *Why Liberalism is Now Obsolete: An Interview with the Nobel Laureate Milton Freedman*. Forbes: 176.
Dahl, R.A. (1988), *Democracy and Its Critics*. Yale University Press.
Kateb, G. (1992), Whitman and the culture of democracy. In: *The Inner Ocean: Individualism and Democratic Culture*. Cornell University Press: 240–266.
Mazzucato, M. (2025), *Resisting Digital Feudalism*. Project Syndicate.
Microsoft Bing Blogs (2023), The new Bing and Edge – learning from our first week. Available online at: https://blogs.bing.com/search/february-2023/The-new-Bing-Edge-Learning-from-our-!rst-week. (Last accessed March 15, 2026).
Schattschneider, E.E. (1975), *The Semisovereign People: A Realist's View of Democracy in Am*erica [1960]. Harcourt Brace Jovanovich.
Slobodian, Q. (2023), *Crack-Up Capitalism: Market Radicals and the Dream of a World Without Democracy*. Metropolitan Books.
Thiel, P. (2009), The education of a libertarian. *Cato Unbound*. Available online at: https://www.cato-unbound.org/2009/04/13/peter-thiel/education-libertarian (last accessed March 15, 2026).
Urbinati, N. (2025), The decline and the need of the key force of intermediation. *Philosophy and Social Criticism* 51, no. 4: 559–570. https://journals.sagepub.com/doi/full/10.1177/01914537251316829.
Zimmermann, A. (2026), *Democratizing AI*. Manchester University Press.

11

AI governance at a crossroads: Renovating democracy in the age of AI

Allison Stanger

Artificial Intelligence (AI) is reshaping societies at a breakneck pace, raising profound questions about power and governance. Will AI be wielded by a few to control the many, undermining democratic institutions? Or can we harness AI to strengthen democracy and human flourishing for all? As someone who has studied technology's impact on governance, I believe the answer depends on how we choose to govern AI *now*. This chapter examines the twin faces of AI governance – its daunting challenges and its transformative opportunities – and outlines a strategy to ensure AI reinforces democracy rather than eroding it.

Drawing on critiques of today's approach to AI, optimism about AI's democratic potential, and a dual-track governance strategy my colleagues and I have developed, I argue that proactive, power-sharing governance can channel AI for the public good. We stand at a crossroads not unlike a constitutional moment: much as the United States once moved from a loose Articles of Confederation to a stronger constitutional federal union, we must now evolve from ad hoc, oligopoly-driven tech rule to an alternative tech framework that secures the blessings of AI for We, the People rather than We, the Billionaires. The stakes could not be higher – if we get this wrong, we risk entrenching digital oligarchy; if we get it right, AI can serve a revitalized democracy. The path forward demands clear-eyed recognition of the dangers, a hopeful vision of what is possible, and actionable policies from the local to the global level. In what follows, I explore these elements in depth, making the case that with foresight and courage, AI governance can indeed fortify democratic institutions and protect human dignity.

The democratic deficit in AI development

Current trajectories of AI development suffer from a troubling democratic deficit. A handful of private tech companies and executives wield disproportionate control over AI's direction (Allen et al., 2025).

This *de facto* oligopoly means decisions with far-reaching social consequences – what kinds of AI to build, how fast to deploy them, what risks to take – are being made by a small elite, rather than through democratic deliberation. As Annette Zimmermann points out, recent AI deployment has been characterized by an asymmetry: risks are widely dispersed among the public, while benefits are narrowly concentrated in the hands of these few actors (Zimmermann, 2026: Chapters 3–4). In a democracy, when everyone bears the risks of a technology but only a select few reap its rewards and make its choices, something is fundamentally amiss.

Moreover, the epistemological challenge posed by generative AI deepens this democratic deficit. As recent scholarship emphasizes, the creators of generative AI systems like ChatGPT themselves 'do not fully understand exactly how these models arrive at their outputs', creating unprecedented governance uncertainty and risk. Dangerous capabilities can emerge spontaneously, making democratic oversight even more essential (Stanger et al., 2024: 3).

Public concern over this state of affairs is growing – there are increasing calls to subject AI decisions to democratic control (Zimmermann, 2026: 8). Some AI CEOs have called for regulation in abstract terms but often continue deploying powerful AI systems on their own terms. Zimmermann incisively asks: 'When it comes to AI, who has the power to determine what we make collective decisions about in the first place, and at what point in time?' (Zimmermann, 2026: 40). Right now, it is largely the tech companies setting the agenda – deciding which AI applications 'simply happen' and only then asking society to react. We have, in her words, shown 'undue deference to powerful actors who simply deploy and make it our problem later' (ibid.). This agenda-setting power of tech elites is an underappreciated pressure point in AI governance (ibid.). If we want to democratize AI, we must seize back some control over what problems AI is used to solve, for whose benefit, and under what constraints. Otherwise, we risk a future in which, as Zimmermann warns, benevolent-sounding 'caretakers' in Silicon Valley chart our collective path without real public accountability (Zimmermann, 2026: 25). Such a technocratic paternalism, even if well-intentioned, is at odds with democratic equality, treating citizens as 'clueless masses' to be managed rather than empowered participants in shaping our future (ibid.).

In short, Zimmermann is right that a core challenge for AI governance is correcting this democratic deficit. The people whose lives will be affected by AI should have a say in how AI is developed and deployed. Achieving that will require changes at multiple levels: increasing transparency, breaking information monopolies, and building channels for public input on AI. But before turning to solutions, it's important to examine a concrete and pressing example of how concentrated AI power can threaten democracy from within.

Oligopolistic AI control and the Trump–Musk alliance threat

The dangers of oligopolistic control over AI are starkly illustrated by the recent convergence of political and tech power in what we might call the Trump–Musk alliance. A notable example is the creation of a US federal initiative called the Department of Government Efficiency (DOGE) – an innocuously named agency with extraordinary reach. DOGE has secured unprecedented access to at least seven sensitive federal databases, including those of the Internal Revenue Service and Social Security Administration (Swan et al., 2025). What makes this especially alarming is that DOGE operates under the influence of Elon Musk, who has been simultaneously in charge of this government agency and his private AI company, xAI (Stanger, 2025).

In practice, DOGE's entanglement with Musk's enterprises creates a direct pipeline of government data into private hands. Reports revealed that DOGE personnel hold dual positions with Musk's companies; for example, SpaceX employees at the Federal Aviation Administration have government email addresses (Hawkins, 2025). This dual employment blurs the lines of accountability and allows data to potentially be siphoned from federal systems to Musk-owned ventures, including xAI's cutting-edge models. Tellingly, xAI's latest chatbot, Grok, pointedly refuses to clearly deny whether it is trained on this trove of government data (Otterbein and Wren, 2025). Such evasiveness heightens suspicions that public data is enriching private AI development behind closed doors. Recent analyses warn of a quiet, AI-driven 'political coup' occurring incrementally across federal agencies, wherein automation and privatized control displace democratic deliberation. For instance, DOGE's implementation within federal agencies has explicitly bypassed traditional Congressional oversight by using AI to automate budgetary and administrative decisions (Salvaggio, 2025).

Why is Elon Musk sacrificing his net worth in the short term to serve in the Trump administration? Because government databases are a Holy Grail for AI training – immensely valuable in a way that web-scraped data is not. Tech companies like OpenAI and Google currently rely heavily on internet data, which is vast but often messy, biased, and reflective of what people say or share online. By contrast, confidential government records represent verified, longitudinal data on actual human behavior across entire populations (Zhao et al., 2019). Every Medicare claim, every IRS tax filing, every Social Security payout is a real, ground-truth data point about how policies affect people's lives. These datasets are comprehensive (covering even people who never use the internet) and reliable (audited and quality-controlled). For an AI developer, gaining access to this would be like finding a treasure trove. As I noted in my analysis of the DOGE situation, this isn't just 'more data' – it's fundamentally different data, the kind that could allow an AI system to understand society at an unprecedented depth.

A private company armed with such data would have an almost insurmountable advantage over any competitors (Stanger, 2025). Imagine an AI model trained not only on internet text, but also on decades of outcomes of policies, health treatments, financial decisions, and education pathways. It could discern which healthcare interventions truly work best across different demographics or predict economic trends by seeing the real flows of money through the economy in Treasury data. Such a model could dominate entire industries – healthcare, finance, urban planning – by virtue of its superior insights. More troublingly, it could influence how society is governed and understood. If one private actor – Musk, in this scenario – controlled an AI that effectively 'knew' how America runs at a systems level, that actor could shape policy debates, business decisions, even elections, with frightening efficacy. The AI could simulate the impact of policies or messages and find levers to pull in order to manipulate public opinion or market behavior.

This is not just speculation. The DOGE saga raises the specter, right here and now, as I write, of AI being used to concentrate power in anti-democratic ways. When Musk (a private billionaire with open political agendas) holds the keys to America's data vault, the checks and balances of democratic governance are subverted. Concentrating such unprecedented data power in any private entity with a political agenda 'represents a profound challenge to the republic'. Absolute data corrupts absolutely. It creates the possibility of 'democracy-shattering corruption'; for instance, using AI-driven insights to manipulate electoral outcomes or public opinion at scale. Voters could be micro-targeted or socially engineered based on predictions no one else even knows exist. This goes beyond individual privacy violations; it is a wholesale power shift. Without exaggeration, if Americans fail to reclaim control over such data and the AI built on it, we may wake up to find ourselves digital subjects rather than human citizens – our lives nudged and nudged again by an AI Leviathan serving a narrow interest (Stanger, 2025).

The Trump–Musk alliance exemplifies in real time how this could happen. Former President Trump's political brand has included open disdain for traditional checks and balances, and an affinity for strongman tactics. Elon Musk, for all his innovative brilliance, has shown a penchant for flouting regulations and norms that inconvenience him. Together, they present a one-two punch: a government willing to hand vast power to a favored private actor, and that actor willing to use it in unaccountable ways. Notably, the very acronym 'DOGE' seems chosen as a wink to Musk's internet fandom (Dogecoin cryptocurrency is often referred to as DOGE) – a meme coin moniker adorning a federal department. This almost satirical detail underscores the absurdity of letting governance be captured by tech mogul whims. But as absurd as it sounds, the consequences are deadly serious. It portends an oligarchy where billionaire tech CEOs and sympathetic politicians collude to oversee AI and data, beyond the reach of democratic oversight.

This is a future we must avoid at all costs. It's a future in which the promise of AI – to improve human lives – is perverted into a tool of surveillance and manipulation by the powerful few. Preventing that outcome is a central motivation for rethinking AI governance. We need to ensure no single alliance or faction can wield AI as their private fiefdom. How, then, can we steer away from this dystopia?

AI's democratic potential: a hopeful vision

Despite these real dangers, there is another side to the story – one of optimism that AI, if properly governed, can strengthen democracy and promote human flourishing. It is easy to fall into despair when faced with scenarios like DOGE, but we should remember that technology is not inherently destined for autocracy. It can just as well be a powerful force against tyranny and inequality, if we make it so. AI is a dual-use tool: the same advanced AI that could be misused to undermine democracy could alternatively be used to reinforce and spread democracy.

Anthropic CEO Dario Amodei is one prominent voice articulating this optimistic vision. Amodei argues that in a world where democracies, not autocracies, maintain leadership in AI, the technology may 'structurally favor democracy everywhere' (Amodei, 2024). Consider the global struggle between open societies and authoritarian regimes. If the most powerful AI systems are developed under democratic governments or values, they can be leveraged to counter the tools of oppression. For example, authoritarian regimes rely on controlling information and spreading propaganda. Advanced AI could help democracies win the information war by detecting and countering disinformation at scale, and by providing citizens access to uncensored information through new channels that dictators cannot easily block (Amodei, 2024).

Amodei suggests we imagine a kind of supercharged pro-democracy AI agent – a 'superhumanly effective AI version of Srđa Popović' (the activist who helped topple a dictator in Serbia) in everyone's pocket

(Amodei, 2024). This AI assistant could empower citizens living under authoritarian rule with knowledge and tactics to non-violently resist, essentially automating and scaling the work of dissidents. While this may sound far-fetched, it speaks to AI's potential as a liberation technology. History shows that free flow of information is kryptonite to authoritarianism; AI might amplify that effect by making it impossible for regimes to censor truth without isolating themselves completely. This, of course, assumes that the knowledge AI provides is accessible to all rather than a luxury good.

Even within established democracies, where the threat is less about an overt dictatorship and more about imperfect institutions, AI offers opportunities for improvement. Democratic governments are supposed to deliver justice, equality, and good governance, but in practice we know they often fall short – courts have biases, bureaucracies are slow, misinformation spreads unchecked. Appropriately designed AI could help address some of these gaps. Take the justice system: one perennial dilemma is that human judges and juries can be biased or inconsistent, yet pure algorithmic decisions have historically been too rigid or opaque. Amodei posits that advanced AI might finally thread this needle by combining impartiality with nuanced understanding. AI systems, under strict transparency requirements, could assist judges by highlighting inconsistencies or checking human biases, leading to fairer outcomes. Imagine an AI that has digested millions of past legal cases and can point out when a judge's pending sentence for a defendant is unusually harsh or lenient compared to similar cases and can explain that suggestion. The judge remains in charge, but they now have a data-driven second opinion that might reduce outlier decisions. Such AI tools, if carefully implemented with appropriate oversight by the full plurality of the human species, could help fulfill the promise that everyone is equal under the law – a promise our human-only system has struggled to fully keep. The goal is not to replace judges or officials, but to augment their decision-making with breadth of perspective and freedom from prejudice that humans alone rarely possess (Amodei, 2024).

Another area is the information ecosystem of democracy. Democracies depend on informed citizens, yet today we are drowning in misinformation and division. Could AI help create a healthier public sphere? Potentially, yes: AI systems might be used to fact-check claims in real time, to mediate online discussions (identifying bots or malicious actors, for instance), or to provide personalized civic education – e.g., an AI that explains how a proposed policy would impact you, in plain language, using truthful data. If done right, this could counter polarization by grounding debate in shared facts and reducing the spread of falsehoods. Indeed, Amodei's optimism stems partly from the idea that AI-driven improvements in quality of life – better education, healthcare, economic opportunity – will make societies more resilient and less susceptible to demagogues. Historically, rising wellbeing and education tend to increase demand for democratic participation (Amodei, 2024). Authoritarianism often feeds on fear and desperation; if AI helps diminish both by curing diseases, creating jobs, or easing daily burdens, people will be less drawn to extremist alternatives.

To be clear, this optimistic scenario is in no way guaranteed. It requires deliberate effort to imagine, design, and deploy AI in ways that support democracy rather than undermining it. The kind of future Amodei envisions – what he calls an 'entente strategy' among democracies – would involve democracies banding together to ensure they collectively maintain an edge in AI capabilities and use that advantage to promote liberal values. He even suggests an approach akin to a new 'Atoms for Peace', where democracies share AI benefits widely (the carrot) while jointly restricting authoritarian regimes' access to the most powerful AI tech (the stick). In his words, success could mean an 'eternal 1991' – a lasting global environment where liberal democracy has the upper hand (alluding to the post-Cold War moment of democratic expansion). This is admittedly ambitious and would be difficult to coordinate, especially in the Trump era. But it underscores a crucial point: we are not helpless. Musk imagines one vision of the future in which he is dominant; we can apply our collective wisdom, harnessing AI, to imagine another. Through smart policy and alliances, we can tilt the balance in favor of democracy.

In sum, AI can be a democracy-enhancing tool. It could help democracies out-compete autocracies by enhancing economic prosperity and military defense in line with democratic norms, rather than through repression. It could also revitalize democracies from within by making institutions more effective and just. None of this happens by default, however. It hinges on governance. That leads us to the question: What kind of governance model can simultaneously guard against the dystopian risks and realize the utopian possibilities? My colleagues and I have advocated for a 'dual-track' strategy grounded in 'Power-Sharing Liberalism'.

A dual-track governance strategy based on Power-Sharing Liberalism

To navigate between the Scylla of oligarchic control and the Charybdis of unrealized potential, we need an AI governance approach that pursues two tracks in parallel: mitigating the risks of AI while maximizing its benefits for society. In a recent collaborative study, my co-authors and I argued that most AI governance efforts so far have been one-sided – overwhelmingly focused on preventing harms, with relatively little emphasis on actively steering AI toward public good uses (Allen et al., 2025). Important as it is to address risks like bias, privacy invasion, or misuse of AI, we believe that an exclusive focus on red lines and prohibitions misses the larger opportunity. AI is a transformative technology; the right approach to governance should not merely be about saying 'no' or 'slow down', but also about enabling positive outcomes that advance human flourishing. This philosophy is rooted in a normative framework that Danielle Allen calls Power-Sharing Liberalism (Allen, 2023).

Power-Sharing Liberalism builds on thinkers like Amartya Sen, Elizabeth Anderson, and Elinor Ostrom and puts human flourishing and participatory rights at the heart of liberal democracy. Unlike Classical Liberalism that focuses primarily on protecting individuals from harm (negative liberties), Power-Sharing Liberalism gives equal weight to positive freedoms – the rights of people to actively participate in shaping their society (Allen et al., 2025). It holds that for individuals to truly flourish, they must have a voice in the decisions that affect them and a stake in communal power. In practice, this means our institutions should be designed to share power broadly rather than concentrate it. A healthy democracy isn't just about electing leaders and then leaving them to it; it's about continual engagement, inclusion of diverse voices, and investing in the common good so that everyone has the opportunity to thrive. Crucially, Power-Sharing Liberalism also emphasizes that stability and justice in a society are secured not only by safeguarding rights, but by actively cultivating the material and social conditions for people to exercise those rights effectively. In other words, it's not enough to have free speech on paper if extreme inequality or tech oligarch media prevent many from being heard; true liberal democracy must foster an environment where power is genuinely distributed and shared.

Applied to AI, this framework urges us to ask: How can AI be governed in a way that expands people's agency and wellbeing, while reducing the chance that it will be used to concentrate power and cause harm? The answer lies in the dual-track strategy. One track is protections – rules and norms to prevent AI from undermining fundamental rights, democracy, and safety. The other track is proactive empowerment – policies to ensure AI is used to enhance public welfare, equity, and democratic participation.

This dual-track approach not only addresses domestic governance challenges but is also crucial in navigating complex international dynamics, as it promotes 'cooperation and coordination among open societies' while simultaneously building 'institutions and norms for cooperation on areas of mutual concern in the broader global community'. Such pragmatic cooperation can significantly reduce existential risk scenarios resulting from miscommunication or technical malfunctions, fostering both democratic resilience and global stability (Stanger et al., 2024).

Let's break down some key components of each track at the domestic level.

Risk Mitigation Track (protection): This involves the classic guardrails often discussed in AI ethics, but with a democratic twist. We certainly need strong measures to prevent the kinds of abuse highlighted earlier (mass privacy violations, algorithmic discrimination, manipulation of the public, etc.). This means requiring transparency and auditability of AI systems, especially those used by government or in high-stakes domains, so that independent auditors and the public can understand how decisions are being made (Allen et al., 2025). It means implementing security and oversight practices such as red-teaming (simulating attacks to find vulnerabilities) and rigorous testing to ensure AI models can't be easily misused or induce harm (Allen et al., 2025). It also means international coordination on AI safety standards – since AI threats can cross borders, democracies should share information on emerging risks and best practices to handle them. For example, countries might agree on protocols for AI research labs to report when they create a model with capabilities that could pose societal threats, similar to how we track dangerous pathogens. Additionally, this track includes legal and regulatory tools: enforcing privacy laws so that companies cannot just seize personal or government data for AI training without consent or oversight, and updating antitrust policies to address the unique market power that large AI firms might hold (e.g. control of critical computing resources or data). In short, the protective track is about safeguarding democracy – ensuring AI doesn't become a black box of authority or a weapon against the public.

Opportunity Maximization Track (empowerment): The flip side is deliberately steering AI towards public interest uses. One of our key recommendations is that AI policy should 'attend as much to opportunities as to potential harms' (Allen et al., 2025). This means governments should ask not only 'How do we stop bad outcomes?' but also 'How can we achieve good outcomes with AI that won't happen on their own?' Many beneficial applications of AI may be under-provided by the market, because they serve broad social needs rather than private profit. Think of AI for public health (e.g. early warning systems for pandemics), for climate and sustainability (e.g. optimizing energy grids, climate modeling), for social services (e.g. improving access to benefits, personalized education for underserved communities), and indeed for democratic processes themselves (e.g. tools to help legislators draft better laws or citizens to engage with government). These are areas where commercial AI development might not invest heavily, since the returns are diffuse. Therefore, our strategy calls for significant public investment in AI R&D for public goods. Just as governments fund basic scientific research that the private sector finds too long term, they should fund

AI initiatives aimed at societal wellbeing. For example, a national institute could develop open-source AI models tailored for use by local governments or NGOs – perhaps an 'AI for Cities' program that helps cities of all sizes deploy AI in traffic management, resource allocation, and civic engagement while respecting privacy and equity. By investing in these areas, we not only get useful tools, but also broaden who benefits from AI beyond the usual Silicon Valley stakeholders (Allen et al., 2025).

Another critical aspect of seizing opportunities is building human capacities and institutions for democratic oversight of AI. Right now, governments often struggle to hire and retain experts who understand AI, resulting in a knowledge gap between regulators and the regulated. To close this gap, we recommend strategies like creating a 'tech talent pipeline into public service' (Allen et al., 2025). This might include scholarship programs that fund STEM students in exchange for a stint in government, or rotational fellowships that bring AI engineers into agencies for public-interest projects. It could also mean updating curricula to blend engineering with ethics and public policy, so the next generation of AI developers are trained to think about social context from the start. Additionally, to empower citizens, we need broad-based AI literacy and public engagement. Just as democracies benefit when citizens have a baseline understanding of economics or law, we will need to educate people about AI's capabilities and pitfalls in an accessible way. Public deliberation forums (like citizens' assemblies on AI) could give representative groups of people the chance to learn and debate AI policy options, feeding their conclusions into policymaking. All this echoes the ethos of power-sharing: it's not just experts and politicians who should shape AI's future, but the public itself.

The dual-track approach can be summarized simply: protect society from AI's threats, while proactively directing AI to achieve societal goals. These two tracks are interdependent. By articulating a positive vision for AI (e.g. AI that helps solve our hardest problems and improves quality of life), we create political momentum and public support for the hard work of enacting tough protections (because people see there is much to gain, not just things to lose). Conversely, by establishing strong guardrails, we build the trust and stability needed to safely deploy AI in innovative ways for public benefit. In implementing this strategy, we must be pragmatic and prioritize. Not every good use of AI can be foreseen or funded by government, and not every risk can be eliminated. But a governance regime guided by the principle of power-sharing will consistently ask: Does this policy/action broaden the distribution of AI's benefits and the inclusivity of oversight? If yes, it's likely on the right track.

From local laboratories to a federal framework

How do we get from our current situation to this envisioned future of democratic AI governance? History provides a useful analogy. In the early United States, the first attempt at national governance (under the Articles of Confederation) left most power to individual states and had a weak central authority. This patchwork governance proved inadequate for problems that transcended state lines – issues of trade, defense, and currency that no single state could handle alone. The solution was the US Constitution, which created a stronger federal government while still reserving significant autonomy for states. This evolution – from loose local efforts to a more unified framework – has parallels in today's quest for AI governance.

Right now, in the absence of comprehensive federal policy, we see a blossoming of state and local initiatives on AI. US states, fulfilling their role as 'laboratories of democracy', have indeed become first movers in AI governance (Kohler, 2025). As of this writing, dozens of state laws on AI have been proposed or passed, covering issues from AI in hiring, to automated driving, to AI use in government agencies (Norden, 2023). Cities like New York have implemented algorithms task forces to audit municipal AI systems (such as those used for allocating public services or policing), and states like Connecticut and Colorado now require government offices to inventory and assess their AI tools (Anex-Ries, 2025). These efforts are incredibly valuable. They generate knowledge about what works and what doesn't on the ground. They also reflect local values – for instance, one state might emphasize privacy strongly, another might focus on preventing algorithmic bias in employment. As one policy analyst put it, statehouses are 'fizzing with AI initiatives' and are turning the classic laboratories of democracy into laboratories for AI policy innovation (Sanders, 2024). In a sense, each state is a mini test case for democratic AI governance approaches.

However, just as the Articles of Confederation era taught us, a purely local approach is not enough for a challenge of this magnitude. National coordination is essential. Without some federal standards or infrastructure, we risk incoherence and inequality. For example, if State A has strict AI transparency laws and State B has none, a company could deploy a system affecting both states but only residents in A get to know how it works. Or companies might flock to the most permissive jurisdiction (a 'race to the bottom'), undermining stricter states' protections. Additionally, many AI issues – like autonomous weapons, interstate commerce involving AI products, or AI-driven financial markets – simply cannot be managed by states alone. We are already seeing concerns about a patchwork of AI rules. In fact, a recent analysis warned that in the absence of clear federal direction, states may struggle with an incoherent 'patchwork' governance that leaves gaps and inconsistencies (Sanders, 2024). Another risk is that individual states can be more easily pressured by powerful tech lobbies; a fragmented approach might let companies play jurisdictions off each other (Grillaert et al., 2025). These are strong arguments for why a unified framework – a 'federal constitution' of AI governance, if you will – is needed to tie together the various local efforts and ensure baseline democratic safeguards everywhere.

What might a federal AI governance framework look like? For starters, it should establish nationwide standards on core issues: transparency requirements for AI that significantly affects people's rights, a prohibition on the most egregious harmful uses (for instance, social scoring of citizens by government, or AI for illegal mass surveillance), and protections for civil rights in automated decisions (building on things like the Biden Administration's AI Bill of Rights principles). It could create a federal agency or expand an existing one (such as the National Institute of Standards and Technology or the Federal Trade Commission) to oversee AI developers and deployers, auditing them for compliance and handling public complaints. Notably, this doesn't mean micromanaging all AI innovation from Washington – far from it. It means setting guardrails and goals that apply uniformly, so that the fruits of state experimentation can be shared and scaled, and so that no state falls woefully behind on protecting its citizens.

Crucially, a federal framework should be built in a collaborative, power-sharing manner with states and cities, not be mandated from on high. Just as the US Constitution reserves powers to the states, the ideal AI governance regime will maintain room for local innovation and stricter rules where communities deem necessary. Federal law might set a floor of protections and rights (for example, a national rule requiring people be informed when an AI system is making significant decisions about them), but states could go further if appropriate (perhaps one state pilots a requirement for algorithmic impact assessments that others watch and later adopt). There should also be formal channels for state and local input into national AI strategy – e.g. a federal AI council that includes governors, mayors, or municipal AI officials, alongside federal regulators and citizen representatives. In other words, multi-level governance is key: local knowledge and experimentation feeding upward, and national resources and consistency supporting the local level.

The evolution shouldn't stop at the national level either, because AI is a global phenomenon. In the twenty-first century, even a strong national governance scheme needs to plug into international coordination – much as the US Constitution had to eventually engage in treaties and international law. AI algorithms trained in one country can be deployed in another; data flows across borders, and so do AI research talents and investment. Democracies worldwide should find common cause in managing AI. We are already seeing nascent efforts: the European Union is finalizing a comprehensive AI Act that will regulate AI systems based on risk levels, and the US and EU had begun to collaborate through venues like the Trade and Technology Council on AI standards. The G7 has launched the 'Hiroshima AI process' to harmonize principles among leading democracies. These are like the early conventions and compacts – useful, but not yet binding or universal.

What's needed is movement toward an international framework where democratic nations agree on basic norms and guardrails for AI, analogous to how they have agreements on human rights or nuclear non-proliferation. That could include sharing best practices for safe AI development, coordinating export controls on the most dangerous AI tech (to prevent it from getting into the hands of rogue regimes or terrorists), and committing to use AI in ways that uphold democratic values (for instance, not using AI to censor the press or discriminate against minorities). Some experts even propose a treaty on AI, though realistically it may start as a softer alliance of like-minded nations. The optimistic scenario described earlier, where a coalition of democracies leads on AI, is essentially a geopolitical extension of this idea (Amodei, 2024). By banding together, democracies can create a *de facto* global standard that nudges others to follow. If enough of the world's innovation and markets adhere to pro-democratic AI norms, it will be hard for outliers to chart a completely different course without facing isolation or backlash.

To sum up, developing AI governance from local to global is a bit like the path of American federalism writ large: we start with diverse, bottom-up experiments, but we must federate these efforts into a coherent whole that can meet the scale of the challenge. Local initiative is indispensable as a source of creativity and democratic engagement. But localities alone cannot govern AI any more than 13 separate states could adequately provide for the common defense of the United States in the early 1780s. The progression should be: local → national → international, each building on the lessons and legitimacy of the previous level. And at every level, the governing philosophy should reflect Power-Sharing Liberalism: including stakeholders, distributing benefits, and ensuring accountability.

Conclusion: AI governance as a democratic renaissance

The coming years will test our collective wisdom and resolve. AI is often portrayed as a threat to democracy – and as we have seen, it certainly could be if left unguided in the hands of a powerful few. But there is nothing preordained about AI leading to Orwellian surveillance or digital dictators.

That outcome is a choice, not an inevitability. With enlightened governance, we can make a different choice: to use AI as a tool to renew and strengthen democracy. In fact, the challenge of governing AI and the unseemly corruption that envelopes everything when the rule of law is bypassed might be just the catalyst American democracy needs to reinvent itself for the twenty-first century.

Consider how grappling with AI could reinvigorate democratic institutions. To manage this complex technology, governments will have to become more agile, informed, and responsive, characteristics that benefit governance overall. Public participation mechanisms introduced for AI oversight could spill over to other areas of policy, giving citizens greater voice in all manner of decisions. By insisting on aligning AI with human rights and dignity, we reinforce those principles across the board. By investing in education and transparency around AI, we double-down on the enlightenment values of knowledge and reason in public affairs. In short, meeting the AI governance challenge can drive much-needed reforms in our democratic processes, making them more inclusive and forward-looking. If anything, the unfolding negative example of AI non-governance and the exploitation schemes it enables should be a catalyst to paint a picture of a radically different democratic future.

We should also take heart in the fact that many democracies have faced existential technological disruptions in the past and emerged all the stronger for it. The printing press, the industrial revolution, the rise of radio and television – each upended how society operated, concentrated new powers, and threatened chaos. Yet, through adaptability and the establishment of new rules of the road (from free press protections to antitrust laws to public broadcasting norms), democracies found ways to bend these technologies toward the public interest. AI is arguably more rapid and wide-ranging in impact, but the principle remains: we can govern what we create, if we have the will to do so. 'We can *choose* the extent to which we want to relinquish decision-making power to corporations, lobbyists, and experts', Zimmermann concludes. 'We can *choose* which risks we are willing to accept, and to which AI-enabled benefits we want to aspire' (Zimmermann, 2026: 104).

The dual-track, Power-Sharing Liberalism approach offers a path forward that is hopeful but clear-eyed. It does not naively assume the market or tech executives alone will get it right, nor does it fearfully reject innovation. It calls for shaping the evolution of AI in line with our highest values: liberty, equality, community, and justice. It also recognizes that in a pluralistic society, this shaping must be done through sharing power, through democratic debate and compromise, not imposed by either an unaccountable elite or a Luddite impulse. It is a grand experiment – but then, democracy itself is a grand experiment, always a work in progress.

In practical terms, success will likely come incrementally, and we must gird ourselves for significant setbacks. We will implement some protections, see what issues arise, adjust course; we will launch pilot projects for beneficial AI, learn from failures, and expand on successes. Internationally, we will hash out disagreements with allies and gradually build norms. The key is to keep the end goal firmly in view: a world in which AI is a force for the common good rather than a money factory for the already super-empowered, embedded in and subjected to democratic oversight from the humans whom technology impacts at all levels. In such a world, scenarios like the Trump–Musk DOGE fiasco would be impossible – no public data troves handed over without accountability, no AI deployment without transparency and consent. Instead, we'd see things like an AI system managed by a public hospital network that helps all clinicians diagnose rare diseases (because it was trained on aggregated and ethically shared health records), or a city AI system co-designed with residents to equitably route public transit. We'd see voters more informed, not less, because AI is steering citizens toward knowledge rather than propaganda, while it potentially illuminates policy impacts. We might even see global collaborations, where, say, scientists from many countries use AI to accelerate climate solutions, guided by an international panel that ensures the tech is shared and its use is equitable.

This is not a utopia; it's within our grasp if we work for it. Yes, there are risks of missteps and the power dynamics are daunting. But as a society, we are not passive spectators to the AI revolution – we are the authors of its trajectory. The governance decisions we make now will echo for decades. We owe it to ourselves and future generations to ensure those echoes resound to enable a thriving democracy rather than a technocratic dystopia.

Ultimately, governing AI effectively means recognizing that AI safety and democratic governance are inseparable. As recent analyses underscore, ensuring technical safety in AI systems is fundamentally about preserving democracy itself. Bridging gaps between theory and practice, and between STEM and humanities perspectives, is not simply an academic task – it is central to the viability of democratic institutions in an AI-shaped future (Stanger et al., 2024: 21).

The recent attempts at technocratic centralization, such as DOGE, serve as an urgent reminder of democracy's fragility. But they also offer a moment of clarity – an opportunity for citizens and policymakers to reaffirm that transparency, deliberation, and accountable governance remain indispensable rather than disposable inefficiencies (Green, 2025). By confronting these risks head-on, we not only protect democracy from erosion but set the stage for its renewal. AI governance, in the final analysis, is about who we want to be in the age of intelligent machines. If we commit to a vision of shared power, human dignity, and collective flourishing, and if we craft policies to match, we can turn AI into a pillar of democratic renewal. It can help us rebuild trust in institutions, solve problems that have long plagued our society, and extend the fruits of prosperity to more people. Far from heralding 'the end of democracy', the AI era – properly governed – can mark a new beginning. It is a rare moment of both peril and promise. By deepening democracy through prudent AI governance, we ensure that the promise prevails.

Let us therefore proceed with both caution and optimism, armed with the knowledge of the pitfalls, inspired by the possibilities, and steadfast in the conviction that democracy, though tested, will adapt and endure. With Power-Sharing Liberalism as our guide and proactive governance as our tool, we can and will fight for an AI that serves We, the people. That is the essence of democratic governance – and it is how we turn AI from a threat into an opportunity for human freedom and flourishing in the twenty-first century.

References

Allen, D. (2023), *Justice by Means of Democracy*. University of Chicago.

Allen, D., Hubbard, S., Lim, W., et al. (2025), A roadmap for governing AI: technology governance and power-sharing liberalism. *AI and Ethics* 5: 3355–3377.

Amodei, D. (2024), Machines of loving grace: How AI could transform the world for the better. Available online at: https://www.darioamodei.com/essay/machines-of-loving-grace (last accessed March 15, 2026).

Anex-Ries, Q. (2025), Regulating public sector AI: Emerging trends in state legislation. *Center for Democracy and Technology* (January 10, 2025). Available online at: https://cdt.org/insights/regulating-public-sector-ai-emerging-trends-in-state-legislation/ (last accessed March 15, 2026).

Green, B. (2025), DOGE plan to push AI across the US federal government is wildly dangerous. *Tech Policy Press* (March 6, 2025) Available online at: https://www.techpolicy.press/doge-plan-to-push-ai-across-the-us-federal-government-is-wildly-dangerous/ (last accessed March 15, 2026).

Grillaert, K., Kennedy, M., and Okolo, C.T. (2025), Risks of state-led ai governance in a federal policy vacuum. *Tech Policy Press* (February 6, 2025). Available online at: https://www.techpolicy.press/risks-of-state-led-ai-governance-in-a-federal-policy-vacuum/(last accessed March 15, 2026).

Hawkins, A. (2025), Starlink poised to take over $2.4 billion contract to overhaul air traffic control communication. *The Verge*. Available online at: https://www.theverge.com/news/620777/starlink-verizon-contract-faa-communication-musk (last accessed March 15, 2026).

Kohler, S. (2025), Technology federalism: U.S. states at the vanguard of AI governance. *Carnegie Endowment for International Peace*. Available online at: https://carnegieendowment.org/research/2025/02/technology-federalism-us-states-at-the-vanguard-of-ai-governance?lang=en (last accessed March 15, 2026).

Norden, L. (2023), States take the lead on regulating artificial intelligence. Brennan Center for Justice. Available online at: https://www.brennancenter.org/our-work/research-reports/states-take-lead-regulating-artificial-intelligence#:~:text=Intelligence%20www,greatly%20increasing%20year%20over%20year (last accessed March 15, 2026).

Otterbein, H. and Wren, A. (2025), What's Elon Musk doing with your data? *Politico*. Available online at: https://www.politico.com/news/2025/02/20/musk-data-ai-00205259 (last accessed March 15, 2026).

Salvaggio, E. (2025), Anatomy of an AI coup. *Tech Policy Press*. Available online at: https://www.techpolicy.press/anatomy-of-an-ai-coup/ (last accessed March 15, 2026).

Sanders, T. (2024), *The Three Levels of Public Interest AI*. Tech Policy Press. Available online at: https://www.techpolicy.press/the-three-levels-of-public-interest-ai/ (last accessed March 15, 2026).

Stanger, A. (2025), DOGE threat: How government data would give an AI company extraordinary power. *The Conversation*. Available online at: https://theconversation.com/doge-threat-how-government-data-would-give-an-ai-company-extraordinary-power-250907 (last accessed March 15, 2026).

Stanger, A., Kraus, J., Lim, W., et al. (2024), *Terra Incognita*: The governance of artificial intelligence in global perspective. *Annual Reviews* 27: 445–465. https://www.annualreviews.org/content/journals/10.1146/annurev-polisci-041322-042247 (last accessed March 15, 2026).

Swan, J., Schleifer, T., Haberman, M., et al. (2025), How Elon Musk executed his takeover of the federal bureaucracy. *The New York Times*. Available online at: https://www.nytimes.com/2025/02/28/us/politics/musk-federal-bureaucracy-takeover.html

Zhao, J., Feng, Q., Wu, P., et al. (2019), Learning from longitudinal data in electronic health record and genetic data to improve cardiovascular event prediction. *Scientific Reports* 9, article number: 717.

Zimmermann, A. (2026), *Democratizing AI*. Manchester University Press.

12

Affirmative not critical: How AI language systems are changing the political public sphere

Regina Kreide

The current diagnoses of the crisis-ridden state of democracy are often similar in one respect. They point to dysfunctionalities in the political public sphere that are linked to the digital media revolution. Large technology companies know our purchasing needs long before we do, bots offer to be our best friend and 'intelligent' language systems promote candidates in the next election and even suggest that we can forget about democracy anyway. The assessments of how best to deal with various forms of digital interference range from the suggestion that AI will quickly become banal through everyday use, to the impressive warning that AI will eventually take on a life of its own (especially in the military sector) and humans will be at its mercy, and to – most realistically – attempts to subordinate AI to democratic regulatory processes.

Annette Zimmermann attempts this and, in her brilliant *Democratizing AI*, impressively shows the obstacles posed by AI development to equal democratic participation, skillfully combining an empirically saturated description of social problems with normative philosophical reflections. She traces the enormous market power of the technology industry and the associated unequal 'risk distribution' experienced by some citizens. While the total wealth of the ten richest tech companies in the world is estimated at around 1.62 trillion dollars, the rest of the population benefits to a far lesser extent. The same extreme disparity is evident in the spread of risk when it comes to the monitoring of behavior, uncontrolled data sharing, and military development – and the barely-foreseeable undermining of democratic conditions.

The strategies Zimmermann proposes based on her diagnosis are particularly impressive. She is one of those who neither trivializes nor diabolizes AI. Rather, her strategy envisages a combination of early detection, analysis, and recurring challenges to AI deployments, relying on a sophisticated and realistic combination of participatory bottom-up mechanisms and regulatory top-down initiatives. In my view, Zimmermann's study leaves little room for fundamental criticism. As befits a well-argued study, she anticipated some of the criticism. For example, what to say to those who do not believe that democracy is the best possible form of government, but who more or less polemically take the position that this predicate belongs to libertarianism, which can be seen to offer solutions to problems more efficiently and with the help of AI. Apart from the fact that one can show how at least the approximation of economic and political equality contributes to a more stable – and just – society, Zimmermann argues that there is in fact not much that can be done to counter authoritarians. Ultimately, while I agree with her voluntarist approach, one needs to reassure oneself about the value of political autonomy.

Irrespective of this, I would first like to address a point that, as far as I can see, Zimmermann has not addressed, but which underpins the thesis of the infiltration of democracy by AI development and drastically demonstrates the scope of increased AI intervention in democratic public spheres. Of crucial importance for assessing the role of AI for democratization are issues in the philosophy of language, and especially the question of whether AI-generated programs and their avatars can be described as rational actors that meet the requirements of reasonable understanding. I will show that AI-generated language programs, which also underlie social media, are *minimally* rational actors, that they can learn up to a certain level and are already part of the public sphere, but that it is also important to know the limits of their competence in terms of understanding symbolic communication. I will argue that AI in its current form primarily reproduces 'affirmative' forms of interaction, which are reactions that adapt to existing conditions and thus exclude self-reflective criticism. And I follow from this that AI's material preconditions steer public debates in an authoritarian direction.

It makes sense to outline what is meant here by a functioning democratic public sphere and by communicative understanding (1), in order to argue in a second step that AI programs do possess a minimal rationality, including basic competences in the generation and understanding of meaning, but fail to fulfil other conditions on the presumptive rationality of communicative exchanges, such as consistency, inclusivity, and equality (2). Third, this leads to the assessment that language-generating programs primarily promote affirmative user reactions and an authoritarian culture (3). As a supplement to Zimmermann's strategy proposals, a critique of ideology should be pursued on the basis of the previous argumentation, which remains scientifically and politically vigilant against the deceptive maneuvers of AI power (4).

Political public sphere as ideology

As with all decisive normative ideas, what the political public sphere actually means is controversial both in theory and practice. In view of the space available here, I will take as my starting point a deliberative conception of the public sphere that goes back to the work of Jürgen Habermas (1989; 2005), Bernhard Peters (2008), Seyla Benhabib (1992), and Nancy Fraser (2007). Habermas understands the public sphere not simply as a public space such as a marketplace, but as a social space of communicative, rational interaction; a place of collective self-understanding. As the basis for democratic decisions, debates in the public sphere form a necessary condition for legislative processes, which can then be said to have come about legitimately. The political public sphere can be imagined as communication and decision-making processes situated between the center and the periphery (Peters, 2008). The center comprises the political system, which consists of parliament, courts, and administration and in which decisions are routinely made, judgements are passed, and clients' cases are dealt with. On the other side of the axis lies the periphery, which is formed by 'civil society'.

Unlike in Hegel or Marx, this concept of civil society includes neither economic nor state organizations. Rather, it is made up of spontaneously formed associations, organizations, and movements that are directly connected to the private spheres of life and that pass on problem-solving discourses on issues of general interest to the public sphere (Habermas, 1996: 354–359). In *descriptive* terms, the public sphere is a resource of meaning for opinion and knowledge formation as well as collective learning. And *normatively*, it serves as a backdrop against which social pathologies that stand in the way of the creation of cultural meaning are highlighted. In this way, the public sphere acts as a starting point and a benchmark for the criticism of social conditions.

There are three decisive criteria that provide information about a legitimate public sphere, which in turn is a prerequisite for successful democratization. First, the conditions for legitimization can already be found in the public sphere itself. Free public spaces are not only places where social problems are discussed, they already possess a *rationalizing power* that generates legitimacy. This happens when the various value orientations come into their own in the process of public deliberation, and an exchange of reasons for or against a controversial position can test its acceptability (Habermas, 2023).

Second, these rational results are achieved by at least two standards of communication practice. First, the possibility of understanding meaning. According to Habermas, the shared linguistic meaning resulting from public debate is an essential cement of societies. The understanding of linguistic signs ultimately also implies agreement with what is generally understood. This is the microstructure of human societies, which makes it possible to compare the interaction between a single person and a language-generating machine on the one hand, and the interaction between two people on the other. Second, and just as importantly, the *inclusion* of all relevant contributions in the public sphere must be achieved on the basis of communicative *equality* of all contributions. Inclusion is not only important in order to arrive at the most original and appropriate solution to a problem (which, quite pragmatically, occurs when the most controversial proposals are discussed). Inclusion also strengthens the idea of a public debate that keeps the common good in mind.

And third, the public sphere itself is a power factor that has both descriptive and normative aspects. Habermas speaks about an 'official' cycle of power that is democratically generated and in which the 'weak' public of the periphery influence the 'strong' public of the political system (Fraser, 1990: 109–142). The political system in turn is supposed to control the administrative apparatuses and the economy. In this cycle, the legitimizing force of *communicative power* is created, which is generated in the public sphere by the public itself and which, ideally, is able to expose, publicize, and criticize communicative distortions, deceptions, abuses, and degradations in general (Habermas, 1996: 359).

These three criteria form the basis of the following analysis, which examines the question of whether and to what extent AI and its avatars have the competences mentioned, and to what extent they are involved in the process of creating critical communicative power – and even whether they possess the technical prerequisites for this.

What AI can do – and what it can't

It is advisable at first to outline how language-generating programs work. Large language models (LLMs) assign word sequences to certain repetition probabilities. As early as the 1950s, words began to be represented as vectors by the frequency of their occurrence in certain texts. Around the same time, the idea emerged that the meaning of a word – and this is exactly how meaning is understood in AI – can be determined by its distribution in language use. This gave rise to the idea of *vector semantics*, which has characterized the processing of natural language (Coeckelbergh, 2022; 2024). The meaning of a word is captured by its word vectors. Currently, the learning and feature-based paradigm of neural networks, also known as connectionism, characterizes AI research. The main task of this 'neural

AI' is to equip systems with learning algorithms and then allow them to continue learning independently with training data (Lyre, 2020: 325–347). The successes of this technology include the image recognition service AlexNet (2012) and the unexpected victory of AlphaGo against the human Go world champion Lee Sedol. It has since been recognized that practical success is achieved when very large and multi-layered neural networks and huge amounts of data are used – the LLMs.

These language programs form the basis for search engines, but also for bots, ChatGPT, and automated fact-checking systems.[1] While chatbots (such as Replika) act as digital friends, partners, or mentors, ChatGPT is primarily an assistance system that answers questions, creates or improves texts, helps with project management, etc. The automated fact-checking system in turn determines whether statements are true and supported by corresponding evidence or not, and provides an explanation for the judgment made – it acts as a corrective. The relationship level of communication is important when interacting with chatbots. With the fact-checking system, however, the content of the communicative statements is decisive. Dialogue interaction with ChatGPT, on the other hand, combines both. This involves complex content that is created in collaboration with the user.

But what can language-generating programs achieve against the background of the normative criteria outlined above and what are their limits? Let's start with the question of whether we can speak of the *rationality* of AI systems and describe them as actors. According to Michael Tomasello, *actors* are the originators of goal-oriented behavior that compares and influences behavioral sequences with those target states that result from a previously defined goal. In this sense, a drone or – in Tomasello's example – a grass-mowing robot are indeed actors ('intentions in action'), even if they lack a common background of world knowledge ('common ground') (McDowell, 2011: 1–18; Tomasello, 2022: 13–20). AI research now goes one step further and speaks of 'minimally rational actors' (Dretske 1999: 19). In the case of a minimally rational actor, the content of the intentions is also the content for the originator of the goal-oriented behavior, the robot. The actor therefore acts for a reason; that is, what takes it in the direction of its goal. The performance of recent language-generating programs such as GTP-4 and Gemini therefore go beyond the stage of Holger Lyre's 'stochastic parrots' and have a certain learning potential (Lyre, 2020: 325–347). One problem, however, is that bots (including Replika) become entangled in contradictions and cannot be fully responsible for their knowledge of

1 Thanks are due to Lisa Schurrer, whose doctoral thesis on 'Automated Public Spheres and Artificial Communication. Political public sphere and communicative action in the light of AI-based technologies' was submitted to ETH Zurich in 2023.

the world. An example is that although the bot Replika appears to adapt its beliefs to a factual question (What colors are there?), it does not do so in a reflective way. Replika has no insight into the contradictions of its self-generated statements. Replika believes both that swans are blue and – after the statement was corrected by the user – that they are white. The rationality of the actor therefore already has some weaknesses at the consistency level. The AI-generated language practice remains *minimally* rational.

The next question is to what extent language-generating systems can pursue a *meaningful* language practice as minimal rational actors and to what extent they can participate in inclusive, justificatory practices in the public sphere. If the language-generating systems are equal participants in communicative interactions, then they promote or hinder the functioning of the political public sphere – something that can be regularly experienced in espionage scandals, election interference, fake news, etc. Wittgenstein's idea of the language game is relevant here. What is crucial is that LLMs are increasingly becoming participants in the language game themselves as we incorporate them into our linguistic practices. If linguistic meaning manifests itself in language use, this also applies to LLMs (and their avatars). The more useful or entertaining they are for us, the more they become our communicative partners and integrate themselves into our language game – and the more they acquire a *social semantic basis* (Lyre, 2020: 325–347). Meaning and representation take place in and through speech in a social context. If a language game exists beyond a social context, such as a game of chess, then one can speak of a *functional* semantics, which remains limited to the respective rules of the particular language game. A more sophisticated concept of meaning therefore requires at least an indirect reference to *world knowledge*, which can develop through the learning processes of the machine (Lyre, 2020: 325–347).

However, AI language systems still only offer a *simulation* of intelligible language. This is because language models such as ChatGPT have so far only restricted contact with the world. They operate in a limited language context, a context that is always pre-structured and from which they themselves cannot generate any new meaning. This could change, however, as they learn from enormous amounts of text that have been and continue to be generated by us grounded beings in the form of large internet archives, the entire Wikipedia resource, and world literature. So far, however, the machine learning process has focused on *representing* the meaning of words, which is done using vectors and feedback control mechanisms (Shanahan, 2024). Machine learning is therefore not just about the physical properties of texts, but about a *minimal generation of meaning* that results from the co-occurrence and calculated relevance of words (Lyre, 2020). The language programs can be described as minimally rational actors with language-like competencies in understanding meaning. This does not come close to the previously developed criteria for a normatively functioning political public sphere. The distance to generating meaningful communication among equals is too great, the neuronal, technical preconditions that exist between humans and machines are too different. The crucial point here, however, is that meaning is indeed generated in the interaction between humans and machines – in the reciprocal use of language. The indistinguishability of the interventions of humans and machines requires a new conceptual tool to understand the influence that language-generating programs have on our public sphere. Despite the fact that they are minimally rational actors with minimal semantic potential, they have become serious actors.

But do LLMs also aim to be inclusive and allow all contributions equally? In the years after the turn of the millennium it was argued that the emergence of digital media supports deliberative democracy. Access was unrestrictedly open, there were no restrictive guidelines regarding the choice of topic, all participants had equal rights in the exchange, and the circle of all participants was also unrestricted. As Joshua Cohen and Archon Fung note, one of the most radical transformations of the public sphere has been the transition from a one-to-many model of communication to a many-to-many model (Cohen and Fung, 2021). The gatekeepers, however, have by no means disappeared. Rather, it is no longer quality media and trained journalists who ensure truth and balance, but tech companies who have redistributed the network and become private and politically active providers and gatekeepers all in one. The fact that language-generating programs explicitly leave room for invective plays into their hands, as does the fact that they place certain content more prominently than others through corresponding algorithm formations. The originally normative idea of a barrier-free, inclusive digital public sphere is thereby transformed into its opposite.

And finally, the self-learning programs and their avatars shut down the potential for the development of communicative power. Why is that? Communicative power, to paraphrase Hannah Arendt, is a form of political power, a power that no one possesses, but that arises between people when they act politically – beyond a narrow focus on asserting their own interests, realizing collective goals, or even making administratively binding decisions (Arendt 1970: 45). Jürgen Habermas has taken up this idea and reinterpreted it as *communicative power*. Generally speaking, communicative power refers to the unhindered exercise of public freedom by citizens. More specifically, communicative power has a cognitive side, through which free, deliberative processing, a free public exchange of information, and arguments on important topics can take place and results can be achieved through a fair procedure.[2] Communicative power also makes it possible to question existing relationships and at the same time enable a new view of things and relationships.[3] It unfolds, as one could describe it, a power of world disclosure, which can direct our gaze to the new in the world through creative connections and experimental forms of communication (Habermas, 1996: 149). This power of questioning and negation can give rise to something new and, ideally, emancipatory.

But to what extent can language-generating programs achieve this? We have seen that exchanges in the public sphere are rational to the extent that they critically scrutinize existing statements, one's own as well as those of others. The programs, on the other hand, are *affirmative*; they reinforce established (conventional) norms without subjecting them to critical scrutiny. This can be seen in at least three aspects. First, in the generally narcissistic communication with bots, the attitude of reciprocity necessary for social cohesion and a civic mindset is lost – as with Replika, for example (Schurrer, 2023: 159). Replika plays the role of 'best friend' without having to be asked how she is doing – because the answer is known: She's doing very well. Always. And Replika in turn supports every statement made by her counterpart with approval, reinforcement, and repetition. There are no questions, critical objections or queries, or even other positions.

Second, the attention of citizens is gained according to their ability to pay – whether as advertisers on platforms or as ongoing citizens. Just recently, shortly before the federal elections in Germany on 23 February 2025, so-called 'micro-targeting' was discussed again, in which tech companies bring products and political advertising to users based on algorithms, depending on financial investment and profit optimization opportunities (Votta et al., 2024: 1–73). Political party advertising is treated as if it were a profitable product that is being sold. In this way, political parties hand over the power to decide who sees which content to the corporate players. Zimmermann speaks of the power of oligopolistic tech actors (pp. 29–30). In the end, the parties do not know who receives their messages and who they influence – despite the money they pay. Democratic parties are handing over their communicative power, placing it in the hands of tech companies and thereby also violating the European Union's data protection rules.

These developments reveal that self-learning programs are becoming increasingly innovative, but only *within* the vector framework; they are not able to create something new that could then function as a unique critique of the existing world or programs used. This is why language systems

2 For the concept of noumenal power, see also Forst (2024). For the concept of communicative power, see Habermas (1996: 148).

3 I would like to thank Peter Niesen for this hint.

solidify a certain world view and the preferences and prejudices of their creators. There is a lack of confrontation and thus a lack of development of alternative imagination. Taken together, the language-generating programs only fulfil the normative requirements of a fully-fledged member of a democratic public sphere in a very limited sense. They can act solely in a targeted manner with restrictions and expand their relationship to the world by learning in exchange with human language, thus generating minimal meaning. Against this background, the pressing question arises about the consequences for the public sphere and its democratizing role.

The erosion of the democratic public sphere

We are dealing with a highly ambivalent picture. From a linguistic–philosophical perspective, the legitimization conditions of an AI-supported democratic digital public sphere are only partially fulfilled. The use of AI systems can in some cases lead to a topic-specific increase in the rationality of opinion formation. And this in turn indirectly lowers the psychological barrier to political participation, as access to material is decentralized and technically easy (Schurrer, 2023: 303). On the other hand, however, AI-generated language interventions undermine democracy in the long term, as can be seen from four examples.

i) 'Littering' of the public sphere and artificial visualization.

The low access requirements lead to a high incidence of communicative intervention – mostly intentional. The political public sphere is virtually flooded with misinformation and 'noise' via social media. Simone Chambers and Jeffrey Kopstein show that digital information chaos is often a deliberate strategy by mostly far-right actors seeking to disrupt information through noise, nonsense, and sheer volume (Chambers and Kopstein, 2023: 225–240). In this way, the ideal of journalistic objectivity is turned against itself by tempting the mainstream media to show 'the other side', thereby calling the truth into question in the first place. Another aspect of this littering is that public spheres have become spaces in which various forms of disparagement and fake news are spreading like a rhizome. The concept of 'invective' is a helpful way to describe this. Invective encompasses all aspects of communication, verbal and non-verbal, that denigrate, insult, and exclude, both in terms of social theory and as a formal category (Müller-Mall, 2020: 86). Examples of invective range from cyberbullying (digital contexts in which many individuals concertedly disparage someone), to phenomena such as swarming and doxxing. In the case of swarming, many users deliberately post bad reviews in order to harm people – such as doctors or teachers – psychologically or economically. Doxxing involves searching for, collecting, and publishing as much data as possible about a person online, which can lead to public humiliation, belittling, and insults (Müller-Mall, 2020: 86). The current constitutional situation is not prepared for this at all.

The other side of littering is that it is now possible to demonstrate an artificially created visibility and reach that does not originate from an actual demand created by clicks and does not reflect the interests of the public. The visibility of certain political messages (in the case of the AfD in Germany, for example) is manipulated by algorithms, while on the other hand, hidden interference tactics can be demonstrated, as seen in the case of Cambridge Analytica or the Russian disinformation campaigns.[4] This can happen, for example, through targeted boosting of content by AfD supporters (Knüpfer et al., 2023). These developments are then picked up by the algorithms, which promote the content to specific groups of people who previously had nothing to do with the topic. Even if the direct effect on voting behavior has not yet been investigated (though neither has that of election posters), it can be assumed that there is a signaling effect.

ii) Fragmentation and degradation.

Access to the new social media and also to programs that generate language is only superficially barrier-free. Age limits, technical illiteracy, but also a still uneven global distribution of the internet and roaming access point to a persistent *digital divide*.[5] The new social media such as X, Tiktok, Snapchat, and others also have another marginalizing function. As Eli Pariser saw early on, they create a personalization that, through the individualized and sales-oriented algorithms of most search engines, leads to an infinite fragmentation and dispersion of what was once a *shared* public sphere (Pariser, 2012). AI systems thus contribute to the fragmentation of public space and reinforce mechanisms of exclusion. Furthermore, there are now studies (such as the UNESCO study *Challenging Systematic Prejudices: Bias Against Women and Girls in Large Language Models*, 2024) that clearly show that exclusionary mechanisms that promote a male, white, European perspective persist in the language-generating programs. This is

4 Katja Muñoz, Research Fellow, Centre for Geopolitics, Geo-Economics and Technology at the German Council on Foreign Relations (DGAP). Personal communication with the author (2004).

5 According to studies, a third of the world's population is still cut off from access to the internet (AlYahya, 2024).

because some of the data used to train GPT3 (the predecessor of ChatGPT) comes from Wikipedia, where 90 per cent of the entries are from white, middle-class European men. One can speak of a *digital colonialism* that is reaching the whole world via a 'path dependency' in relation to knowledge.

iii) Loss of trust in a democratic public sphere.

The aforementioned processes lead to a loss of trust in the power of the public sphere as a space that promotes the common good and generates truth. On a collective level, littering, artificial visualization, hate speech, and hierarchization lead to a division not only in social media itself, but also in the real public sphere. In the social sciences, this is referred to as 'affective polarization' and refers to the tendency of party supporters to publicly denigrate and distrust members of other parties (Druckman et al., 2021). On a more fundamental level, this leads to a loss of trust in democratic institutions. The American philosopher Daniel Dennett sees the biggest problem not in the fact that AI could take away jobs in the long term, but in the danger of imitating human communication so that it can no longer be distinguished from real people in the new digital context (Dennett, 2023). It is this uncertainty over whether statements are authentic, true, and correct that destroys trust in human interaction and ultimately in human freedom.

iv) On the road to authoritarianism.

These processes of a progressive infiltration of democratic public spheres become clearly visible, as we have seen, when the social context and the material foundations of AI's linguistic competence are taken into account. In addition to the basic capitalist structure, technical materiality, which has become a new structural component of linguistic communication, also plays a decisive role here. What is new is that both economic and technical power currently go hand in hand with political power and are reshaping the rational understanding of meaning in the public context to such an extent that it seems difficult to speak of a possible democratization of the public sphere (Risse, 2023). AI is perfectly adapted to the functionalities of a monopolistic and also oligopolistic market and undermines an important aspect of democracy in a fundamental way. There *appears* to be reason-guided communication, but it remains within the framework of vector logic; it is human-like and yet stops at the boundaries of inclusion and equality in public discourse, undermining trust in public debates. The structural conformism of AI language systems is a companion on the path to a techno-autocratic regime that promises freedom without democracy and only feigns equal participation and economic freedom.

This is because decisive changes have taken place in the relationship between capitalism and democracy – a development that plays into the hands of AI power. For a long time, it was believed that with the establishment of democratic conditions (e.g. after the fall of the so-called Iron Curtain), democratic development would follow economic growth. This thesis of self-perpetuating democratization has not held true. Instead, we are dealing with neoliberal surveillance capitalism, for which a new maxim applies: the more prosperity for some, the more democracy gets in the way. To a certain extent, as Quinn Slobodian has shown, a planned economy is good for economic growth. Countless special economic zones that puncture nation states like smallpox and manage venture capital (on the basis of a low-wage sector) beyond democratic co-determination while creating tax havens are even better, for the few.[6] If capital flows into new, unregulated low-tax zones, economies that want to control capital will be forced to imitate these anomalies. Following Adorno, one can speak of a *mimicry of techno-autocracy*. The fragmentation and polarization of the public sphere, the loss of trust in democratic institutions, and AI-generated affirmation and servility are in line with these developments.

In conclusion: What to do?

Through its minimally rational avatars, AI influences the formation of opinion and will, it floods the digital public with 'information rubbish', becomes entangled in self-contradictions, reproduces and reinforces racist, sexist, and other forms of exclusion, emphasizes disagreeable political content, undermines trust in democratic institutions, and yet is completely real, present, and uncritical. The material basis, its vector-relatedness, makes AI submissive and a learning 'tech soldier'. But what, according to this analysis, can be done to counter this path dependency on the undemocratic public sphere?

I want to close by focusing on a few proposals that complement Annette Zimmermann's sophisticated strategies. Zimmermann places a strong emphasis on analyzing possible counter-strategies (Zimmermann, 2025: 69–85). She clearly sees various short- and long-term risks that will arise from the unreflective use of AI. And she is aware of the 'Oppenheimer moment' of AI (pp. 7, 103), an irreversible point where human beings are no longer able to control the technology. Rather, she calls on all conceivable actors, but above all the democratic constituencies worldwide, to level out the existing asymmetry in the use of AI as far as possible.

6 In his impressive study on crack-up capitalism, Quinn Slobodian describes how there are already 5,400 extraterritorial territories worldwide (Slobodian, 2023).

She discusses a number of possibilities as particularly promising and divides her proposals for democratizing and regulating the use of AI into two broad strategies that are already present in both US and EU AI policy (pp. 55–61). In this way, the ideas for a democratic mastering of AI appear neither abstract nor unrealistic. The first – top-down – strategy consists of a heterogeneous bundle of approaches to regulating decisions about the use of AI itself. These include licensing regulations, institutionalized mechanisms for security checks before or after use by newly created public institutions, imposed either by the respective government or by industry players from the top-down. The latter could include, for example, labeling AI-generated content as such, a proposal that is already mentioned in the EU's Artificial Intelligence Act. Bot-generated content must be made transparent and clearly labeled as such. Systems should not only point out the limits of their knowledge, but also make the limits of their ability to act transparent. Bots, for example, should have to indicate when something is not within their scope of action.

Zimmermann's second strategy focuses on changing the way democratic electorates respond to the already deployed – or currently ongoing – use of AI, as exemplified by the bottom-up activism that led to the temporary local banning of facial recognition programs in parts of the US (p. 57). This type of strategy is a countervailing force, encompassing bottom-up agenda-setting, political activism, lobbying, or advocacy, with the aim of changing the goals and constraints of AI deployment as far as technically possible. One can also imagine new forms of politics (such as digital civil disobedience). A number of AI projects and initiatives have already emerged in response to the stereotypical, disparaging portrayal on the internet, which not only draw attention to the problems of AI, but also attempt to develop their own non-discriminatory technologies. In this way, citizens would be given meaningful opportunities to reclaim some of the decision-making power currently concentrated in the hands of large tech companies and to publicly challenge the wealth accumulation associated with these technologies (pp. 103–105).[7]

On the basis of the analyses presented here, one more general point could be expressly added to Zimmermann's suggestions. The economic power of oligopolistic corporations would have to be contained and the transformation of economic power into political power completely eliminated – an aspect that Zimmermann also clearly has in mind, but which, with the growing strength of the extreme political right almost worldwide, has

7 One example is Q, an attempt to create a voice assistant with a genderless voice; another example is F*xa, a feminist chatbot developed by a diverse team from the British organization Feminist Internet.

moved into the distant rather than near future.[8] Ultimately, however, the analysis also results in a challenge for academia. The main point that emerges from the above analysis, and which also provides information on what to do, is that more than ever, a critique of ideology is of crucial importance. The language-generating programs promise low entry thresholds, equal participation, transparency, and rationality – but, as we have seen, they are incapable of keeping their promises. This contradiction is the starting point for a critique of ideology. The work of Habermas, from *The Structural Transformation of the Public Sphere* to his recent publications on the subject, are entirely in the tradition of a critique of ideology; they are based on the assumption that the critical public sphere has become a sham and democratic politics a farce.

Ideology is a deception that has a firm grip on us. It is, in Adorno's words, true and false, affirmative and critical. It is true because a transcending idea (which may be religious, moral, or even technocratic–futuristic) is extracted from the existing world and projected onto another world that appears to be perfect, so that it completely contradicts the first, real world. In this way, difficult-to-solve problems (the climate crisis, for example) of late capitalist society are shifted *into the future*. And at the same time, ideology is wrong. You can see this when you analyze how the nature of such conditions determines thinking and what role ideology plays. Then the social contradictions become clear, and it is possible to see who benefits from them – in our case primarily the tech oligarchies. You can see neoliberalism's economic promise of freedom, which turns out to be hyper-control, the spread of poverty, and futile individual responsibility. And ideology is false precisely because it ignores social conflicts. It is the responsibility of critical science to analyze the decline of the democratic public sphere in such a way that possible alternative, emancipative counter-strategies emerge. Annette Zimmermann's essay is a great example of this and inspires hope.

References

AlYahya, D. (2024), Comment: Together we can end the digital divide that disenfranchises 2.6 billion people. *Reuters*. Available online at: https://www.reuters.com/sustainability/society-equity/comment-together-we-can-end-digital-divide-that-disenfranchises-26-billion-2024-09-17/ (last accessed February 1, 2025).

Arendt, H. (1970), *On Violence*. Harvest Books.

Benhabib, S. (1992), Models of public space. Hannah Arendt, the liberal tradition, and Jürgen Habermas. In: *Habermas and the Public Sphere*, ed. Craig Calhoun. MIT Press: 73–98.

8 See also Reich et al. (2021: 24).

Chambers, S. and Kopstein, J. (2023), Wrecking the public sphere: The new authoritarians' digital attack on pluralism and truth'. *Constellations* 30: 225–240.
Coeckelbergh, M. (2022), *Political Philosophy of AI: An Introduction*. Polity.
Coeckelbergh, M. (2024), *Why AI Undermines Democracy and What to do About it*. Polity.
Cohen, J. and Fung, A. (2021), Democracy and the digital public sphere. In: *Digital Technology and Democratic Theory*, eds. Lucy Bernholz, Hélène Landemore, and Rob Reich. University of Chicago Press.
Dennett, D.C. (2023), The problem with counterfeit people. *The Atlantic*. Available online at: https://www.theatlantic.com/technology/archive/2023/05/problem-counterfeit-people/674075/ (last accessed March 15, 2026).
Dretske, F.I. (1999), Machines, plants and animals: the origins of agency. *Erkenntnis* 51, no. 1: 19–31.
Druckman, J.N., Klar, S., Krupnikov, Y., et al. (2021), Affective polarization, local contexts and public opinion in America. *Nature Human Behaviour* 5: 28–38. https://doi.org/10.1038/s41562-020-01012-5
Forst, R. (2024), *The Noumenal Republic. Critical Constructivism After Kant*. Polity Press.
Fraser, N. (1990), Rethinking the public sphere: A contribution to the critique of actually existing democracy. In: *Public Space Reader*. Routledge.
Fraser, N. (2007), Transnationalising the public sphere: on the legitimacy and efficacy of public opinion in a Post-Westphalian World. *Theory, Culture and Society* 24, no. 4: 7–30.
Habermas, J. (1989), *The Structural Transformation of the Public Sphere. An Inquiry into a Category of Bourgeois Society*. MIT Press.
Habermas, J. (1996), *Between Facts and Norms: Contributions to a Discourse Theory of Law and Democracy*. William Rehg (trans.). MIT Press.
Habermas, J. (2023), *A New Structural Transformation of the Public Sphere and Deliberative Politics*. Wiley.
Habermas, J. (2005), Concluding comment on empirical approaches to deliberative politics. *Acta politica* 40, no. 3: 384–392.
Knüpfer, C.B., Schwemmer, C., and Heft, A. (2023), Politicization and right-wing normalization on YouTube: A topic-based analysis of the 'alternative influence network'. *International Journal of Communication*. https://ijoc.org/index.php/ijoc/article/view/20369/4381
Lyre, H. (2020), The state space of artificial intelligence. *Minds and Machines* 30, no. 3: 325–347.
McDowell, J. (2011), Some remarks on intention in action. *The Amherst Lecture in Philosophy* 6: 1–18.
Müller-Mall, S. (2020), The public sphere of disparaging statements: Constitutional perspectives along digital transformations of the public sphere. In: *Digital Transformations of the Public Sphere*, eds. Jan-Philipp Kruse and Sabine Müller-Mall. Velbrück: 78–102.
Pariser, E. (2012), *Filter Bubble: What the Internet is Hiding from You*. Penguin.
Peters, B. (2008), *Public Deliberation and Public Culture: The Writings of Bernhard Peters*, 1993–2005. Palgrave Macmillan.
Reich, R., Sahami, M., and Weinstein, J. (2021), *System Error. Where Big Tech Went Wong and How We Can Reboot*. HarperCollins.

Risse, M. (2023), *Political Theory of the Digital Age: Where Artificial Intelligence Might Take Us*. Cambridge University Press.

Schurrer, L. (2023), Automated public spheres and artificial communication. Political public sphere and communicative action in the light of AI-based technologies. Doctoral thesis, ETH Zurich.

Shanahan, M. (2024), Talking about Large Language Models. *Communications of the ACM* 67, no. 2 (February 2024): 68–79. https://doi.org/10.1145/3624724

Slobodian, Q. (2023), *Crack-Up Capitalism: Market Radicals and the Dream of a World Without Democracy*. Penguin.

Tomasello, M. (2022), *The Evolution of Agency: Behavioral Organisation from Lizards to Humans*. MIT Press: 13–20.

Votta, F., Kruschinski, S., Hove, M., et al. (2024), Who does(n't) target you? Mapping the worldwide usage of online political micro-targeting. *Journal of Quantitative Description: Digital Media* 4: 1–73. DOI: 10.51685/jqd.2024.01

Zimmermann, A. (2026), Democratizing AI. Manchester University Press.

13

On the variety of ways of making philosophical sense of AI

Mathias Risse

The owl of Minerva in times of rapid technological change

One thing that stands out as far as recent developments around Artificial Intelligence (AI) are concerned is the sheer pace of change. The very term 'Artificial Intelligence' appears first in a research proposal for a project at Dartmouth in 1956. This project occurs in the aftermath of enormous breakthroughs in previous decades, both in mathematical understanding of computation and in the design of digital computation devices. Its goal indeed was to create *artificial intelligence*: for a group of smart men (sic) to congregate and imitate the mind in programming language. That project failed, but the ambition has remained alive among thinkers and entrepreneurs alike (Risse, 2023: Ch. 1).

Over the decades the AI field has been through ups and downs, but there has been considerable acceleration in the last fifteen years or so. During this period the predominant mathematical approach to imitating natural intelligence has been in terms of neural networks, a network of interconnected nodes, called neurons, that solve complex problems. These networks are inspired by the structure and function of the brain. Conceptual breakthroughs have been accompanied by breathtaking advances in the hardware domain, as well as availability of an ever more encompassing amount of data, especially images. A much-discussed working paper by AI-researcher Leopold Aschenbrenner from June 2024 argues that within the next few years this approach will either lead to General AI that outperforms humans not just in specific tasks but comprehensively, or else reach its limits and be understood not to generate such an outcome (Aschenbrenner, 2024). If there will be an entity that with some plausibility counts as General AI, then this event might well be the most important thing that ever happened in human history.

But to be sure, the range of disagreement among knowledgeable people about where these developments might take us is formidable. In any event, for scholars who look at large-scale societal trends from the standpoint of philosophical detachment, any such trends characterized by rapid change pose considerable challenges. Hegel famously pointed out that the 'owl of Minerva flies at night' (Hegel, 1967): philosophical questions appear in greatest clarity and lend themselves to the best answers once we can see where such developments are going. After all, such questions are not about predicting technological advances, but about assessing human possibilities that arise here, about concepts we use to capture them, and about what is desirable for future life on this planet in an era when much in that regard depends on human activity.

The pace of change notwithstanding, in recent years the sheer significance of these technological developments has given rise to a burgeoning philosophical literature on topics around AI. Some of this literature is grounded in the philosophy of mind. After all, the possibility of a non-organic entity doing anything that resembles thinking gives new relevance to long-standing questions about the nature of the mind; the best accounts of notions like intelligence, reason, thought, or rationality; as well as about consciousness and its place in nature. For moral philosophers the ever growing need to encode value judgments in the behavior of entities endowed with AI capacities (ranging from decision-making algorithms to robots and self-driving cars) reminds us of perpetual disagreements about right action and practical reasoning. Philosophers of technology might ask large-scale questions about what possibilities of human life recent technological trends advance or foreclose. Alternatively, they might ask more specific questions about deployment of currently available or anticipated technologies in the fabric of existing societies, and would thereby then operate at the intersection to moral or political philosophy.

Annette Zimmermann's 'Democratizing AI' is an exercise in political philosophy, and the title identifies its focus: Zimmermann offers philosophical reflection not on human possibilities once AI is out in society to a much larger extent than now, or on how AI shapes what it means to be human, but on how AI ought to be rolled out to begin with (Zimmermann, 2026). A brief reference to the Amish, as surprising as their appearance might be, might be useful to put in perspective what Zimmermann is doing.

Descending from radical sixteenth-century European Protestants and named for influential leader Jakob Ammann, the Amish are pacifist Christians who fully separate church and state. They seek to maintain close control over how technology shapes their affairs. They inhabit houses disconnected from the electric grid, cultivate land with horse-drawn machinery and get around in buggies, renounce insurance schemes including social security, do without TV and radio, and limit the use of phones. Though some communities are more open than others, all bar technologies they suspect of weakening community ties, strengthening dependence on government or surrounding communities of non-believers, or threatening their pursuit of virtuous lives. If for something to be 'political' means it pertains to how institutions, practices, or actions shape human living arrangements, use of technology is among the most central political issues for the Amish. Whatever else one might think about them, clearly large territorial democracies like the US or also countries in Western and Central Europe cannot deliberate about technology quite the way Amish communities can. One way of thinking about Zimmermann's essay is as an effort to assess what a *democratically driven* deployment of technology (in this case AI) could even mean, and how it would be appealing, in such democracies.

My main interest in discussing Zimmermann's essay is in what kinds of philosophical questions the author highlights (or does not highlight) in the ongoing intellectual efforts to grapple with the arrival of AI. I am interested in this matter partly because it is an enduring question, in a century of technological disruption, what the role of philosophical inquiry could and should be; and partly because I myself have worked on philosophical questions about AI from a somewhat different angle. This is not a competition: clearly there are different ways for philosophers to weigh in on questions that arise around technological disruption, and it seems Zimmermann would readily agree. Still, some reflection on the role of philosophy in this context might be useful given that we are just at the beginning of much technological disruption in digital technology, but also in genome editing, synthetic biology, as well as geoengineering, nano and pharmaceutical technologies, etc.

I also take it that by exploring various ways of tackling philosophical questions about technological disruption we are not limited to assessing what scholars with degrees in philosophy or employment in philosophy departments should do. The concern is with the vastly more interesting question of how one ought to interrogate human possibilities in the face of rapid technological change in ways that touch on the nature of personhood (e.g. questions around mind and body), on normative questions that arise in the domain of interpersonal relations, and on questions around societal ideals and how they are informed or driven by technology. I mostly look at Zimmermann's approach in comparison to Shannon Vallor's 2024 *The AI Mirror*, Audrey Tang and Glen Weyl's 2024 *Plurality: The Future of Collaborative Technology and Democracy*, and my own 2023 *Political Theory of the Digital Age* (Vallor 2024) (Weyl et al., 2024) (Risse, 2023). But while my main goal here is a contextualization of Zimmermann's work, I end by pointing out a striking convergence between a central theme in her work and one in mine. This convergence makes clear how much agreement there is between our approaches.

Prioritizing democratic practice – or what else?

What is arguably at the heart of Zimmermann's view is a set of proposals for a 'playbook' for democratizing AI deployment. It is a 'playbook' in the sense that these are relatively high-level proposals that are not developed in great detail for particular situations, but that nonetheless capture the broad outlines for how to put the democratic public in charge of how AI enters society. So these are broad guidelines to explain how large territorial democracies can deliberate on new technologies, parallel to how a small Amish community could do so during a sequence of assemblies.

Zimmermann's first proposal is to empower informed sub-constituencies to enforce accountability and make binding decisions. 'Informed' sub-constituencies include people with technical expertise, but also with relevant experiences in being exposed to technologies. There would have to be mechanisms through which these groups actually make binding decisions. Such an approach contrasts with leaving AI deployment to a combination of private-sector initiatives and high-level regulation, whatever that might amount to in a given country. Zimmermann also envisages ballot propositions and other referenda mechanisms to involve democratic publics in AI deployment, as well as a strengthening of voice and exit opportunities for tech workers. Empowering tech workers, after all, strengthens an especially well-informed sub-constituency with multiple reasons to want companies to serve the public well. Most radically, perhaps, Zimmermann envisages massive investments in publicly owned open-source AI models. Given the enormous amounts of private funding tied up in the larger companies in the AI field, it would indeed take public investments of an extraordinary caliber to make such models competitive.

I return to these proposals below, but for now I am interested in Zimmermann's choice of philosophical questions in the domain of AI. Zimmermann acts as a philosophical consultant on democratic processes, specifically in the context of technological innovation. This consultant offers advice on how to deploy AI in meaningful democratic ways, in contrast to leaving it to the private sector to shape the future with technology.

One recent work that has proceeded in similar spirit is Tang and Weyl's *Plurality* (Weyl et al., 2024). The idea behind "plurality" is that social complexity and diversity are resources to be harnessed for innovation and progress. Digital technology at its best helps us create systems that transform potential social conflict into mutual growth, much like industrial engines harness physical fuels. They frame the social world as a network of diverse and intersecting affiliations, highlighting interconnectedness between individual identities and collective organizations. Some of the work Tang and Weyl do is to spell out philosophical foundations for this idea, drawing on Hannah Arendt, Danielle Allen, and Sun Yat-sen. They also take a keen interest in foundational questions about mathematical concepts they use to capture the dynamics of diverse collaborations. Still, much of their work is dedicated to making very concrete proposals for how to use digital technology to improve collaborative behavior, ranging from workplace integration, health and healthcare, and media; to the environment, improvement of life-long learning, simplified administrative processes, political participation, etc. For instance, restructured work environments and inclusive communication strategies are posited as mechanisms to enhance economic outputs and employee satisfaction.

This work draws on Tang's experience as a cabinet member in the Taiwanese government. It also draws on the fact that in Taiwan, democracy and the internet are of just about the same age. As Tang likes to say, in Taiwan it has always been plausible for democracy advocates to see the internet as a technology of democracy. Zimmermann's playbook is not typically focused at the same level of concreteness that Tang and Weyl (and, I should add, the many collaborators who contributed to this unusual work) are in a position to offer. The basic ideas Zimmermann presents operate as mid-level principles for shaping the role of the citizenry in designing its future with technology. Such differences notwithstanding, Zimmermann and Tang and Weyl share the same approach to philosophical questions around deployment of digital technologies in our lives here and now: they articulate ideas on how to develop a strong democratic ideal.

Selecting this kind of philosophical question in the context of AI also contrasts with thinking about these matters from the standpoint of justice. Zimmermann attends to this point and formulates the 'Justice Objection': 'The implementation of democratically legitimate political processes – including democratically legitimate agenda-setting – is not sufficient for ensuring that democratic constituencies will reach decision outcomes that move us closer to a more just society. In fact, democratization may undermine justice' (Zimmermann, 2026: 89).

This objection is well-taken. Private-sector capture is among the biggest concerns about the deployment of technology that we should have these days, to be sure. But in addition, digital technologies also have ways of bringing out people's more pernicious sides, and populist politicians in turn have ways of turning these tendencies to their advantage. Just how the role of private industry and these other matters are related is an interesting question by itself that we cannot pursue. Shoshana Zuboff would say they are problems from the same cloth and has offered a 'unified field theory' to this effect. (Zuboff, 2022). And for roughly the last decade there has been a good deal of literature on how wealthy elites turn digital technologies to their advantage, how these technologies undermine democratic discourse by enabling large-scale distribution of misinformation and disinformation, how racist and gender stereotypes are reinforced online, etc. (O'Neil, 2017; Eubanks, 2018; Noble, 2018; Benjamin, 2019; Broussard, 2019; Zuboff, 2019).

To be sure, what philosophers and other intellectuals can do about these tendencies in the short run is limited regardless of whether they focus on democratic theory of other matters. But it is worth emphasizing that the philosophical questions here really cannot be limited to democratic theory. Zimmermann's response to the Justice Objection begins by emphasizing the close conceptual connection between democracy and justice. She also turns to Danielle Allen's work that makes this very point in the title of a recent book: *Justice by Means of Democracy* (Allen, 2023). This matter is of some general interest. In debates about AI an approach from the standpoint of democratic theory is a relatively new move just because this whole literature itself is new. But reflection on justice in the post-Rawlsian area has not only increasingly fallen by the wayside, it has also been severely criticized as the wrong kind of thing to focus on altogether. One driving theme among those who think philosophers should refrain from making pronouncements on justice is that, one way or another, it would be presumptuous for intellectuals to offer prescriptions (Risse, 2020: Ch 1).

But for one thing, philosophers and other intellectuals should only ever understand themselves as contributors to societal debates (Risse, 2020: Chs. 2–3.). Once that is understood we can see that pronouncements on justice are as intellectually legitimate as pronouncements on the shape of the democratic process. Moreover, while the ideal of democracy as such can plausibly be understood as guided by more than just procedural ideas, it would be wrong to think of matters of justice as somehow becoming redundant or otherwise irrelevant if only we focus on democracy the right way. The perennial quest for justice, I have proposed, is about making sure each individual has an appropriate place in what our uniquely human capacities permit us to build, produce, and maintain and is respected appropriately for her capacities to hold such a place in the first place. Reflection on these matters goes into a new round in this digital age. At the very least we should engage in such reflection in ways that are supplementary to reflection on democracy. After all, we need to have ways of saying that even perfectly legitimate democratic decisions can be *wrong*. The most plausible manner for that to happen is by falling short of justice.

There is nothing here Zimmermann seems to disagree with. In fact, her well-balanced discussion leads to this very conclusion, that 'justice and democracy *can* reinforce each other – but they need not' (Zimmermann, 2026: 93). Still, it is worth emphasizing this point given that the overall intellectual climate is moving away from doing work on justice, which to my mind is a serious flaw in contemporary philosophical work. Fortunately, it is not a flaw shared by Zimmermann even though they have their priorities elsewhere.

Alternative ways of pursuing philosophical questions about AI

Shannon Vallor's recent book *The AI Mirror* offers a very different engagement with AI from Zimmermann's (Vallor, 2024; Risse, 2024).[1] Vallor's 2016 book *Technology and the Virtues* is something like a virtue–theoretical counterpart to the work done by Zimmermann and Tang and Weyl with their starting point in democratic theory (Vallor, 2016). After all, that earlier book spells out what virtue theory (with a Buddhist and Confucian rather than Aristotelian emphasis) advises in times of technological disruption. Vallor's 2024 book continues these themes but also captures a sense of frustration with what she perceives to be too much hype around AI.

Vallor deploys the analogy between AI and the mirror to diagnose how we are going wrong in our relationship with AI. AI reflects our individual and collective appearance much as a mirror does. This means several things for Vallor. First of all, there is *nothing more* to AI than reflection of ourselves. In 2022, then-Google-engineer Blake Lemoine concluded that Google's LaMDA (Language Model for Dialogue Applications) had become sentient and thus had developed capacities for independent thought and agency. Vallor thinks Lemoine was basically talking to himself, or in any event, he was talking to a device that was channeling what numerous humans had said. Lemoine's mistake was to think there was genuine agency to this device, instead of its being a mirror.

Second, in virtue of being a mirror, AI reflects multifarious ugly realities about how we interact with each other. As we noted, authors such as Ruha Benjamin, Cathy O'Neil, Safiya Noble, Virginia Eubanks, Meredith Broussard, Shoshana Zuboff, and others have drawn attention to phenomena such as that the accumulated human data reflect a whole range of rather hateful human stereotypes, that algorithms either unwittingly or often rather wittingly perpetuate inequalities in society, or that our whole era of capitalism is driven by surveillance and mining of data to such an extent that it makes sense to speak of Surveillance Capitalism. Third, mirrors also distort, instead of reflecting everything faithfully and without distortions. As far as AI is concerned, it might seem it does all sorts of good things for us because those who want us to believe that find ways of creating

1 I am drawing here on – and in fact duplicating some paragraphs from – my recent review of this work, see Risse (2024).

that impression. So often, instead of actually seeing these pernicious tendencies we should associate with AI – per this second use of the mirror analogy that I just mentioned – we see something else entirely, namely some kind of short-term benefit.

There is again nothing here that Zimmermann would need to disagree with or even have a view on. At the same time, the sheer existence of the intellectual context in which Vallor's recent book was written also highlights how in this age of rapid change in technology many philosophical questions must be addressed in tandem with questions of democratic theory. A dissent I have myself with Vallor is that I am not as convinced that Lemoine was wrong. Or that is, I do not think what matters is if he was wrong about his statements in 2022. What matters is whether he might be right *eventually*. Vallor articulates one strong position on being skeptical about that, critically analyzing a mindset from within which we might think he could be right one day. She also suggests a powerfully different way of thinking about technology that would not let us look at it in ways that make it tempting to agree with Lemoine. My doubt is how we can be sure. If we cannot be sure, we need to consider, politically and philosophically, that there might in fact be much more to AI, at least eventually.

We need to *consider*, I say. I am obviously in no position to predict how technology will develop and, again, such predictions are not among the philosophical issues that arise about AI. But the approach I have chosen in my own work, especially in *Political Theory of the Digital Age*, is that it behooves us to take seriously the possibility that we are on the brink of entering what Max Tegmark has called Life 3.0 (Tegmark, 2017). That would be a version of life where we also have entities that can choose the design of both the shape of their bodies and the details of their learning behavior (paradigmatically, uploaded brains).

There are so many philosophical questions to which we do not have conclusive answers, especially in the philosophy of mind. Is there only matter, or is there also something immaterial? If there are two kinds of things, how do they connect? What is the nature of consciousness? How do consciousness, intelligence, practical rationality, and possibly other features like emotions relate? That is, can they appear separately in different creatures, or do some supervene on some combination of the others? Just what is the best way of conceptualizing intelligence in the first place? Is it really not possible for non-carbon-based entities to have minds (whatever minds are) given that carbon-based entities clearly can? For religious people one question might be if machines can eventually have souls. If we are worthy enough of having them, how do we know machines might not eventually also be?

The sheer pace of change in the domain of AI speaks somewhat in support of those who think our lives on this planet will be revolutionized through the development of a new kind of intelligent entity. I think we should see the future as open in ways other than those Vallor discusses, and we should organize the overall ensemble of our philosophical work around technology accordingly.

Again, Zimmermann need not disagree with anything here, but if I may push the point a bit further: That we get democracy right always matters, and the idea can and should be spelled out in every context. Quite plausibly it matters especially now that we are getting democracy right because democracy is going wrong in so many places right now. The sheer existence of this disagreement between Vallor and myself I just articulated might do two things. It makes clear again how important democratic attention to these matters is, but then also how hard it will be for democracy to get these matters right given how much is at stake and how complex these matters are.

The point can be pushed yet further. In their final section, Zimmermann points out that 'the goal of democratizing AI is not necessarily linked to any particular evaluative view about whether further technological innovation in this area is all-things-considered *desirable*: the latter plausibly depends, in part, on the specific values and preferences of the democratic constituencies directly affected by AI' (Zimmermann, 2026: 101–2). This discussion makes contact from afar with the large techno-skeptical themes that have shaped twentieth-century philosophy of technology. Zimmermann does not mention these authors, but readers who approach their work from the philosophy of technology rather than ethics, political philosophy, or philosophy of mind will think of authors like Martin Heidegger, Jacques Ellul, or Lewis Mumford. Let me briefly talk about them.

One of the most distinguished German philosophers of the twentieth century, Heidegger argues that technology shapes humankind's experience of its very existence by making things show up in certain ways, in a manner focused on use or consumption (which is, roughly speaking, what he means by *Gestell*). Digital lifeworlds complete the alienation from nature that has become increasingly dominant since the Industrial Revolution. A French philosopher and Christian anarchist, Ellul thinks the development of technology is driven by its own internal logic, regardless of anybody's will or desires. Digital lifeworlds complete this development through the emergence of a super-intelligence that could dispense with human input altogether. Finally, American polymath Mumford – who is broadly-based in the humanities – interprets human engagement with technology as the deliberate if slow-moving construction of a vast control-system ('megamachine'). The megamachine imposes a stifling and increasingly irreparable conformity on humankind. Our present digital lifeworlds complete incorporation of all human life into such a megamachine.[2]

These authors touch on themes so large that it is hard to assess how to refute them. After all, they are offering overall approaches to just about anything that happens around us. If they are right, democracy will not save us from the troubles they identify, no matter how well-developed an ideal of democracy we develop to see through the deployment of AI. But nothing else will either.

Conclusion

My point so far has been to contextualize Zimmermann's work by clarifying its relationship with other major publications and themes around philosophical questions about AI. Let me conclude by articulating a substantive agreement on a matter I approach from a standpoint of justice and Zimmermann from a standpoint of democratic theory. As noted earlier, a radical proposal Zimmermann makes is massive investments in publicly owned open-source AI models. Given the enormous amounts of private funding tied up in larger companies in the AI field, it would indeed take public investments of an extraordinary caliber to make such models competitive.

In *Political Theory of the Digital Age*, I have taken a position on data ownership, organized around the claim that what makes data valuable to the private sector in an era of Surveillance Capitalism (in Shoshana Zuboff's sense) is that they are social facts (Zuboff, 2019; Risse, 2024: Ch. 9). The basic idea is that the value of data does not reside in individual items but in collectively generated patterns that allow for predictions regardless of whether people's actions have aided the identification of the pattern, as long as those people who have not are relevantly like the ones who have. Unlike personal data that reveal something important about someone, the data that drive Surveillance Capitalism do not matter piece by piece but for the patterns they reveal.

By a collectively generated pattern, I mean something like this:

> Under social parameters $P_1, \ldots, P_n$ as they prevail in country C (or perhaps in countries $C_1, \ldots, C_n$), individuals with features $F_1, \ldots, F_n$ will with probability p do action A under circumstances $CI_1, \ldots, CI_n$.

2 For these authors and their importance for the philosophy of technology, see Mitcham (1994). For the works of these authors, see in particular Heidegger (1977); Ellul (1964); Mumford (1967; 1974).

This could be anything from people with certain features hailing a cab or ordering pizza to them participating in marriage, home-buying, or loan-taking behavior or political actions. Past behavior predicts what happens next, at least probabilistically. Data generated from behavior of numerous people are valuable to the extent that they permit such inferences. In increasingly sophisticated ways, data-mining techniques use large quantities of data to identify such patterns.

Collectively generated patterns are 'social facts' in Emile Durkheim's sense in virtue of being facts about group behavior that are systematic enough to generate predictions about the future. For Durkheim, a social fact is 'any way of acting, whether fixed or not, capable of exerting over the individual an external constraint; or: which is general over the whole of a given society whilst having an existence of its own, independent of its individual manifestations' (Durkheim 1982: 59). This definition makes it possible to study behavior of societies per se, parallel to and unreducible to behavior of individuals.

For those who collect or mine data, it might be perplexing that what they deal with is anything other than vectors in multi-dimensional spaces that would not exist (in any interesting sense) were it not for certain platforms and hardware to connect them, and that would yield no insight were it not for analytical techniques. But such work yields results because those vectors reflect an underlying social reality. So, there is more to them than their mathematical existence *as* such vectors and the work that leads to their presence in the data miner's storage.

The current default is that data are controlled by whoever gathers them, normally companies that provide phones, tablets, personal computers, digital assistants, electronically linked household appliances, positioning systems, or search engines. However, as I argue in *Political Theory of the Digital Age*, the default should be that collectively generated patterns are also collectively controlled. Chapter 3 of that earlier work explores some ideas around democratic reforms in terms of which this kind of control should occur. Zimmermann's proposals, including and especially the one I just revisited, are perfectly suited to do this kind of work. For all their radicalness, I welcome them wholeheartedly. For this reason I have had little to offer here by way of criticism.

References

Allen, D. (2023), *Justice by Means of Democracy*. University of Chicago Press.

Aschenbrenner, L. (2024), Situational awareness: The decade ahead. Available online at: https://situational-awareness.ai/ (last accessed March 15, 2026).

Benjamin, R. (2019), *Race After Technology: Abolitionist Tools for the New Jim Code*. Polity.

Broussard, M. (2019), *Artificial Unintelligence: How Computers Misunderstand the World*. The MIT Press.

Durkheim, E. (1982), What is a social fact? In: *The Rules of Sociological Method: And Selected Texts on Sociology and Its Method*, ed. S. Lukes, trans. W.D. Halls. The Free Press: 59.

Ellul, J. (1964), *The Technological Society*, trans. John Wilkinson. Vintage Books.

Eubanks, V. (2018), *Automating Inequality: How High-Tech Tools Profile, Police, and Punish the Poor*. St. Martin's Press.

Hegel, G.W.F. (1967), *The Philosophy of Right*. Oxford University Press.

Heidegger, M. (1977), *The Question Concerning Technology, and Other Essays*, trans. William Lovitt. Garland Publishing.

Mitcham, C. (1994), *Thinking through Technology: The Path between Engineering and Philosophy*. University of Chicago Press.

Mumford, L. (1967), *Myth of the Machine: Technics and Human Development*. Harcourt, Brace Jovanovich.

Mumford, L. (1974), *Pentagon of Power: The Myth Of The Machine*, Vol. II. Harcourt, Brace Jovanovich.

Noble, S.U. (2018), *Algorithms of Oppression: How Search Engines Reinforce Racism*. NYU Press.

O'Neil, C. (2017), *Weapons of Math Destruction: How Big Data Increases Inequality and Threatens Democracy*. Broadway Books.

Risse, M. (2020), *On Justice: Philosophy, History, Foundations*. Cambridge University Press.

Risse, M. (2023), *Political Theory of the Digital Age: Where Artificial Intelligence Might Take Us*. Cambridge University Press.

Risse, M. (2024), Review of Shannon Vallor, *The AI Mirror: How to Reclaim Our Humanity in an Age of Machine Thinking*. *Notre Dame Philosophical Reviews*, no. 2024.12.10.

Tegmark, M. (2017), *Life 3.0: Being Human in the Age of Artificial Intelligence*. Knopf.

Vallor, S. (2016), *Technology and the Virtues: A Philosophical Guide to a Future Worth Wanting*. Oxford University Press.

Vallor, S. (2024), *The AI Mirror: How to Reclaim Our Humanity in an Age of Machine Thinking*. Oxford University Press.

Weyl, E.G. and Tang, A. (2024), Augmented deliberation. In: *Plurality: The Future of Collaborative Technology and Democracy*. Independently published: 276–290.

Weyl, E.G., Tang, A., and □ Community (2024), □ 數位 *Plurality: The Future of Collaborative Technology and Democracy*. Independently published.

Zimmermann, A. (2026), *Democratizing AI*. Manchester University Press.

Zuboff, S. (2019), *The Age of Surveillance Capitalism: The Fight for a Human Future at the New Frontier of Power*. Public Affairs.

Zuboff, S. (2022), Surveillance capitalism or democracy? The death match of institutional orders and the politics of knowledge in our information civilization. *Organization Theory* 3, no. 3.

Part III

Reply to critics

14

Reply to critics

Annette Zimmermann

'The powerlessness of the individual is perhaps the most dangerous illusion a human being can possibly have.'
– Joseph Weizenbaum, computer scientist & creator of ELIZA[1] (1987: 51)

I am deeply grateful to my interlocutors for their philosophically charitable and analytically rigorous engagement. Their contributions show how much political philosophy, democratic theory, and technology law can offer – and how many urgent research questions remain for scholars and the public. Fittingly for a book about agenda-setting, their observations help shape a compelling agenda for future work on the political philosophy of AI. I'm honored to respond to their critiques, clarify my position, and build on emerging areas of agreement.

Several contributions probe the normative foundations of my view and propose alternative framings, extending the argument beyond Part I. These include concerns about AI's potential trajectory toward AGI and impersonal domination (as raised by Cordelli), as well as the opposite concern – raised by Kreide – that AI may never acquire essential human capacities like genuine understanding, remaining a 'stochastic parrot' (Bender et al., 2021) while continuing to mislead the public and politicians alike.

Others take up institutional questions – domestic and global – as well as structural barriers to democratization, such as capitalism's economic incentives. Several responses align strongly with my view that democratizing AI must be part of a broader effort to strengthen democratic control across society. My interlocutors connect these issues to long-standing debates in political philosophy, especially the problem of mobilization in elite-dominated, apathetic, and polarized contexts – here, interlocutors like

1 My translation. The original quote is: 'Die Ohnmacht des Einzelnen ist vielleicht die gefährlichste Illusion, die ein Mensch haben kann.'

Urbinati, Agrawal, and Christiano emphasize the democratic potential of workers, scholars, intermediary organizations, and civil society.

My interlocutors fall on different points of the 'AI optimism/pessimism' scale, though I think that we all agree that neither AI's future nor humanity's future is predetermined. Neither the doomsday scenario nor the tech utopia scenario is inevitable (yet). This makes our shared future especially hard to forecast at this moment characterized by such significant political and technological complexity, and by an increasingly overt and direct incursion of powerful tech oligarchs into our democratic institutions.

The natural conclusion to draw from this, in my view, is to resist the two extremes of apocalyptic despair and blue-sky thinking. Instead, we are called to face the future as it is: *fundamentally open*, and therefore up to us to shape. Several interlocutors join me in emphasizing this perspective: Stanger is clear that the 'optimistic scenario is in no way guaranteed. It requires deliberate effort to imagine, design, and deploy AI in ways that support democracy rather than undermining it,' because 'the same advanced AI that could be misused to undermine democracy could alternatively be used to reinforce and spread democracy'. Similarly, Risse joins me in 'see[ing] the future as open in ways other than those [other scholars in the philosophy of AI literature have done]', and in particular in calling for a turn beyond a purely ethical focus on AI towards a more distinctly political focus on questions of democratic institution-building and of public ownership of innovative technologies when exploring the philosophical implications of accelerating AI deployment.

Yet the claim that an open future implies a responsibility to shape it faces implementation challenges. As Joseph Weizenbaum warned, people often fall into learned helplessness – whether in bureaucratic politics or when overwhelmed by rapid technological change. Even back in the 1960s, users of his early chatbot ELIZA overestimated its intelligence and anthropomorphized it – a phenomenon now known as the 'ELIZA effect'.

This helplessness is understandable – but dangerous. As Parts I and II argue, citizens and representatives must reject it. Weizenbaum criticized researchers who evade ethical responsibility by appealing to expertise – 'that's not my department' (2001: 117) – a deflection that ignores the social embeddedness of research. Research is shaped by funders with political and economic interests. Just as money distorts democratic deliberation through campaign finance and lobbying, it also shapes which kinds of research receive support.

While Part I focused on the tech industry's growing influence in regulatory spaces, recent developments show the same risk in academia: research agendas and funding structures can also be captured by anti-democratic or oligarchic interests. This is especially true when (i) public investment into, and thereby control over, the direction of AI innovation could counterbalance corporate power but (ii) public institutions are already captured; for instance, because elected officials actively relinquish control to unelected tech industry leaders, and/or (iii) public institutions are unwilling, often for politicized reasons, to invest public resources in support of free academic inquiry into pressing scientific and social problems.

With that in mind – and building on an inspiring call to action by Urbinati in this volume for scholars and intellectuals to acknowledge their own responsibility to contribute to positive social change – let me take the opportunity in this final part to highlight that not only tech workers and elected officials, but also academic researchers across all disciplines, must be highly attuned to 'siloed expertise' thinking giving rise to an artificial division between ostensibly pure research and politically messy applications and consequences of that research. Though convenient, that division is less clear than some might wish. Weizenbaum rightly warns that insistence on one's own domain of expertise must not be used as a shield from public accountability, even when individuals – researchers, citizens, and workers – are part of complex social systems that seem too big to influence (Weizenbaum, 2001: 104–132). Even when we operate within vast social, legal, economic, and technological incentive structures, there are opportunities for active participation and even for principled refusal: academics and tech workers alike can choose not to perform, or to professionally reward, work on projects that set back human welfare and democratic values.[2]

2 Where *exactly* the line for principled refusal should lie is obviously a subject of enduring societal disagreement – Weizenbaum, informed by his lived experience of escaping Nazi Germany and of later, as an MIT professor, protesting against the Vietnam War, drew the line at military applications of technology, which he defined broadly so as to include technologies like computer vision: 'if it is at all possible to integrate a research result, e.g. in computer vision, into a weapon in order to "improve" it, then it will be done' (Weizenbaum, 2001: 124). There may be some ethical gray areas, of course, and people will disagree about them. However, Weizenbaum persuasively argues that on the edges of those gray areas, there will be *clear* cases of technology use cases that are obviously ethically defensible, and those that obviously are not. Much like dawn or dusk can make it hard for all of us to converge on an unequivocal, precise judgment about when daytime ends and nighttime begins, we do all have a firm grasp of the concept of '(clearly) day' and '(clearly) night' (Weizenbaum, 2001: 126). For Weizenbaum, the mere fact that there are some technology use cases of debatable ethical status does not imply that there cannot be cases firmly located in the 'night' territory. A contemporary policy example of a similar view is the EU AI Act, which lists prohibited AI deployments necessarily falling into the 'night' territory, such as 'the use of an AI system that exploits any of the vulnerabilities of a natural person or a specific group of persons due to their age, disability or a specific social or economic situation' (European Union, 2024).

Elected officials and bureaucrats can choose to forcefully resist policy agendas that funnel public support of research into unduly narrowly scoped, possibly short-sighted, and corrosive areas of inquiry. Citizens, as citizen-activists or even citizen-scientists, can choose to empower themselves to ask questions that the institutions around them are not able or willing to ask.

Cordelli

It is impossible to do a critique as original and as nuanced as Chiara Cordelli's powerful commentary justice in this narrowly scoped part of the book, though I am grateful to be able to tackle a small number of points of immediate philosophical and policy relevance in what follows, and to highlight areas that I plan to explore in future work.

Cordelli worries that democratizing agenda-setting concerning AI deployment decisions will be insufficient for rectifying the asymmetrical concentration of power, wealth, and information amongst oligopolistic actors coupled with a widespread and democratically unjustified dispersion of risk. Here, Cordelli introduces an important two-pronged problem that she frames as more fundamental than the problem of democratizing AI at the agenda-setting stage: first, the 'problem of collective disempowerment by AI', and second, the 'problem of collective disempowerment beyond AI'.

Cordelli is clearly correct on the insufficiency claim: democratizing AI by targeting the agenda-setting stage is just one of the actions morally and politically required of us as democratic constituencies. For that reason, my line of argument in Part I emphasizes that democracy and justice remain distinct, yet mutually reinforcing, normative goals. They may well come apart, which in turn will plausibly be a clear indicator that democratic constituencies have chosen a path that stands in need of correction. Analogous arguments apply to other distinct normative goals centered by Cordelli, such as the goal of addressing worsening social inequality, of mitigating capitalist market inefficiencies, and so on. And even the goal of democratization writ large is clearly not automatically achieved via successful interventions aiming to democratize the agenda-setting stage: democratizing agenda-setting is necessary but not sufficient for democratization all-things-considered, as anti-democratic forces may still unduly intervene upon societal decision sequences at any point post agenda-setting.

Given that I explicitly make room in my view for the possibility that democratizing AI will not necessarily *resolve* all or even some political and moral problems directly, and indeed that efforts to democratize AI must be weighed carefully against countervailing normative goals because they may in some instances even run *counter* to those goals, I take the point that democratizing AI deployment agenda-setting is 'insufficient' as straightforwardly compatible with the view defended in Part I rather than opposed to it. The idea that motivates my view is that agenda-setting is simply a particularly *attractive pressure point* – and one that has been – presumably due to the disproportionate economic and political influence of tech oligarchs – largely untapped by 'regular' citizens and their representatives. This does not imply that other pressure points need not be explored; that democratizing agenda-setting will be sufficient for addressing the democratic legitimacy deficit created by the ASYMMETRY.

Let us return to Cordelli's two-pronged problem itself. The second prong is easier for my existing account to address than the other: Cordelli's insightful observation that we need to democratize economic structures more broadly to address the problem of collective disempowerment *beyond* AI. I take the parts of the PLAYBOOK that explicitly call for major anti-oligopolistic legal and institutional transformations coupled with major investments of public resources into collective ownership models over AI as well as significant measures to mitigate exploitative labor conditions in the tech industry to offer a response to exactly this concern. I share Cordelli's concern that capitalist market structures wrongfully 'depoliticize or privatize transformative [investment] decisions that determine the future course of a society' and leave production to be 'determined by largely uncoordinated [and undemocratic as well as possibly irrational] investment markets' (see also Cordelli, 2025). My claim that democratically legitimate AI deployment requires that not just co-authorship, but also co-ownership of the future, is aligned with Cordelli's normative analysis.

Cordelli's other concern about future collective disempowerment *by* AI points to a thornier issue. Cordelli worries that democratic constituencies may choose to disempower themselves by deliberately choosing to relinquish control to advanced AI, thus subjecting themselves to the impersonal *rule of none*. Again, I cannot disagree with Cordelli's analysis, and I welcome the opportunity to highlight this important risk, which receives insufficient attention in Part I. While I do explicitly address the problem that democratic constituencies may reach unjust or otherwise broadly bad decision outcomes, *anti-democratic* decision outcomes are a qualitatively distinct instance of bad democratic decision-making, and thus merit particular scrutiny.

My rationale for de-emphasizing this particular issue in Part I was that I have the following background assumption: I think that, in the near term, it is much more likely that a small group of human decision-makers will disenfranchise and exploit the rest of the *demos* by deploying and benefiting from advanced AI tools, than it is that *demoi* will choose to delegate significant authority to AI proper. For this reason, I see the threat of widening economic inequality, ideological radicalization, and regulatory capture and corruption, all enabled straightforwardly by human agents using their power over the direction of AI for their own ends, as the most pressing threat to democratic constituencies. This analysis pushes against a trend in the interdisciplinary AI safety literature to focus on threat scenarios involving much more advanced AI agents, which is clearly important yet risks distracting us from the undemocratic actions of our fellow humans here and now.

Nonetheless, Cordelli is entirely right that the more medium-term future may present us with a different threat landscape. Therefore, I see her call to explore the implications of collective disempowerment *by* AI as a central part of the larger research agenda for the political philosophy of AI. It is infeasible to address all implications of this concern comprehensively in this short response, though let me highlight one possible safeguard that both Cordelli and I endorse: the introduction of constitutional constraints – which the risk-sensitive moderate proceduralist framework labels 'minimum outcome standards' – that act as guardrails against democratic constituencies' decision to disempower themselves, for instance by relinquishing control to AI in unduly deferential ways, which would violate their members' core civic rights.[3] Cordelli's illuminating discussion shows how my existing account in Part I can be fruitfully extended to tackle the possible risk of collective self-disenfranchisement. When tech oligarchs evangelize about techno-solutionist uses of AI in government and public life for the sake of greater efficiency, agenda-setting *counterpower* is our first line of defense against emerging collective tendencies to voluntarily hand over control either to oligopolistic market actors or to their impersonal tools.

Cordelli's discussion of the 'impersonal rule of none' problem leads me to an even more complex issue: Cordelli's claim that public equality geared at fair co-authorship and co-ownership is not enough, and that only collective alienation can explain why current forms of AI deployment call out for greater democratic control. Building on – but significantly going beyond – philosophical accounts connecting alienation to individual and collective self-rule developed by Jaeggi (2014) and Stilz (2015), Cordelli argues that the 'value of public equality is insufficient to support a case for a right to collective self-rule' because only her preferred non-alienation account '(1) picks rule of all over rule of none and (2) can ground a positive case for (equally) shared control rights'.

3 An additional safeguard, which I develop at length below, is increased political mobilization around the cultivation of a stronger pro-democratic mindset in society.

I share Cordelli's concern that any plausible account of democratic legitimacy must block rule over none in Kolodny's (2014) sense, and I agree that impersonal rule would be wrongfully alienating in Cordelli's collective alienation sense. But I insist that my risk-sensitive moderate proceduralist account, which emphasizes citizens' ability to rule over their affairs as free equals and as part of fair procedures, tracks autonomy interests that logically *precede* our interest in non-alienation, in the sense that people will feel alienated just if those autonomy interests are set back by authoritarian or oligarchic rule or by wildly unchecked capitalist market dynamics. This suggests that autonomy interests tracked by the co-authorship and co-ownership of the future that risk-sensitive moderate proceduralism seeks to enable are the higher-order normative concern, not non-alienation – though admittedly a more thorough philosophical defense of my stance in future work is warranted. For now, suffice it to say that, as I argued in Part I, what matters on my risk-sensitive moderate proceduralist account is *actual participation*, not just hypothetical participation in the form of top-down political representation of citizens' interests or in the form of impersonal preference aggregation via AI, and not just a thin conception of public equality compatible with some benevolent dictator ruling over everyone equally. Through actual participation, citizens assert themselves as stewards of their shared future, which is our best bet against a sense of alienation that develops under impersonal or oligarchic rule.

Agrawal & Christiano

Like the other insightful responses to my argument, Agrawal and Christiano's philosophically incisive and empirically grounded critique merits a much more comprehensive discussion than that which I can provide here. I thus reserve the completion of this challenge for future work, especially regarding specific matters of institutional design. For now, let me begin with a clarification. Agrawal and Christiano attribute the view to me that AI poses *philosophically unique*, qualitatively distinctive problems for democratic legitimacy. This is a welcome opportunity to explain one of my core background assumptions in more detail. My interlocutors state that, on my view, the Asymmetry 'involves a deep inequality in the abilities of individuals to influence the larger society. She claims that this effect of AI is distinctive of AI.' Call such a view the *Uniqueness View*. They move on to critique the *Uniqueness View* at various junctures in their response, likening various features of the highly concentrated AI market and their respective normative implications to other, more familiar market and policy domains, which obviously casts doubt on any type of *Uniqueness* claim.

I am actually sympathetic to my interlocutors' worries about the *Uniqueness View* – a position that I do not in fact hold. As I say in Part I, 'generative AI deployment in particular illuminates the familiar problem of a democratic legitimacy deficit with *unprecedented* urgency, thus rendering a well-understood problem space at the same time more salient and less straightforwardly feasible to intervene upon', but (crucially) I also say that 'rapid, large-scale generative AI deployment risks undermining democratic legitimacy in a way that resembles other, less mysterious threats to this core political value'. In short: the problem is novel in scale, not in kind. This is a feature, not a bug, of the argument: lack of philosophical uniqueness does not imply lack of political urgency.

Denying the *Uniqueness View* for the purposes of my argument in this book does not preclude other AI developments raising philosophically entirely novel questions – for instance, in the philosophy of mind, as Risse plausibly suggests. But the AI-related questions with which I am concerned here are distinct in scale, not kind.

This reasoning leads me to explicitly reject the phenomenon that I call 'AI exceptionalism' in Part I, and thus to reject the *Uniqueness View* directly. As I argue in Part I, overinflated claims about AI's supposed distinctiveness in comparison to other technologies can be highly misleading and counterproductive, as it may push democratic constituencies to embrace 'an attitude of learned helplessness premised on the assumption that AI is simply too unique, too novel, too complicated for us to try to grasp and direct'.[4]

Let us turn to another worry raised by Agrawal and Christiano. They agree in principle with the 'mixed approach' recommended by 'one of [my] main innovations' – the idea that informed sub-constituencies will offer an agenda-setting pathway that bridges the gap between exclusively top-down and exclusively bottom-up models by harnessing both 'the democratic potential of people's movements as well as the power of the regulatory state'. However, they worry that this view gives rise to a *dilemma*: if informed sub-constituencies cannot make binding decisions, it is unclear how they can effectively set agendas; yet if they can, they, too, will over time become vulnerable to regulatory capture much like other bureaucratic government agencies, which diminishes the degree to which informed sub-constituencies plausibly count as truly democratic.

We can get the first horn out of the way swiftly. As I noted in Part I, I reject a merely consultative model: without the ability to make binding

4 I first develop this thought in Zimmermann et al. (2020). Other scholars have recently embraced a somewhat similar view: see, for example, Narayanan and Kapoor (2025), who argue that we ought to resist AI exceptionalist hype/doomsday rhetoric by viewing AI as a 'normal' technology like other technologies.

decisions or enforce real accountability through audit and critique, such bodies fail to meet the bar I set – and, as Christiano and Agrawal rightly say, they would lack meaningful agenda-setting power. The second horn is trickier. As I argue in the Introduction, even nominally independent academic institutions and researchers can be captured in ways resembling traditional regulatory capture. Therefore, informed sub-constituencies conducting third-party audits are not immune – and neither are ordinary citizens participating in long-term municipal assemblies or task forces.

Several design solutions come to mind: First, we could impose short, non-renewable term limits on members of auditing bodies, possibly including post-appointment bans on industry employment or research funding. Second, we might enforce radical transparency – not just about final decisions but also about deliberation processes, reducing the risk that industry-aligned views are quietly adopted. Third, multiple sub-constituencies could work in parallel to red-team each other, applying a common AI design practice applied to the policy world. Fourth, we could choose to invest significant public resources such that whistleblowers acting in the public interest are rewarded – for example via monetary awards, coupled with social support and legal protections. Finally, I see sub-constituencies necessarily as but one part of a plurality of possibly imperfect though mutually reinforcing strategies. No design can eliminate all risks of anti-democratic interference, but we can build more inclusive and resilient checks and balances.

Christiano and Agrawal continue to make three persuasive strategic proposals, on which they request my response. First, they join me in calling for strengthening antitrust law. I explicitly recommend this in the fourth part of the PLAYBOOK, where I argue that recent US efforts are encouraging but require more sustained action and broader popular support. Their original suggestion in this context – to curb media ownership by tech oligopolies – is well taken. As they note, tech firms increasingly shape public discourse by acquiring media outlets. Restricting this form of ownership would complement the anti-oligopolistic interventions I advocate. While the normative justification and institutional mechanisms for such restrictions require further development, I welcome the proposal as consistent with the framework I propose.

Second, echoing highly impactful earlier work by Christiano (1996; 2012), they recommend tighter campaign finance regulations to lessen the problem of regulatory capture. This too is consistent with the anti-oligarchic and pro-democratic thrust of my argument. But I remain skeptical that curtailing money in politics directly is the best or the main solution here. One of the most troubling forms of regulatory capture in the AI space occurs without large donations: elected officials *voluntarily* cede authority to tech CEOs, often as part of unduly high deference to technical experts and their preferred policy proposals, as in the exchange between Sam Altman and Senator Kennedy discussed in Part I. It is possible for regulators to be effectively captured without violating campaign finance laws, even if the grip of those laws were to be tightened significantly.

Third, Christiano and Agrawal agree with my argument in favor of the transformative power of tech unions as an instrument of democratic counterpower (see also O'Neill, 2012). I note that on my view, tech unions can provide the scaffolding of exactly the kinds of *informed sub-constituencies* for which other parts of my PLAYBOOK advocate, and about which Christiano and Agrawal express some degree of skepticism. Against that, I insist that the instrumental value of unions in a democratic system is not only one of *information* and one of *representation* (Christiano, 2019), but also – and even more importantly – one of *direct deliberation and participation*: in that way, tech unions are akin to other democratic intermediaries. What makes unions particularly *appealing* intermediaries, of course, is that they combine the advantages of representative structures that are already fairly well-established in democratic societies with one of the strongest features of the informed sub-constituencies approach: the fact that they are comprised of people with particularly direct domain-relevant expertise, technical or otherwise.

Urbinati

Nadia Urbinati offers a deeply constructive commentary, expertly balancing clear-sighted political realism about old and new threats to democratic legitimacy with an inspiring account of how citizens navigating complex democratic societies can empower themselves and others. Her *tour de force* clarifies key aspects of my argument, while extending the discussion to broader terrain within democratic theory.

Despite its seemingly meek label, the risk-sensitive moderate proceduralist view defended in my lead essay is not *politically* moderate – in fact, as Urbinati's astute contribution shows, it has radical political implications, and it would be an oversight to understate this feature of the view. Urbinati is correct when she says that my argument:

> proposes to apply democratic rules to a realm that libertarians have traditionally kept out of the political domain: individual freedom and research. This move makes [my] strategy radical, even if I present it as 'moderate proceduralism' [...] democratizing agenda-setting can hardly be a moderate strategy. It is not the logic of research that radicalizes it but the monopoly–money–technology nexus. This knot of 'absolutes' makes AI different from the many other complex arenas democratized in past decades.

Like Risse, who similarly identifies and 'wholeheartedly welcome[s]' the 'radical' nature of my proposals, Urbinati is right to point out that realizing my AI democratization PLAYBOOK, and its normative foundations, in practice will require far-reaching political, legal, and economic transformations. This includes not just making more space for regulatory guardrails and diverse direct pathways of civic participation in AI deployment-related decisions, but also bigger-picture structural transformations and investments that enable real public ownership and control over emerging technologies. Here, too, Urbinati's commentary eloquently identifies the normative center of the view: 'Democratic equality rejects the logic of the zero-sum game (no compromise) with which the AI oligarchs regulate the risk/benefit ratio in their favor. *Democracy is not risk averse but asymmetry of power averse.*'

Urbinati and I also fundamentally agree on the democratic power of intermediaries in conditions of entrenched inequality (Urbinati, 2025), including innovative models of direct participation and representation like mini publics (Lafont and Urbinati, 2024; see also Landemore, 2020). Here, I especially welcome Urbinati's insight that my 'informed sub-constituencies' proposal concerning the role of third-part experts resonates with a theoretical resource not explicitly discussed in Part I: Gramsci's view that intellectuals can play either a liberating or an oppressive role in societal processes of transformation.

Here and elsewhere, Urbinati gives voice to what we both see as one of the PLAYBOOK's most innovative ideas, articulating it with greater clarity and force than my own exposition. She frames my proposal as 'an invitation to democratic theorists to open a new chapter of research on the civic/democratic education of technical experts', in alignment with my view that technical knowledge alone is insufficient for democratically legitimate AI policy. I hope many in the field will take up that invitation. Kreide's contribution also emphasizes the scholars' responsibility to resist disciplinary silos and Big Tech's ideological capture: 'a challenge for academia [...] more than ever, a critique of ideology is of crucial importance'.

Of course, intermediaries are themselves vulnerable to oligopolistic capture, as are academic institutions – an issue I raise in the introduction to Part III. On this, too, I suspect Urbinati and I share instincts. In fact, Urbinati's vast body of work on the transformative power of intermediaries is instructive on the point of the threat of academic capture as a parallel to regular capture, too: only a robust system of *multiple* well-functioning intermediaries can keep antidemocratic forces at individual junctures of democratic society in check (Urbinati, 2006; 2014; Lafont and Urbinati, 2024).

Finally, Urbinati's contribution compellingly highlights the distinctive importance of mobilizing political will and of cultivating a democratic mindset that stands a chance at countering oligopolistic influence on agenda-setting. Urbinati argues that 'Zimmermann does not pay sufficient attention to the consent fabrication, which germinated from the structural relations of power and poisons deliberation at the start [...] We live in what scholars call "a democracy of the public" or audience democracy. Zimmermann seems to believe that this kind of democracy, which so profoundly relies on social media replacing parties, can curb the will of the oligarchs.' To some extent, Urbinati's concern is shared by Kreide ('AI influences the formation of opinion and will', possibly turning 'democratic politics [into] a farce') as well as Agrawal and Christiano ('referenda would be captured by big money interests [...] they can hardly play the role of countering ASYMMETRY in agenda-setting power that Zimmermann wants them to').

Urbinati and other interlocutors aligned with Urbinati's worry are, in my view, right to press the point that an insufficient attention to the issue of oligarchic actors polluting public deliberation about technology, and simultaneously possibly chilling democratic enthusiasm in favor of technocracy more generally, may render any AI democratization PLAYBOOK 'utopian', not just radical, if it remains proceduralist without offering a strategy for effectively protecting the integrity and content of participatory procedures from oligarchic power: 'proceduralism risks being ineffective since it would be utopian to think that procedures have the strength to correct the structural asymmetry of power, which underlies the distribution of risks and benefits in AI deployment'.

More specifically, Urbinati underscores the importance of addressing inegalitarian distributions of *material* resources as well as of social powers of speech and deliberation, *before* the proceduralist approach can be implemented effectively: 'We have seen that compromise is *de facto* out of place in the monopolistic environment of AI production and deployment. It is, therefore, fatal for a reformist strategy to stop at the door of such a radical conflict. It doesn't have the teeth to face it. In this context, the predictable condition for a reformist strategy to remain in play is accepting a level of inequality beyond discussion.' On this point, too, Urbinati is joined by other interlocutors, namely Agrawal and Christiano, who raise questions about the *realistic feasibility* of my preferred approach to democratizing AI deployment.

Still, I want to stress that the PLAYBOOK's pro-democratic implications are not excessively idealistic. Democratization of any kind faces serious feasibility constraints: propaganda, polarization, misinformation, political corruption, entrenched inequality, and more. And indeed, Urbinati identifies what may very well be the most serious obstacle of all when it comes to democratizing *AI* specifically: consent manufacturing by powerful tech actors, which often promotes fear-driven, hyped-up public deliberation on AI, while serious inequalities remain in place. This is indeed a major obstacle, but also the very problem the strategies in the PLAYBOOK are designed to address by offering multiple pathways for hedging against feasibility risks: just because one participation pathway is marred by serious obstacles at a given moment, that does not mean *all* of them will be.

Notably, the PLAYBOOK also includes a strategy geared at larger-scale economic and institutional transformation, such as antitrust measures and possibly broader distributive justice policies designed to address material inequality in society more directly. This is best done in *conjunction* with, not exclusively *before*, meaningfully ramping up civic participation opportunities through various intermediaries. We cannot defer democratic agenda-setting 'until after the revolution', to echo Urbinati's, and in turn Dahl's, words. Democratization becomes viable when democratic publics decide to act – as Urbinati rightly says, when citizens mobilize beyond AI hype or doomsday narratives and refuse to remain passive observers.

Messy, imperfect participation is better than no participation while we wait for conditions of economic equality to improve, and the former in itself may have a mobilizing effect on the citizenry, emboldening citizens to develop and push for their own normative preferences about AI's societal role. In Weizenbaum's spirit, the main illusion that democratic societies must combat when it comes to democratizing AI is the illusion that they are fatally uninformed and ultimately powerless against oligopolistic AI deployers.

Citizens boldly deciding to take responsibility for this weighty area of collective decision-making, even under highly imperfect political and economic conditions, is our best shot at providing a counterweight against the ASYMMETRY that both Urbinati and I find highly politically and morally troubling.[5] As meek as risk-sensitive moderate proceduralism may sound terminologically, I hope to have clarified that substantively it implies that enabling serious political *contestation* and productive *conflict* over what we decide on collectively, and which conclusions we reach in our civic deliberations, is what moves the needle for a more democratically legitimate landscape of AI deployment.

5 Political mobilization geared towards cultivating a stronger pro-democratic mindset will also help address and combat a number of other 'public bads' linked to AI deployment, diagnosed by Agrawal and Christiano, which establish bad incentive structures and erode the democratic character of a polity. As they rightly say, such public bads include plagiarism and disinformation, as well as negative environmental consequences of AI innovation. My view is that cultivating a stronger pro-democratic mindset in the demos will make it more likely that 'regular' citizens will take it upon themselves to build different incentive structures, and to choose modes of expression that are conducive to learning and genuine deliberation rather than those that undermine these goals.

Stanger

Allison Stanger's contribution offers a distinctively hopeful yet grounded intervention informed by cutting-edge AI policy and governance debates. Power-Sharing Liberalism, as positioned as the normative heart of Stanger's response, is an alluring political ideal (see also Allen, 2023; Allen et al., 2025):

> unlike Classical Liberalism that focuses primarily on protecting individuals from harm (negative liberties), Power-Sharing Liberalism gives equal weight to positive freedoms – the rights of people to actively participate in shaping their society. [...] Power-Sharing Liberalism also emphasizes that stability and justice in a society are secured not only by safeguarding rights, but by actively cultivating the material and social conditions for people to exercise those rights effectively [...] it's not enough to have free speech on paper if extreme inequality or tech oligarch media prevent many from being heard.

Unsurprisingly, I am sympathetic to much of this picture. Liberal democracy without real power-sharing, not just politically but also economically, misses the heart of what is so appealing about a system of government by free equals. But recent political developments highlight that Power-Sharing Liberalism, for all its philosophical appeal, has an image problem. Democratic fatigue is rising globally. A significant sector of citizens in Western democracies, and especially young and male citizens, do not believe that democracy is the best way to govern society. While I leave a more comprehensive analysis to empirical political scientists, it is noteworthy that in 2024, 52 per cent of Gen Z citizens in the UK polled by Channel 4 said that 'the UK would be a better place if a strong leader was in charge who does not have to bother with parliament and elections', with 33 per cent endorsing the view that 'the UK would be a better place if the Army was in charge' (Channel 4, 2025). Across the pond, 57 per cent of college students surveyed by *Inside Higher Ed* in November 2024 said that they believed their vote 'does not much or at all make a difference in elections' (Mowreader, 2024). The cross-generational picture is rather bleak, too: 72 per cent of US citizens of all ages sat that 'the U.S. used to be a good example of democracy, but isn't anymore' according to a 2024 survey by the Pew Research Center (Pew, 2024).

To make matters worse, elected officials across Western democracies increasingly stoke democracy skepticism with populist appeals, promoting far-right authoritarian models in which a strong leader presides over a feudal system of corporate and political vassals, free from real checks and balances. As Stanger's discussion of Elon Musk's role at DOGE shows, this arrangement suits growing public–private enmeshments. Even tech CEOs with a more even-keeled reputation have not shied away from signaling overt support for newly elected political leaders, even when those leaders noticeably disrupt established democratic norms and principles. Sam Altman, in a January 22, 2025 post on X, states that 'watching @potus more carefully recently has really changed my perspective on him (i wish i had done more of my own thinking and definitely fell in the npc trap). i'm not going to agree with him on everything, but i think he will be incredible for the country in many ways!'[6]

The problem here is not just mere regulatory capture by Big Tech: instead, it is a more general and widespread problem of eroding a healthy democratic mindset in society. When authoritarian rhetoric and elite consolidation go hand in hand with tangible institutional failures – unreformed campaign finance, gerrymandering, suppression of dissent, and anti-majoritarian structures like the Electoral College (Levitsky and Ziblatt, 2023: 4) – it becomes harder to mobilize citizens around democratic ideals.

To be sure, this is not a problem unique to Power-Sharing Liberalism; rather, it reflects the broader crisis of democracy. The fatigue problem is also a problem for – and, troublingly, due to – democracy more generally. As Stanger herself persuasively shows, recent political developments in different nations have been significantly shaped by the rise of forces that flout democratic norms, including but not limited to democratically unchecked direct alliances between tech oligarchs and elected officials. Still, in order to democratize AI, be it in accordance with my PLAYBOOK and/or in alignment with the principles of Power-Sharing Liberalism Stanger recommends, mass pro-democratic *mobilization* through a revived sense of democratic responsibility and active participation is indispensable. This is in principle *compatible* with Stanger's Power-Sharing Liberalism, but it does imply that achieving shared power requires a strategic focus on countering democratic fatigue. We should be wary of overstating how easy that will be under current conditions.

This leads me to a larger point on which Stanger and I agree: the claim that democratizing AI is about safeguarding democracy *as a whole*, and that whether AI as such will threaten democracy is up to us to decide – as I emphasize in Part I, democratic constituencies should capture the current window of opportunity for meaningful political action, given that it is unclear how long that window will remain open. If democratizing AI promotes broader democratic resilience, the reverse is also true: democratic

6 Altman (2025a). 'npc' stands for 'non-playable character', suggesting that Altman thinks that his earlier hostility to Trump ('I think Trump is terrible and few things would make me happier than him not being president', Altman [2017]) was a result of merely following others' opinions, and that his new-found enthusiasm about Trump, by contrast, is the result of independent reflection.

decay will make AI democratization increasingly difficult. The more authoritarian a society becomes, the less feasible it becomes to implement reforms like those outlined in the PLAYBOOK. In such contexts, direct political resistance is needed first.

Stanger optimistically appeals to all of us to remain 'steadfast in the conviction that democracy, though tested, will adapt and endure'. I am far less sure than Stanger about this *predictive* claim – I think that without a significant increase in civic pushback and mobilization, democratic backsliding in various Western democracies may well accelerate, with no guarantees of a straightforward recovery. While Stanger is admirably measured in assessing the prospects for optimism, I believe an even more solemn reckoning with rising constraints is urgently needed.

Here, I find it instructive to bring Stanger's view in conversation with Kreide's observation that:

> decisive changes have taken place in the relationship between capitalism and democracy – a development that plays into the hands of AI power. For a long time, it was believed that with the establishment of democratic conditions (e.g. after the fall of the so-called Iron Curtain), democratic development would follow economic growth. This thesis of self-perpetuating democratization has not held true. Instead, we are dealing with neoliberal surveillance capitalism, for which a new maxim applies: the more prosperity for some, the more democracy gets in the way.

Equally, I share a related worry voiced by Cordelli: democratic constituencies may make small incremental decisions that seem unobjectionable, but that end up relinquishing too much power to technology, and that ultimately have a self-disenfranchising effect.

Despite my skepticism of the predictive claim, I agree with a possible *normative* version of the claim that democratization – of AI, and of other decision domains – remains more desirable than any non-democratic alternative. Whether that goal, and the associated PLAYBOOK I recommend, remains attainable will depend on democratic constituencies' ability and willingness to fight for it.

Kreide

In her original and wide-ranging response, Regina Kreide compellingly builds on a Habermasian conception of communicative power, which she brings into conversation with an analysis of generative AI's communicative shortcomings from the perspective of the philosophy of language. These two components of her contribution jointly point to a conclusion clearly aligned in spirit with my own conclusions in Part I, although Kreide, of course, arrives at that conclusion by mobilizing useful conceptual resources not employed by me originally. That conclusion is the claim that AI deployment can (and does!) have deeply corrosive effects on a well-functioning public sphere, the latter of which is integral to the legitimacy of democratic institutions.

I can see why Kreide draws complex connections between her Habermasian-inspired view and mine. Habermas's broader philosophical contributions contain elements that align with my position, as defended in the lead essay, that democratic legitimacy requires that citizens possess meaningful opportunities to be the *equal co-authors and co-owners of their shared future*. The strongest theoretical connection I see here is not primarily Habermas's account of communicative power itself – though I welcome Kreide's illuminating discussion of the latter – but Habermas's *co-originality thesis*, according to which democracy on the one hand, and a system of individual rights protections enabled by the rule of law on the other, are co-constitutive. On this view, 'the addressees of law are simultaneously authors of their rights' (Habermas, 1996: 104): unsurprisingly, I am sympathetic to this view.

Importantly, the co-originality thesis implies that democracy and the rule of law are *irreducible* to each other. As I argue in Part I, democratic legitimacy cannot be reduced to other normative goals – such as goals of substantive justice. In that way, I take the co-originality thesis to successfully track political and moral intuitions not far removed from my own. Further, both Habermas's view and my own view connect democratic co-authorship directly to the concept of *legitimacy*: as Habermas' principle of democracy in *Between Facts and Norms* states: 'only those statutes may claim legitimacy that can meet with the assent of all citizens in a discursive process of legislation that in turn has been legally constituted' (Habermas, 1996: 110).

The Habermasian perspective does add a novel lens on my work despite these theoretical parallels. In offering an innovative extension of a Habermasian analysis, Kreide's contribution identifies an analytically distinct way AI risks undermining democratic legitimacy. The problem is not only that AI deployment often pre-empts legitimate agenda-setting – via unilateral deployment by oligopolistic actors or via regulatory capture – but also that AI, and generative AI in particular, may skew and corrupt the public sphere itself. By obstructing citizens' reasoning and deliberation, AI can degrade the discursive basis of agenda-setting. In short, Kreide's argument shows that erosions of civic communicative power, alongside oligopolistic concentrations of power, are central to understanding the legitimacy deficit AI creates.

One particularly interesting feature of Kreide's response is her observation that generative AI's *affirmative* nature fortifies and calcifies particular sociopolitical viewpoints that are not representative of the democratic constituency at large 'without subjecting them to critical scrutiny'. This alone, she argues, poses a significant threat to democratic institutions. Generative AI may reinforce anti-democratic views aligned with tech authoritarianism, while placating the constituency by affirming input rather than enabling critical deliberation beyond the status quo.

Against the (in my view misguided) position that widespread AI access will 'democratize' technological progress purely by putting AI at all of our fingertips, Kreide warns that 'the structural conformism of AI language systems is a companion on the path to a techno-autocratic regime that promises freedom without democracy and only feigns equal participation and economic freedom'. Mere uncritical widespread use of AI corrodes the communicative sphere while obfuscating its own corrosive effects.

I agree with much of this: Kreide's argument offers welcome support for the view that generative AI deployment has created a democratic legitimacy deficit. Nonetheless, I have doubts about whether Kreide's focus on AI's communicative *capacities* ultimately helps us overcome that deficit. I think she is correct in her *descriptive* assessment of language models (as 'minimally rational actors with language-like competencies') and in her account of how AI erodes public spheres – by spreading harmful content, eroding trust, promoting polarization, and so on. A worry about the *normative implications* of this view arises, however, if we imagine a future AI with significantly more sophisticated capacities. Suppose such an AI constructively supports democratic deliberation – helping citizens understand diverse views, countering manipulation, and mapping marginalized policy preferences. Suppose it exceeds the bar required to promote, not hinder, democratic discourse.

Would the legitimacy deficit then disappear? Not so fast. *Capacities* are not the normative difference-maker, strictly speaking. After all, the deployment of such an agent is compatible with a state of affairs in which a small subset of oligarchic actors benefits from an ongoing concentration of wealth, power, and information. Thus, democratically illegitimate ASYMMETRIES can persist irrespective of how far AI's capacities advance. A strong focus on what AI can and cannot do risks diverting our attention away from the normatively decisive issue of how power and resources are distributed in society – between ordinary humans, and the vast structures they build. Kreide need not disagree with this: her analysis is compatible with mine so long as AI deployment's negative or (hypothetical) positive effects on *communicative* power count as one, but not the only, way in which democratic legitimacy is threatened.

Let me end with an observation about what I take to be one of the most generative aspects of Kreide's response: the point that legitimate communicative power is a 'power of world disclosure', which bears emancipatory potential in that it allows us to critically interrogate our past and future collective decisions. I agree that questioning the status quo; contesting existing social, economic, and political arrangements; and constructively arguing with our fellow citizens is crucial for safeguarding healthy democracies. Harnessing this potential, however, will require moving beyond the ideal of strictly rational deliberation that many, including Habermas, have found appealing.

Radical or *contestatory* democrats have long criticized rationalist approaches, urging us to embrace the constructive potential of conflict rather than replace it with mild-mannered deliberation (Pettit, 2000; Celikates, 2021; cf. Cohen and Fung, 2011). A full defense of such a view is beyond the scope here, but given rising tech authoritarianism, it is important to learn from contestatory democrats. Powerful tech leaders, invoking tropes like the 'boy genius' or 'chaotic disruptor', often frame their views as rational and data-driven, dismissing opponents as irrational or uninformed. But this is often false. Reasonable disagreement exists about guardrails for tech or acceptable levels of societal risk. These different positions should not be dismissed so easily, lest we miss important opportunities to effectively contest the Asymmetry. Although rational deliberation remains an important ethical and political ideal, it merits stronger critical scrutiny, since the *pragmatic effects* of centering that ideal may enable the exclusion of perspectives that challenge those who most loudly claim to speak in reason's name.

Risse

Mathias Risse's erudite response situates my work in the vibrant and rapidly growing field of philosophy of AI, as well as adjacent disciplines. But it does much more than that: it offers an insightful roadmap of the research questions and approaches around which the field – not just my work – has coalesced. This is a good moment to take stock in this way: philosophy of AI has entered a new phase of maturity, following a renewed wave of interest sparked by the algorithmic fairness boom in computer science – boosted by influential work on fairness 'impossibility theorems' (Kleinberg et al., 2016; Chouldechova, 2017) – and an associated AI ethics boom in philosophy. That boom followed earlier waves of philosophical engagement with technology, as well as related currents in STS, history, economics, law, and political science. Risse's contribution successfully zooms in on the state of play in the current philosophy of AI wave, without ignoring that larger contemporary and historical context.

Much of his generous discussion identifies points of agreement between my work, his, and others'. Let me highlight three areas where his analysis is especially perceptive. First, Risse links my work to Weyl and Tang's (2024) *Plurality:* 'Zimmermann and Tang and Weyl share the same approach to philosophical questions around deployment of digital technologies in our lives here and now: they articulate ideas on how to develop a strong democratic ideal.' I agree that concerns over AI deployment and democratic legitimacy are a key parallel. However, I am less convinced than they are that decentralization will bolster democratic aims, on the grounds that a mere *distribution* of power does not necessarily imply democratic control over that distribution. In fact, decentralization might sometimes hinder legitimacy by introducing feasibility constraints – for instance, when deliberation becomes prohibitively complex or slow. On my view, decentralization is desirable *conditional* on it actually enhancing democratic control over some domain.

Second, Risse engages with Shannon Vallor's *The AI Mirror* (2024), a powerful intervention that centers near-term justice in AI ethics, even as others focus on speculative AI superintelligence. Yet, shifting the focus in a different direction than Vallor, Risse warns that 'in this age of rapid change in technology many philosophical questions must be addressed in tandem with questions of democratic theory', *including* the issue of AI's *longer-term future* status. Risse worries that if AI achieves sentience or other significantly advanced capabilities, democratic systems may not be able to effectively address matters of justice because we will be faced with a Mumfordian 'megamachine' (Mumford, 1967): Risse wonders:

> how hard it will be for democracy to get these matters right given how much is at stake and how complex these matters are. [Mumford and others see] human engagement with technology as the deliberate if slow-moving construction of a vast control-system ('megamachine') [which] imposes a stifling and increasingly irreparable conformity on humankind. [...] If [authors like Mumford are] right, democracy will not save us from the troubles they identify, no matter how well-developed an ideal of democracy we develop to see through the deployment of AI. But nothing else will either.

I agree that this risk is underexplored in current AI ethics scholarship, and I welcome Risse's emphasis on this gap, which parallels Cordelli's concern about self-disenfranchising democratic constituencies blindly enamored by advanced technology. I share Risse's concern and believe enhancing democratic control over AI's trajectory, paired with political efforts to foster a stronger pro-democratic ethos, is our best shot at averting megamachine dynamics. While imperfect, this strategy seems far preferable to hoping that tech elites will impose democratic constraints on themselves.

Finally, Risse identifies an important point of agreement between his work and mine. This is the claim, developed in the final part of my PLAYBOOK and across various chapters of Risse's *Political Theory of the Digital Age*, that democratic constituencies ought to engage in massive investments to enable the public ownership of data and data-driven technologies, rather than relinquishing control of these domains to the private sector entirely.

This is a politically visionary claim: Risse and I agree that democratization cannot succeed without deep changes in the fabric of society's economic incentive structures, and without meaningful material backing behind any effort geared at the collective co-authorship of decisions. As Risse argues in his earlier book (2023) and this commentary, 'the default should be that collectively generated patterns [such as the kinds of data that allow far-reaching inferences about people and that thereby sustain surveillance capitalism] are also collectively controlled'. And as I have argued, the demos should have far greater control not just over collectively generated patterns, but also over the material and technological infrastructure making pattern generation possible in the first place, which is why the PLAYBOOK recommends significant public investment into AI research and development, akin to public investments in other kinds of infrastructure. In future work, I look forward to exploring additional political strategies for realizing my view in practice, such as tech worker-owned cooperatives, or investment pooling initiatives at local and domestic levels. In agreement with Rawls, I am concerned that 'inequalities in the ownership and control of wealth, income, and property can reduce the fair value of basic liberties' (Rawls, 2001). Effectively safeguarding these basic liberties of democratic citizens will plausibly require rethinking how current ASYMMETRIES can be tackled so as to move closer to the ideal of a real *property-owning democracy*, in which key resources are not only redistributed but also pre-distributed.

Inspired by Risse's emphasis on shifting what we as a society consider the 'default' when it comes to data ownership, let me now push his point further and end with a more general reflection cutting across different critical responses in this volume. Beyond shifting the economic and political ownership structures surrounding AI innovation, true 'co-authorship and co-ownership of the future', as per my arguments in Part I, also requires shifting our default views about what constitutes *progress*, and to what extent *speed* is essential in this context. Risse's contribution serves as a powerful reminder to critically interrogate more general, widely shared background assumptions in this area.

Many citizens, and interlocutors like Stanger, Agrawal, and Christiano, are acutely aware of the potential risk of us missing out on the benefits of AI innovation if we are too trigger-happy in our attempts to put guardrails on AI deployment, possibly overlooking opportunities to use AI for good. Agrawal and Christiano are reasonably concerned about 'possibly slowing down innovation, progress, and even creativity in the development of algorithms by over- or mis-regulating a nascent industry', emphasizing that we must 'find ways to adequately incentivize investments that spur innovation while safeguarding the needs of democratic constituents'. Similarly, Stanger says that:

> to navigate between the Scylla of oligarchic control and the Charybdis of unrealized potential, we need an AI governance approach [of] mitigating the risks of AI while maximizing its benefits for society. [...] Most AI governance efforts [have] overwhelmingly focused on preventing harms, with relatively little emphasis on actively steering AI toward public good uses. [...] An exclusive focus on red lines and prohibitions misses the larger opportunity. [...] The right approach to governance should not merely be about saying 'no' or 'slow down'.

While I am sympathetic to these general concerns, I think that we are far too close to the Scylla side – oligarchic control and largely unchecked, potentially harmful AI deployment – at the moment. We should remain vigilant about too hastily softening AI deployment guardrails. There is a particularly pernicious problem at play here, which I imagine both Stanger as well as Agrawal and Christiano will find troublesome as well. That problem is that the Scylla side has been highly effective in *instrumentalizing* the Charybdis claim – the concern that too much control over AI deployment will mean that we will miss out on unrealized innovation potential – for their own purposes.

As Marc Andreessen states in the aforementioned *New York Times* podcast interview, when prompted to explain Silicon Valley's unprecedented shift in support of the right: 'They came for business in a very broad-based way. [...] [I]t happened in a bunch of other industries, but the C.E.O.s felt like they couldn't talk about it. [...] They just ran this incredible terror campaign to try to kill crypto. Then they were ramping up a similar campaign to try to kill A.I. That's really when we knew that we had to really get involved in politics' (Douthat, 2025). In response to such complaints, many politicians and parts of the public eagerly fall in line, for fear of stifling the tech geniuses promising to push society to an abundant future.

This is exactly the problem of 'consent manufacturing' compellingly identified both by Urbinati and by Kreide. Consent manufacturing leads to a hyped-up status quo in which, as Urbinati says, 'millions of people enthusiastically welcome AI products and do not perhaps perceive acceleration as a problem: those very people that democracy would like to protect from the exploitation that the asymmetrical distribution of risks and benefits generates'. When Sam Altman prophesies on X that 'this is gonna be more like the renaissance than the industrial revolution' (Altman, 2025b), masses of people buy into the message that they must do whatever is necessary not to miss out on the magical benefits of AI innovation, even if that means that the distribution of those benefits will be fundamentally unequal and outside of democratic control.

Democratic constituencies must resist AI-FOMO – fear of missing out – and instead more rigorously question the underlying logic of accelerated capitalist optimization – coupled with increased collective alienation, in Cordelli's sense – driving the bulk of AI industry. In my view, the fear that regulation will necessarily stifle innovation has been vastly overstated by industry actors. It is worth noting that the United States *still* lacks comprehensive AI regulation at the federal level: whether having a federal framework in place would be quite as stifling as tech oligarchs perceive it to be actually remains untested. In fact, in a return to more overt anti-regulation ideology possibly emboldened by recent political shifts, both industry actors and right-wing politicians are now pushing back even against much smaller-scale AI regulation at the state level; for instance, by pushing for a heavy handed ten-year ban on any state AI regulation (Bhuiyan, 2025) – again citing concerns about unduly constraining innovation – and adopting patchy regulatory frameworks that are hard for companies to navigate.

There are at least two reasons to resist this type of thinking. First, smaller-scale regulation can serve as a form of *innovation* itself – stress-testing different models in low-stakes environments. This is analogous to AI sandboxing: trying things out in limited, controlled settings. Early examples include stronger protections in hiring, housing, and policing. Far from stifling Big Tech entirely, as AI FOMO suggests, such effective state-based and local approaches offer a less heavy handed way of responding to the rapidly evolving field of AI. They allow us to engage in 'learning by doing' when it comes to AI regulation, while at the same time minimizing the risk of policy failure by constraining it to a part of the democratic constituency only.

Second, even if meaningful democratic control over AI slows down AI deployment, it is not clear that slowness is necessarily *objectionable.* Inspired by Risse's earlier call to reconsider what we take to be the *default*, we should consider shifting the default here, too: it is an open question whether a slower deployment pace in some domain of AI may be what is needed not just to innovate, but to innovate in the right direction.

It has become commonplace to say that 'AI is just a tool' – often by those trying to downplay ethical risks associated with AI. But those of us who are interested in a fairer and more even-handed assessment of the democratic stakes of relevant risks and benefits can learn from this slogan, too. After all, tools are measured by what they can do *for us*, not by how much they matter in and of themselves. So, democratic constituencies should not uncritically accept the view – popular in the tech industry – that speed and novelty in AI innovation are *intrinsically* desirable in some way no matter what. They will be better served by empowering themselves to demand and contest explanations from AI deployers about why speed in some particular domain of AI innovation is *instrumentally* valuable in our collective pursuit of other desirable societal goals and purposes, such as human welfare, freedom, and equality.

References

Allen, D. (2023), *Justice by Means of Democracy*. University of Chicago Press.

Allen, D., Hubbard, S., Lim, W., et al. (2025), A roadmap for governing AI: technology governance and power-sharing liberalism. *AI and Ethics* 5: 3355–3377.

Altman, S. (2017), @sama 'I think Trump is terrible and few things would make me happier than him not being president'. March 8, 2017. Available online at: https://x.com/sama/status/839618895585562624 (Accessed: May 30, 2025).

Altman, S. (2025a), @sama 'watching @potus more carefully recently has really changed my perspective on him (i wish i had done more of my own thinking and definitely fell in the npc trap). i'm not going to agree with him on everything, but i think he will be incredible for the country in many ways!' January 22, 2025. Available online at: https://x.com/sama/status/1882234406662000833 (last accessed: May 30, 2025).

Altman, S. (2025b,) @sama 'i think this is gonna be more like the renaissance than the industrial revolution'. April 18, 2025. Available online at: https://x.com/sama/status/1913320105804730518 (last accessed: May 30, 2025).

Bender, E.M., Gebru, T., McMillan-Major, A., and Shmitchell, S. (2021), 'On the dangers of stochastic parrots: Can language models be too big?🦜'. In *Proceedings of the 2021 ACM Conference on Fairness, Accountability, and Transparency*, 610–623.

Bhuiyan, J. (2025), 'Republicans propose prohibiting US states from regulating AI for 10 years,' the *Guardian*, May 14, 2025. Available online at: https://perma.cc/JK4A-MMSH (last accessed: May 30, 2025).

Celikates, R. (2021), Radical democratic disobedience. In: *The Cambridge Companion to Civil Disobedience*, ed. W.E. Scheuerman. Cambridge University Press: 128–152.

Channel 4 (2025), Gen Z: Trends, Truth and Trust. Channel 4. Available online at: https://perma.cc/4XGJ-4KRS (last accessed: May 30, 2025).

Chouldechova, A. (2017), Fair prediction with disparate impact: A study of bias in recidivism prediction instruments. *Big Data*, 5, no. 2: 153–163.

Christiano, T. (1996), *The Rule Of The Many: Fundamental Issues In Democratic Theory*. Routledge.

Christiano, T. (2012), 'Money in politics'. In: *The Oxford Handbook of Political Philosophy*, ed. D. Estlund. Oxford University Press.

Christiano, T. (2019), Democracy, participation and information: Complementarity between political and economic institutions. *San Diego Law Review* 56, no, 4: 935–960.

Cohen, J. and Fung, A. (2011), Radical democracy. *Raisons politiques* 4, no. 2: 115–130.

Cordelli, C. (2025), What is the wrong of capitalism? *American Political Science Review*: 1–16.

Douthat, R. (2025), How Democrats drove Silicon Valley into Trump's arms. *Interesting Times with Ross Douthat (The New York Times)*, April 6, 2015. Available online at: http://tiny.cc/oqz3101 (last accessed May 30, 2025).

European Union (2024), 'Regulation (EU) 2024/1255 of the European Parliament and of the Council of 13 March 2024 laying down harmonised rules on artificial intelligence (Artificial Intelligence Act) and amending Regulations (EC) No 300/2008, (EU) No 167/2013, (EU) No 168/2013, (EU) 2018/858, (EU) 2019/2144 and (EU) 2019/881 and Directives 2014/90/EU, (EU) 2016/797 and (EU) 2020/1828.' *Official Journal of the European Union*, L 150, 8.5.2024, 1-269.

Habermas, J. (1996), *Between Facts and Norms: Contributions to a Discourse Theory of Law and Democracy*. William Rehg (trans.). MIT Press.

Jaeggi, R. (2014), *Alienation*. Columbia University Press.

Kleinberg, J., Mullainathan, S., and Raghavan, M. (2016), Inherent trade-offs in the fair determination of risk scores. *arXiv preprint arXiv:1609.05807*.

Kolodny, N. (2014), Rule over none I: What justifies democracy?' *Philosophy & Public Affairs* 42, no. 3: 195–229.

Lafont, C. and Urbinati, N. (2024), *The Lottocratic Mentality: Defending Democracy against Lottocracy*. Oxford University Press.

Landemore, H. (2020), *Open Democracy: Reinventing Popular Rule for the Twenty-First Century*. Princeton University Press.

Levitsky, S. and Ziblatt, D. (2023), *Tyranny of the Minority: Why American Democracy Reached the Breaking Point*. Crown.

Narayanan, A. and Kapoor, S. (2025), AI as Normal Technology. 25-09 Knight First Amend. Inst. (Apr. 14, 2025). Available online at: https://perma.cc/HVN8-QGQY (last accessed May 30, 2025).

Mowreader, A. (2024), Survey: Majority of college students believe their vote didn't matter in the election. *Inside Higher Ed*, December 4, 2024. Available online at: https://www.insidehighered.com/news/student-success/college-experience/2024/12/04/57-college-students-my-vote-doesnt-make (last accessed: May 30, 2025).

Mumford, L. (1967), *Myth of the Machine: Technics and Human Development*. Harcourt Brace Jovanovich.

O'Neill, M. (2012), Free (and fair) markets without capitalism: Political values, principles of justice, and property-owning democracy'. In: *Property-Owning Democracy: Rawls and Beyond*, ed. T. Williamson. Wiley-Blackwell: 75–100.

Pettit, P. (2000), Democracy, electoral and contestatory. In: *Designing Democratic Institutions: Nomos XLII*, eds. I. Shapiro and S. Macedo. New York University Press: 105–144.

Pew Research Center (2024), 72 % of Americans say the U.S. used to be a good example of democracy, but isn't anymore. July 10, 204. Available online at: https://perma.cc/SB7Q-JLBK (last accessed: May 30, 2025).

Rawls, J. (2001), *Justice as Fairness: A Restatement*. Harvard University Press.

Risse, M. (2023), *Political Theory of the Digital age: Where Artificial Intelligence Might Take Us*. Cambridge University Press.

Stilz, A. (2015), Decolonization and self-determination. *Social Philosophy and Policy* 32, no. 1: 1–24.

Weyl, E. G., Tang, A., and ⿻ Community (2024), *⿻ 數位 Plurality: The Future of Collaborative Technology and Democracy* (Independently published). Available online at: https://www.plurality.net/ (last accessed February 1, 2026).

Urbinati, N. (2006), *Representative Democracy: Principles and Genealogy*. University of Chicago Press.

Urbinati, N. (2014), *Democracy Disfigured: Opinion, Truth, and the People*. Harvard University Press.

Urbinati, N. (2025), The decline and the need of the key force of intermediation. *Philosophy & Social Criticism* 51, no. 4: 559–570.

Vallor, S. (2024), *The AI Mirror: How to Reclaim Our Humanity in an Age of Machine Thinking*. Oxford University Press.

Weizenbaum, J. (1987), *Kurs auf den Eisberg: Die Verantwortung des Einzelnen und die Diktatur der Technik*. Piper.

Weizenbaum, J. (2001), *Computermacht und Gesellschaft: Freie Reden*. Suhrkamp.

Zimmermann, A., Di Rosa, E., and Kim, H.S. (2020), Technology can't fix algorithmic injustice. *Boston Review*. Available online at: https://www.bostonreview.net/articles/annette-zimmermann-algorithmic-political/ (last accessed May 30, 2025).

Index

abundance 16, 25
academia xii, 81, 85, 94, 191, 210–19
accelerationism, effective 16–26, 78
accountability xiv, 11, 31, 38, 42, 61, 65, 69–78, 83, 99, 121, 148–9, 156, 162–3, 173–5, 197, 211, 217
  see also disclosure obligations of tech companies; sanctions
activism, bottom-up *see* participation
Adorno, Theodor W. 189, 191
agenda-setting 42–9
  via AI deployment 45–7
  via direct political influence 56–60
AI consciousness 7, 195, 201
AI ethics 12, 79–80, 85, 88, 121, 169, 227
AI exceptionalism 11, 13, 67, 102, 147, 152, 216
  see also normal technology; Uniqueness View
AI literacy *see* expertise
AI safety 7–8, 13, 17, 21, 23, 56–60 *passim*, 63, 72, 80, 85, 143–4, 168–9, 175, 214
AI winter 101
algorithmic bias 24, 27, 73, 87–92, 121, 136, 163–171 *passim*, 187
alienation 122–132, 202, 214–15, 231
  see also discrimination; racism; sexism
Allen, Danielle 30, 91, 94, 168–70, 198–9, 222
Alphabet Workers Union 82
AlphaGo 192
Altman, Sam 6, 10, 40, 48, 57–60, 80, 218, 223, 231
  equity in OpenAI 59
  ousting of Altman during OpenAI leadership struggle 58
  statements about Donald Trump 223
  policy conversations with US public officials 58–9
altruism, effective 7, 16–7, 21–6
  see also accelerationism, effective; AI safety; longtermism; TESCREAL
Amazon 30, 34, 45–7, 149
  deal with FBI concerning facial recognition capabilities 64
  deployment moratorium, facial recognition 58
  labor conditions in Amazon warehouses 78–80
America PAC *see* campaign finance
Amish 195–7
Amodei, Dario 24–5, 165, 167, 173,
anarchy 131–2, 202
Anderson, Elizabeth 79, 81, 168
Andreessen, Marc 15, 20–6, 36, 147–8, 230
Anthropic 5, 7, 24, 45, 69, 72, 165
anticipation in AI regulation xii, 65–6, 85, 100, 150
anticompetitive
  anticompetitive agenda-setting 12, 41, 148
  anticompetitive markets 30, 52
    see also antitrust, oligopoly
antitrust xv, 30, 84, 98–9, 144, 169, 174, 217, 221

approval regulation *see* FDA for algorithms; licensing
arms race 7, 68, 173
Asymmetry, The 29
  public justification and xi, 12, 29, 36, 50, 53, 55, 148
  the democratic legitimacy deficit and 144, 148, 152–4, 158–9, 162, 189, 219–20
auditing xiii, 70–2, 164, 169, 171–2, 217
authoritarianism xiii, 20, 55, 68, 156, 165–7, 179, 188, 215, 222–3, 226–7

backsliding, democratic 79, 80, 224
  see also authoritarianism
ballot propositions *see* referendum
ban *see* moratorium
Barlow, John Perry 19
Bezos, Jeff 27, 30, 34–5
Big Five *see* FAANG
Bostrom, Nick 7, 21
boy genius 227 *not to be confused* with Altman, Sam; Bezos, Jeff; Karp, Alexander, Musk, Elon; Thiel, Peter; Zuckerberg, Mark
Brave New World *see* Huxley, Aldous
bribery *see* corruption

Californian Ideology 19, 147–8
campaign finance 20, 43–9, 130, 137, 145, 152, 217–8, 223
capitalism xiii, 17, 19, 23, 81, 123, 129, 130–2, 154–5
  incompatible with democracy 67
  surveillance capitalism 5, 172–3, 189, 200, 203, 224, 220
    see also Zuboff, Shoshana
  venture capitalism 20, 27, 189
capture
  academic capture 211
  civic capture via ideology 158–9, 223
  media capture 145, 220
  regulatory capture 52, 68, 83–5, 143, 165, 214–8
caution 3–5, 12, 19–22, 55–6, 176
  see also uncertainty
ChatGPT 5, 9, 15, 87, 134, 141, 162, 182–3, 188
checks and balances 38, 42, 47, 78, 164, 217, 222
China 6, 46, 141, 155
chips 45, 141
citizen assembly xiii, 72, 170, 197, 217
civic mindset *see* ideology and political mobilization
Clarke, Arthur C. 97
Claude 5, 141
co-authors and co-owners of our shared future 103–5
colonialism, digital 188
complacency, political *see* passivity
conflict, productive 221
  see also contestation, democratic; democracy, models of: contestatory/radical
connectionism 181
consent fabrication *see* antidemocratic ideology
consumer protection 52, 64
contestation, democratic xii, 45, 47–8, 51, 61–77 *passim*, 89, 99, 102–4, 220–1, 227
corruption
  as distortion 54, 164, 210, 225
  as political influence 20, 49, 210, 214, 220–1
counterpower *see* agenda–setting
coup 163
  see also electoral interference
cryptocurrency 165, 230
cryptonormative judgment 48

Dahl, Robert A. 44, 148, 159, 221
data center 4, 28, 46, 79, 140–1
decentralization 186, 228
Declaration of the Independence of Cyberspace
  see John Perry Barlow
deepfakes 4, 91, 136
DeepSeek 141

deference, undue
by citizens to AI 93, 123, 129–130, 214
by regulators to tech industry 40, 93, 104, 162, 217
deliberation
augmented deliberation 70, 197–8
deliberation under capture *see* deference, undue
Dell 30, 46
democracy, models of
audience democracy 158, 220
consultative democracy 43–4, 70, 216
contestatory/radical democracy 227
deliberative democracy 49, 53, 69, 91, 126, 132, 180, 184
representative democracy 41–3, 49, 125, 144–8, 156–7, 170, 210
Thick vs. Thin Democracy 41–45
democratic authorization, direct vs. indirect 11–2, 36, 41, 44–9, 65, 99, 102, 121–3, 148–9
democratic control
ex ante vs. ex post 43, 47, 60, 65–6, 122 150–2
meaningful democratic control 13, 47, 197, 217, 223, 231
deployment
deployment pace *see* move fast and break things
unilateral power to deploy 16, 37–9, 46, 101, 121, 149, 225
determinism *see* inevitability
dictator, benevolent 50, 121, 124–7, 165–6, 173, 215
disclosure
disclosure obligations of tech companies 64, 76, 98–9, 121, 162, 166, 171
world disclosure *see* power of world disclosure
discrimination 90–2, 121, 169–72, 190
see also algorithmic bias
DOGE (Department of Government Efficiency) 163–5, 175, 222
domination 39, 124–9, 157, 209
donor, political *see* campaign finance
doom 8, 26, 32, 35, 100, 104, 210, 216, 221
Durkheim, Émile 204
dystopia *see* utopia

education 140
of the public by technologists 40, 60
see also expertise
of technologists, civic 157, 219
see also Gramsci, Antonio
Education of a Libertarian, The *see* Thiel, Peter
electoral interference 49, 183, 187, 217
elites 19–26 *passim*, 30, 35, 95, 104, 150, 162, 174, 198, 209, 223, 229
ELIZA 209–10
see also Weizenbaum, Joseph
emancipation *see* liberty
entente strategy 167
see also Amodei, Dario
ethics pledge *see* voluntary self-regulation
EU AI Act 6, 55, 59, 63, 98, 139, 155, 173
experiment 3–4, 12, 19, 27, 34, 69, 147–9, 151–2, 172–4, 185
expertise
moral expertise 93–96, 156–7, 197
see also education of technologists, civic
technical expertise xv, 25, 71–4, 81, 86, 93–96, 100, 156–7, 170, 187, 197, 218
exploitation xiii, 4, 15, 28, 69, 78, 99, 153, 174, 211, 213, 231
externalities 136

FAANG (Facebook Amazon Apple Netflix Google) 45
fake news *see* public sphere
fascism 20, 87, 104
see also authoritarianism; ideology

FDA (Food and Drug Administration) for algorithms 6, 61, 85
feasibility constraints 68, 48, 50, 55, 74, 78, 101–2, 155, 173, 178, 190, 218, 220, 228
  see also cryptonormative judgments
FOMO (fear of missing out) *see* SOTA-chasing
freedom *see* liberty
FTC (Federal Trade Commission) 30, 64, 70, 98–9, 143, 172

Gates, Bill 16, 30
GDPR (General Data Protection Regulation) 144, 185
Gebru, Timnit 7, 8, 22, 80
Gemini 87–8, 182
Generative AI xi, 4–10, 15, 28, 34, 39, 41, 45, 137, 141, 152, 225–6
geopolitics and AI *see* arms race
global justice 21, 23, 28, 61, 142, 154, 159, 161, 165, 173–5
Google 5, 7, 15, 28, 45–6, 57, 59, 64, 79, 87, 98, 163, 200
GPU (Graphics Processing Unit) *see* chips
Gramsci, Antonio 157, 219
Grok 163
growth, economic 21, 131, 142, 189, 224

Habermas, Jürgen
  Co-originality thesis 91, 225
  communicative power 180–4, 191, 224
Hegel, G. W. F. 180, 195
Hinton, Geoffrey 7, 57
Hippocratic Oath 62
  see also voluntary self-regulation
hope *see* optimism and pessimism
Hugging Face 45–6
Humanities 175, 202
Huxley, Aldous 104

IBM 46
  deployment moratorium, facial recognition 58
  UK government deal concerning facial recognition in law enforcement 64
ideology
  antidemocratic ideology 42, 78, 219
    see also fascism, TESCREAL
  ideology and temporality 148–52 *passim*
  ideology and political mobilization 62, 73, 142–4, 152–4, 209, 214–9, 223
  ideology critique and analytic philosophy 18, 179, 191, 219
imagination, collective 13, 16, 104, 153, 186
impersonal rule *see* dictator, benevolent
incremental change 66, 155, 163, 175, 224
industrial revolution 174, 202, 231
inevitability in the context of technology deployment 15, 48, 65, 83, 104, 174, 210
informed sub-constituencies 69–74
injustice, algorithmic *see* algorithmic bias
innovation
  democratic innovations 74, 94, 100
  technological innovation and determinism *see* uncertainty
intermediaries, democratic 13, 69, 81, 157, 218–221
invective *see* philosophy of language; public sphere
isēgoria 61, 76, 148
isonomia 148, 156
ivory tower *see* academia

justice
  by means of democracy 91
  democracy vs. 87–93

Karp, Alexander 7–8, 20, 48

Laboratory *see* experiment
labor unions *see* unions

language models
affirmation in 226
as minimally rational actors 179–89
as stochastic parrots 182, 209
hallucination in language models 27, 33, 88, 136, 139
learned helplessness 102, 210, 216
see also deference
legitimacy
democratic legitimacy deficit 10, 12, 29, 37, 40, 73, 101–2, 154, 161–3, 213–6, 225–6
instrumentalism and legitimacy 50–1, 74, 93–5
in tension with other political goals 87–93, 212–8
proceduralism and legitimacy 51–3, 64, 73, 88, 90–1
libertarianism 16–26, 67, 147, 150, 152, 155, 179, 218
liberty 19, 25, 67, 77, 85, 104, 131, 143, 147–9, 150–9, 166, 168, 176, 184, 188, 191, 218, 222, 226
basic liberties 91, 229
civil liberties 57
positive vs. negative liberty 149–51, 158, 168, 222
licenses for deployment 6, 13, 52, 56–7, 60–1, 84, 190
lobbying 43–4, 59–60, 82–3, 104, 137, 174, 190, 210
longtermism 7–10, 16, 19–24, 27, 150–2, 189, 217
Luddism *see* innovation

MAAAM (Meta Alphabet Amazon Apple Microsoft) *see* FAANG
Magical thinking 3, 4, 97, 104, 147, 231
Manhattan Project *see* arms race; nuclear technology; Oppenheimer, J. Robert; World War II
manipulation 99, 164–5, 169, 187, 226
marginalized groups 34, 45, 51–2, 88–9, 123, 154, 173, 187, 226
market share *see* oligopoly; monopoly
Marx, Karl 131, 180
megamachine 202–3, 228
Microsoft 5, 9, 15, 45–6, 59, 80, 149, 151
microtargeting 164, 185
see also electoral interference
minorities *see* marginalized groups
misinformation and disinformation 4, 7, 27–8, 34, 49, 56, 165–6, 186–7, 199, 220–1
money in politics *see* campaign finance
monopoly *see* anticompetitive; oligopoly; power, market
monopsony 136
moratorium, deployment xii, 4, 6, 13, 16–17, 23, 56–8, 60, 64, 74, 76, 84, 130, 138, 231
move fast and break things 3–6, 10, 16, 141, 171
Mumford, Lewis 202–3, 228
Musk, Elon xii, 6, 19, 23, 30, 57, 80, 163–7, 175, 222
see also DOGE

nationalizing technology companies 99
neoliberalism 189, 191, 224
neo–reactionary 42
network states 20
see also Srinivasan, Balaji
neutral networks *see* Generative AI
normal technology, AI as a 216
novel philosophical problem, AI raising a 102, 216
see also Uniqueness View; AI exceptionalism
novel in scale vs. novel in kind 216
npc (non–playable character) 223
nuclear technology 4, 7, 102, 135, 173
Nvidia 45–6

oligarchy 81, 147–9, 152–5, 167–170, 212–17, 226, 231
oligopoly 9–13, 22, 29–30, 45–8, 72, 162–5, 185, 190, 219
OpenAI 5–10, 45, 56, 58–9, 69, 80, 139, 141, 163

Oppenheimer, J. Robert 7, 103, 189
see also arms race; nuclear technology; World War II
oppression 8, 87, 165
epistemic access to the nature of oppression 92
optimism and pessimism 29, 50, 99, 104, 158, 161, 166–7, 176, 210, 224
see also techno-optimist manifesto, The
ownership of technological resources, public 83–5
data ownership and 99, 141, 203, 229
democratization of investment and 131–2
infrastructure and 98, 229
public investment into AI development 85
worker-owned cooperatives 299

Palantir 7, 20
see also Karp, Alexander; Thiel, Peter; surveillance
participation, democratic
actual vs. hypothetical 215
via bottom–up activism 13, 28, 42–9 *passim*, 57, 60–1, 65, 70, 173, 178, 216
electoral participation 41–4
see also electoral interference; electoral sanctions; Thick vs. Thin Democracy
mere input vs. binding decisions 70
participation pathways see Playbook, The
participatory budgeting 74, 94
in the workplace 81
passivity, political 10, 38, 62, 77, 81, 97, 104, 124, 127–30
active participation vs. 25, 60, 76, 80, 97, 104–5
democratic fatigue and xv, 209, 222–3
patchy regulation 62, 231
paternalism see dictator, benevolent
philosophy of language 179, 224
philosophy of mind 201, 216
philosophy of technology 202
Playbook, The 69–96
different elements of The Playbook working together 65–6, 221
playbook vs. blueprint 68
polarization see public sphere, erosion of the
political wrongdoing see bribery; campaign finance; capture; corruption; electoral interference; lobbying
populism 156, 198, 222
power
agenda-setting power 47–9
communicative power see Habermas, Jürgen
counterpower 13, 45, 62, 80, 83, 158, 214
countervailing power 45, 143–4, 190
market power 12, 23, 30, 134, 136, 140–1, 169, 178, 188
power of world disclosure 185, 227
power to deploy 18, 35, 45–47
prediction, limits of see uncertainty
predistribution see property–owning democracy
preferences
adaptive preferences 92, 129–132, 220, 230
preference aggregation 71, 138, 215
representing and enforcing civic preferences 76, 82, 148, 170
value-based preferences 14, 62, 65, 67, 73, 77, 94, 102–3
pressure point 40, 55, 60, 77, 84, 100, 103, 162, 213
privacy 5, 75, 136, 139, 151, 164, 168–71
proceduralism
constitutional limits and proceduralism 51–2, 90–1, 123, 130, 214

moderate proceduralism 51
moderate proceduralism as a radical strategy 158, 197, 221, 227
risk-sensitivity and moderate proceduralism 52–3, 64–6, 73, 88, 90–1, 214–5, 221
pro-democratic mindset *see* ideology and political mobilization
progressivism, social 19
propaganda 165
property-owning democracy 229
prosperity *see* abundance
protest 28, 42–3, 73, 211
public equality 51–3, 76, 81, 90, 122–8, 156, 188, 215
public sphere
erosion of the 187–8
littering 186–7

racism and racial injustice 5, 8, 24, 34, 58, 64, 87, 187, 199
see also discrimination; fascism; TESCREAL
rationality
deliberation and 78, 179–190, 226–7
language models and *see* language models
Rawls, John 199, 229
recourse in the context of AI decision-making 51, 65, 89, 99
red-teaming 169
referendum 74–8, 145, 197, 220
refusal 65, 211, 221
risk
dispersion of 12, 28, 34
fairness and 34
innovation and risk 27
pure risk 32
risk mitigation vs. opportunity maximization 169
trivial interests and risk impositions 32–3, 43
rule of none *see* dictator, benevolent

salience in the context of agenda-setting 42–3, 48–9, 68, 73, 102
sanctions
electoral sanctions 43–4
legal sanctions 43–4, 52, 84, 155
sandboxing 231
Schmitt, Carl 42
see also fascism
science fiction 97
sexism and gender-based injustice 5, 8, 24, 87, 199
see also algorithmic bias; boy genius; discrimination
Shift, The 16, 26, 41
social facts *see* Durkheim, Émile
socialism 25
SOTA-chasing (state-of-the-art-chasing) 5, 18, 30
SpaceX 163
speed *see* deployment pace
Spengler, Oswald 42
see also fascism
Srinivasan, Balaji 20
start–ups 4, 29, 61
status quo
status quo and political change 66, 98–101
status quo of the AI market
see oligopoly; SOTA-chasing
reasonably just status quo 87
stochastic parrot *see* language models
Strauss, Leo 42
success of democratization strategies, prospects of 13, 43–4, 62–3, 67, 74, 82, 90, 93, 100, 134, 167
superintelligence *see* AGI; doom
surveillance
and authoritarianism 165, 172–3, 200, 229
Stop Secret Surveillance Ordinance 57
surveillance capitalism *see* capitalism
sycophancy *see* language models

Tang, Audrey 70, 198–200, 228
Techno-optimist manifesto, the 20, 25, 94
see also effective accelerationism; Marc Andreessen

technosolutionism 88
TESCREAL (Transhumanism, Extropianism, Singularitarianism, Cosmism, Rationalism, Effective Altruism, Longtermism) 22
see also accelerationism, effective; altruism, effective; Gebru, Timnit; ideology; longtermism; racism
Thiel, Peter 19, 21, 25–6, 42, 77, 148, 150, 152
tinkering *see* experiment
Trump, Donald xii, 20, 163–7, 175, 223
trust 54, 63, 80, 95, 156, 170, 176, 189, 226

uncertainty 8, 24, 27, 103, 162, 188
unemployment due to AI deployment 79, 141–2
unions, labor 82, 143–5, 218
Uniqueness View 215–6
see also AI exceptionalism
utopia
utopian in a political feasibility sense xiv, 149, 158–9, 220
utopian in a technology ideology sense 67, 147, 167

Vallor, Shannon 7, 196, 200–3, 228
voice and exit 78–83, 99, 144, 197
volenti non fit iniuria 37
voluntary self-regulation xii, 13, 62–3, 155
voyeurism *see* privacy

Weizenbaum, Joseph 209–11, 221
Weyl, Glen 30, 70, 197–8, 228
woke 20
work, future of *see* unemployment
workers, technology xv, 4, 78–83, 99, 136–44
and collective bargaining 82, 144
and subordination 79, 99
and whistleblowing 80, 99, 217
workplace democracy *see* participation
World War II 104, 150
see also arms race; Huxley, Aldous; Oppenheimer, J. Robert

X (platform) 80, 223
xAI 163

Zuboff, Shoshana 200, 203
Zuckerberg, Mark 30, 35, 54

EU authorised representative for GPSR:
Easy Access System Europe, Mustamäe tee 50,
10621 Tallinn, Estonia
gpsr.requests@easproject.com

www.ingramcontent.com/pod-product-compliance
Ingram Content Group UK Ltd.
Pitfield, Milton Keynes, MK11 3LW, UK
UKHW021840100926
8556IPUK00004B/455
9781526183613